In the MIDDLE of NOWHERE

In the
MIDDLE
of
NOWHERE

TERRY UNDERWOOD

BANTAM BOOKS
SYDNEY • AUCKLAND • TORONTO • NEW YORK • LONDON

The author wishes to thank: Mrs Marie Megaw for permission to reproduce the extract from Mary Durack's poem 'The Lament for the Drowned Country'; Mrs Olive Quilty for the extract from Tom Quilty's poem 'Ringer in Disguise'; and the Northern Territory Library for the photograph of Pope John Paul II.

IN THE MIDDLE OF NOWHERE
A BANTAM BOOK

First published in Australia and New Zealand
in 1998 by Bantam

Copyright © Terry Underwood, 1998

National Library of Australia.
Cataloguing-in-Publication Entry

Underwood, Terry (Marie Thérèse).
In the middle nowhere.

ISBN 0 7338 0130 7.

1. Underwood, Terry (Marie Thérèse). 2. Ranchers — Northern
Territory — Biography. 3. Women ranchers — Northern
Territory — Biography. I. Title.

636.01092

Bantam books are published by

Transworld Publishers (Aust) Pty Limited
15–25 Helles Ave, Moorebank, NSW 2170

Transworld Publishers (NZ) Limited
3 William Pickering Drive, Albany, Auckland

Transworld Publishers (UK) Limited
61–63 Uxbridge Road, Ealing, London W5 5SA

Bantam Doubleday Dell Publishing Group Inc
1540 Broadway, New York, New York 10036

Typeset by Midland Typesetters, Maryborough, Victoria
Printed by McPherson's Printing Group, Maryborough, Victoria

10 9 8 7 6 5 4 3

This book is dedicated to my husband, John,
my lover, my anchor, my rock.
And to our four extraordinary children,
Marie, Patrick, Michael and Rebecca.
The love, loyalty, courage and resourcefulness of these five
have made for me all things possible.

CONTENTS

ACKNOWLEDGEMENTS

....

From my earliest memories, I was enchanted by the magic of words and the power of the pen. Childhood poems and stories were passionately written and preserved in a special exercise book called *My Book of Beauty*. One day when I was an old lady I would write my autobiography.

At my photographic exhibition entitled *The Cattle Kingdom* in 1995, at the Barry Stern Gallery in Sydney, I was approached by Selwa Anthony, literary agent extraordinaire. I answered in the affirmative to both her questions: 'Do you have a story? Can you write?'

Selwa and I shared the conviction that the story of the outback family whose survival revolves around unity and love was long overdue. I am grateful for Selwa's unfailing faith and support—my good friend knows books; she knows people too.

I thank the other fine members of my publishing team. At Transworld, Jude McGee and Maggie Hamilton in particular, have accommodated with professional ease the bush woman determined to include in her story a tribute to each and every hero and heroine of today and yesterday. My unqualified thanks go to Amanda O'Connell, a sensitive and intelligent editor, who represented 'the rest of the world' from whom I had parted physical company three decades ago.

To my beloved family and dear friends and mere acquaintances, who knowingly or unknowingly have influenced my journey thus far—with heartfelt gratitude I acknowledge you all.

FOREWORD

....

There can never be enough written about the pioneers of Outback Australia. There is a fascination with people who shun modern comforts for a life of hardship in the harshest environment this country can offer.

The story of John and Terry Underwood is as gutsy as it gets. How John Underwood is still alive is simply amazing. It is a testament to the strength of the human spirit and the bond between he and Terry, their children and the land they love so passionately.

I've known the Underwoods for near on ten years now, and having enjoyed Riveren hospitality on several occasions—many a night I've sat under the stars with John and Terry, totally enthralled by their real-life saga—I can even offer my own Riveren experience.

Once, when my departing light aircraft broke down and the young pilot had all but given up, it was left to a fiercely determined John Underwood to get us airborne. Risking life and limb in the blazing hot sun, he gripped the blade of the propeller and spun it for all he was worth, eventually starting the Cessna 410. I guess that's the way of the bush.

On 'Hey Hey It's the Northern Territory' in 1992, there was a huge reaction from viewers to a profile piece on Riveren, especially when Terry casually mentioned that they didn't have a phone for the first thirteen years! Hard for someone in the big smoke to imagine.

'Gee, Terry, you must write a book one day,' I urged. Mind you, many had made that suggestion before me. I've always been in awe of Terry's enormous energy, near photographic memory and a capacity for life rarely matched—what ideal traits for an author!

I feel privileged and honoured to be part of this project and shall always cherish my friendship with this great Australian family. As you read their intriguing story you'll think, 'How can they do it? Why would they do it?' It takes a special breed to accept the challenge. Thank God Australia still produces such sturdy stock.

DARYL SOMERS
February 1998

It is not possible for us to know each other except as we manifest ourselves in distorted shadows to the eyes of others; therefore why should we judge a neighbour? Who knows what pain is behind virtue and what fear behind vice? No-one in short knows his thoughts, his joys, his bitterness, his agony, the injustices committed against him and the injustices he commits.

God is too inscrutable for our little understanding. After sad meditation it comes to me that all our lives, whether good or in error, mournful or joyous, obscure or of gilded reputation, painful or happy, is only a prologue to love beyond the grave, where all is understood and almost all forgiven.

SENECA

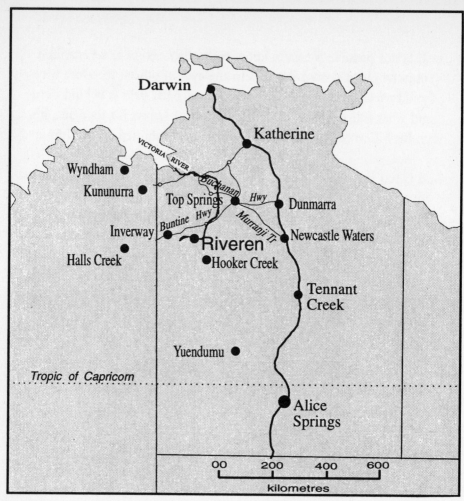

Darwin

Katherine

VICTORIA RIVER

Wyndham

Kununurra

Buchanan

Top Springs

Dunmarra

Hwy

Buntine Hwy

Inverway

Murranji Tr.

Newcastle Waters

Riveren

Halls Creek

Hooker Creek

Tennant
Creek

Yuendumu

Tropic of Capricorn

Alice
Springs

00   200   400   600

kilometres

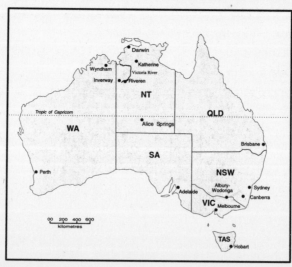

Darwin

Katherine

Wyndham

Victoria River

Inverway

Riveren

NT

QLD

Tropic of Capricorn

Alice Springs

WA

SA

Brisbane

NSW

Perth

Albury-
Wodonga

Sydney

Adelaide

Canberra

VIC

Melbourne

TAS

Hobart

00 200 400 600
kilometres

PROLOGUE

....

The battered, sturdy Willy's Jeep lurched across the drought stricken land. It followed a track visible only to the concerned yet somehow contented stockman, anchored behind the vibrating steering wheel.

Hours later the vehicle shuddered to a halt and, feeling thoroughly shaken, they stepped down beside a parched creek bed.

With a broad grin of excitement he extended huge arms like the giant blades of a windmill and stated: 'See that country in front now? That's the headwaters of the Victoria River. When I get married I'm going to build my place there, my own cattle station.'

She saw only never ending horizons devoid of man-made interruptions. 'Poor bloody woman,' she muttered.

They devoured corned beef slabs trapped between thick, freshly baked chunks of bread in silent contemplation.

'Cup of tea?' the strapping young stockman asked.

He tossed the tea-leaves into the bubbling water, picked up the boiling billy with his well-worn hat, then swung it around vigorously.

She repeated with greater conviction: 'Poor bloody woman.'

CHAPTER 1

NIGHT DUTY
IN WARD 3

....

FEBRUARY 1963

'Good evening, I'm Nurse Augustus. You'll have to help me
with your names.'

The patient directly before me led the response. His smile
was big enough to light the universe. He lay in an extended plaster bed
which engulfed his body but obviously not his spirit.

'I'm big bad John,' he chuckled as he turned his head to fully engage
my attention. Beneath a short blond fringe, his blue eyes seemed to laugh
too and a special kind of boyish charm leapt out at me. According to his
records he was twenty-two; however he looked younger.

In the next bed was Geoff Collits, who tragically had become a quadriplegic
days after his twenty-first birthday. Although quietly spoken, his own brand
of humour surfaced instantly as he quickly returned John's light-hearted
banter. Geoff's gaze followed me with interest before looking up to his friend,
who lay on a higher level than anyone else. The specially designed plaster
cast was superimposed on a normal hospital bed. This meant my contact
with John was at eye level, whereas I had to bend to treat other patients
who were unable to sit up. Even as I moved beyond the two young men to
continue my introductions, I sensed John's positive attitude and influence.

From the window leading onto Burton Street, a voice called with a degree of urgency.

'Nurse, nurse, over here, quickly sweetheart, it's some medicine for the boys.' I was confronted with a carton of beer which someone's visitor shoved through the window into my arms, despite my protests. What to do?

'Don't worry nurse,' my charges chorused, 'it's old Pop's birthday and we are going to cheer him up.' Old Pop was gentle and very frail. I had to lean close to hear his whisper.

'Never touch the stuff, darlin'. Let 'em go though,' and as his paroxysm of coughing took over, I thought I heard, 'They surely need it.'

The senior nurse on duty with me emanated wisdom.

'You work it out and involve me if need be,' she advised.

It was no problem to oversee first and last drinks for those of my patients who relished a cold beer. After completion of the entire thirty-two night temperatures, charts and teas, I commenced hourly backs and pressure points in my ward.

John hurriedly pushed the empty cans under his plaster cast as the night superintendent appeared. On this extended routine ward round, she could not help but notice her normally subdued and often depressed patients were chortling with glee. I withstood her look of inquisition and wondered if she knew our secret. Fortunately, methylated spirits remained the dominant odour and later I scolded my charges as I massaged the nonfunctional areas of their leaden limbs.

'She was a good sort,' observed big bad John. He was incorrigible.

It was great to be back in uniform and even though I was still a junior nurse I now had a second blue stripe on my white belt. With five nursing friends I had only just returned from glittering Surfers Paradise. During that initial taste of freedom for most of us, we'd celebrated twelve months survival at Sydney's best teaching hospital, St Vincent's at Darlinghurst. I felt strongly that my small sense of achievement would swell to a roar in the remaining three years of training. Every patient offered a unique challenge.

During the spontaneous sharing of confidences that holidays evoke, we learned even more about each other than over intimate cups of coffee in the nurses' pantry. Feeling a little like a broken-down record, I repeated my intention to marry a farmer, someone from Moree or Mudgee or another area equally accessible to Sydney. Even though they'd heard it before, my friends wondered if I had a touch of the sun. Country men in moleskins were definitely the rage at the Royal Easter Show, but marriage? What about those good-looking new resident medical officers in white coats, the sun-tanned holidaymakers retorted.

They thought I was being simplistic and idealistic. Perhaps I was remembering my small-town Albury childhood with rose-coloured glasses, and clinging to an impossible dream of a life in the country, far removed from the pressures and turmoil of city life.

It was easy to imagine John on a horse. The young Territorian's medical records identified fractured lumbar vertebrae as a result of a horse riding accident. His subsequent hospitalisation in Darwin had not resolved his back injury. Upon his admission to St Vincent's, skilled orthopaedic surgeon Dr John Roarty had performed a spinal fusion and was pleased with his patient's progress. The current regime was to continue for twelve weeks; six days on his back with a turnover every seventh day.

When the main ward lights were extinguished, my work continued. Each patient required constant and thorough care and understanding. Geoff's wife and baby daughter were of more immediate concern to him than his own future. The man with the tracheotomy insisted on writing frequent messages in the hope of contributing to the philosophical observations of fellow patients. Whatever else happened during their day, it must have included a certain amount of sleep, because there was very little during my shift from 8 pm until 6.30 am.

At midnight our senior nurse stayed on duty while her middle or third-year nurse and I departed for supper. Although adequately lit, the hospital corridors were eerily empty. It was good to have company as we were all familiar with stories of the hospital ghost—the Grey Lady.

Six months earlier in the thoracic unit, Cameron Wing, a very ill patient on the tuberculosis floor had described to me the unusual colour of a nun's habit and the unusual hour of her visit.

'It was about two o'clock in the morning when she glided in, sat on my bed and held my hand reassuringly,' she explained. 'I felt safe and free of my dreadful pain. Nurse, please thank the sister in grey. She made sleep possible for the first time in weeks.'

My goose bumps were like porcupine quills and I had no doubt about the identity of the nun. However, as I continued the unpopular but ever necessary sputum rounds, I confirmed that none of our nursing nuns had been on duty or been involved in pastoral care in the early hours that morning.

Apparently she was a young nun whose love for a doctor had proved all powerful. She succumbed at a time when to leave the convent met with disapproval enough; to exchange her ring symbolic of lifetime dedication to God for a wedding ring was deemed unforgivable. Upon her death bed she had vowed to make restitution by helping all within the hospital she had been accused of deserting. I had good reason not to be among the sceptics who scorned the stories of her appearances.

I managed to extract an extra plate of icecream from the custodian of the night-duty kitchen and quickly returned to Ward 3.

'The only things more scarce than icecream where I come from are single women,' John confided. 'Thanks mate.'

He wanted me to know about his life and the more he explained, the less I could understand. He and his family lived a long way from everywhere. How could anyone work an area of 2400 square miles, I wondered.

'You must have a diversity of skills, John Underwood,' I offered.

'Well, I can fight a bit and skite a bit,' he admitted with the brilliant smile that gave hope and encouragement to Geoff and the others who, unlike John, would never walk again.

Three nights later he answered most of our unspoken questions. How could such a strong young man sustain such serious injuries? Where did his accident happen? Would he ride again? Who rescued him?

'I had been riding a mongrel horse all morning,' he told Geoff and the rest of us. Within our small ward there was not the space nor need for privacy. 'We were mustering a large area and going flat strap.'

'Who's we?' someone asked.

'The blackfellas in the stockcamp with me. Anyway, after dinner camp we all changed horses. I was now on a smart horse called King. I reckoned I was right for the rest of the day. We found the mob on a black soil plain near Peartree Bore. As they headed for the scrub I took off after them, confident because this time I was on a good horse. Without warning, King hit a hole, plaited his front feet and cartwheeled over on top of me. I had landed for an instant on my hands and knees and seconds later he had driven the saddle into the small of my back.'

How on earth did the ambulance system work in the extremely remote Northern Territory Outback, I wondered. As I progressed to my next patient, he continued.

'I knew I'd hurt my back, however I had to be moved. They lifted me onto an old table, lowered me onto the back of the Bedford truck and drove me over the pretty rough road into the station. Our only contact with the outside world was and still is via the Royal Flying Doctor radio. The doctor on call authorised my evacuation following Mum's medical report. Even though the plane was despatched immediately, they ran out of daylight and had to overnight at home.

'When I was eventually admitted to Darwin Hospital I couldn't believe my eyes when the bloke in the next bed turned out to be my old mate Lynny Hayes. He'd also had a fall while mustering. People who ride horses for fun are crazy, especially in our country. It's bloody dangerous because of the cracks in the black soil, gullies galore and the stony terrain.'

In silence I thought about his last comment. When my love affair with books intensified at a very early age, my dream to follow in the footsteps of ballerina Anna Pavlova was overtaken by the galloping hooves of Flicka and National Velvet. I lived to own a horse. My new dream was pursued with riding lessons in Centennial Park. We city folk rode horses not just for fun, but for the incomparable sheer exhilaration.

'How long were you there?' inquired Geoff a little impatiently.

There was no answer. Sleep had overtaken big bad John, representing healing and hope and peace.

The following night I asked John about his hospitalisation in Darwin. By the very nature of my night duty, his story was unfolding like a serial. He explained that with the graduated use of a walking machine, he noticeably improved. After repeated X-rays, John was given the all clear and discharged. Although he walked out of hospital, it quickly became obvious that his back was not right.

'It was my turn to go on holidays,' he continued. 'My destination was

Perth for the 1962 Empire Games. Everyone was worried about my back and Mum reckoned I should drive across to Sydney to see a specialist. So I kept on coming until I arrived here with the address in my pocket of a family relation, a gynaecologist called Dr Storman. He made a few phone calls and organised an appointment for me to see Dr John Roarty.'

Over the ensuing weeks John told me that he had completed his Diploma in Animal Husbandry at Gatton College in Queensland. With unusual resolve for someone his age he recognised his heritage. He called himself a true blue Aussie because his ancestors came out on the third fleet. It seemed important to him that he was sixth generation Australian. Apparently his family founder, James Underwood, was a convict sentenced to seven years in the penal colony for stealing goods to the value of thirty-nine shillings.

My own grandmother had built terraced houses in Windsor Street, Paddington, and we had often journeyed back with Dad through his childhood haunts. We traced his way to St Francis Xavier Church where he'd served early morning Mass. Through Piper's Lane (or Captain Piper's Lane, as it was called then) and down Jersey Road we had wandered. Hence I was reasonably familiar with the suburb not far away from St Vincent's and now wondered if this young man from the centre of Australia could possibly have any family connections with Underwood Street, Paddington. For someone who reckoned he didn't know too much detailed family history, he had an attentive audience.

It was extraordinary to learn that the name of the Sydney suburb Paddington was derived from Paddington House, the English home of the same James Underwood and Underwood Street and Lane in that suburb were also named after him.

'Subject closed,' John stated, extending his arm in my direction. 'Now something far more interesting. I want to know if you have a serious boyfriend.'

'One topic at a time,' I countered as I attended to another patient. 'Let's finish you first.'

His sense of history and sense of heritage really impressed me. So did his good nature as he readily obliged.

'Well, ever since those early years when James Underwood and his brother Joseph invested in wide tracts of farming land with more than a thousand head of cattle on hand, way back in the 1820s I think it was, our family has continued to be farmers and graziers. Both sets of my grandparents were from Queensland cattle stations. Maybe I was born lucky. Anyway, I can't wait to go home and get stuck into it.'

I looked forward to eight o'clock each night. There was an air of expectancy about my patients too and they'd welcome me with wolf whistles and big smiles, anxious for my news and that of the outside world. Even though I read thoroughly each night their daily progressive medical reports, they wanted to share their news with me, what the specialist had said, what the physiotherapist had said. In their darkest moments in the dark of night, I listened to their frustrations and heartaches.

As the busy nights passed, I gradually became a little more familiar with just what John Underwood meant by 'getting stuck into it'. He talked about mustering cattle over vast tracts of land, branding and castrating, bronco panels and Condamine bells. For me these were words with limited meaning and of little consequence. However, his commitment and involvement were more than impressive.

He was like an encyclopaedia and every night we heard something new. Instead of our four seasons they in the Northern Territory had only two. In the Wet Season they awaited sufficient rain to grow new grasses and fill the billabongs and waterholes along the creeks. John would make greenhide ropes, hobbles and counter-lined saddles. In the Dry Season the grasses hayed off and temperatures dropped, signalling the time for working cattle. It was the time when stockmen and ringers willingly responded to the demanding challenges of mustering cattle across unfathomable expanses of unfenced land.

There was never time to hear enough about life on his cattle station that was four hundred miles south-west of Katherine and nearly in Western Australia.

John's cheerful acceptance of his confinement increased my admiration for him. Normally so active, he was uncomplaining about the restrictions imposed by the stiff plaster cast created to accommodate his six foot three and a half inch frame.

I asked him about the rest of his family.

'Mum and Dad were so pleased with me that they kept having babies, hoping for a repeat. Along came Suzanne, then Patricia, then Marion and

Anna and finally Reg. Imagine four daughters before another young John.'

The dimness hid my smile. I had a feeling there could never be another one of his mould.

Before going off duty, I suggested to John that he refrain from winking at the nuns and wait for the arrival of the occupational therapist. He readily agreed. Having already invited her out, he felt it quite appropriate. Little did she know that she was one of fifteen helpful hospital females whom Mr Underwood intended to shout a feed in order to express his gratitude. While the generous spirit and infectious enthusiasm of this young Territory cattleman endeared him to everyone, I decided that I was certainly not going to become his first or last date. The list was long enough.

It was knock-off time. Geoff called me over as I asked for any last-minute requests.

'He reckons he is going to marry you, you know,' he whispered. 'Told me so on your first night here.'

I smiled with understanding at the vulnerability and gratitude of patients and the various ways these feelings surface.

'You better believe it. He's fair dinkum,' Geoff insisted.

I wished them all good day and hurried to my room.

It was a relief to remove the good old nurse's cap. I exchanged it for our unofficial informal uniform item, the ever reliable all-weather coat, and in the company of a fellow nurse headed for a popular breakfast venue at nearby Kings Cross. Many a prostitute from the infamous Cross who had been to Casualty or been treated elsewhere in our hospital recognised the coat-over-uniform brigade. They were always anxious to talk and thank us. As Barbara showed her most recent bruises, her tears disproved her brittleness. She had long been abused by a well-known celebrity singer from whom she knew no escape. Once again I listened. Her desperation increased by an almost fatalistic sense of being trapped reminded me of other kinds of illnesses. The basic needs for recognition and love, as well as shelter and warmth, were never more critically absent than from the tormented lives of those with whom we shared tea and toast on many an occasion that signalled the end of their shift and ours.

Three months after I started in Ward 3, I arrived on duty to meet to my astonishment the patient previously only seen in a horizontal position actually standing before me. John was so tall! With the support of a back brace he walked comfortably. We were all very thrilled by his progress.

One of the day staff recounted the thoughtfulness of John towards fellow patient Geoff, who was spending limited periods in a wheel-chair. Kind Mr Underwood had offered to push his mate out to the lawn area for some fresh air. They were sighted beside the garden seat beneath the statue of the Blessed Virgin, enjoying the sunshine and freedom. Sometime later two ruddy-faced, broadly beaming fellows noisily returned to their ward. I could visualise them so clearly. Less attention was paid to their glowing faces than to Geoff's near-bursting urinal bag. It had been a quick dart across the back road to the famous Wedge Hotel. Though shaped as it was named, it served good cold beer.

John worried about Geoff. Tomorrow John was to be discharged and he wanted desperately to secure from me 'yes' to two questions before leaving hospital. If Geoff was given leave of absence, would I on my night off accompany him to a special party? I agreed and asked what I should bring.

'Don't worry about anything,' he assured me, 'the job is right. Secondly, you have been good to me and I really want to take you out. Please.' There was no need for his disarming grin because I was already acutely aware of the gap his departure would create in the ward. Geoff and I would miss him most of all. We agreed to meet at St Leonards railway station for a cup of tea the following evening before I commenced duty.

John was looking decidedly sheepish when I joined him at the designated meeting place. I was surprised how different he looked dressed in normal clothes. He seemed preoccupied as he guided me down a side street to where a tow truck was attached to a car. It was his car! The tow truck pulled the car forward until all four wheels were back on the road. Having paid the driver, John checked for marks or scratches and then we walked around the corner to the coffee shop.

As I slid into the cubicle, John carefully followed. His bulky brace left little space between the table and the back of the chair. I couldn't wait to hear about his dilemma. He explained that it had seemed a reasonable place to park, particularly as there had not been a lot of choice. For one reason or another he had misjudged the edge of the bitumen, as he called the road, and as he backed in, the two passenger-side wheels had dropped over the edge of a steep bank and started spinning. There was no way he could move the car. The only good thing was the proximity of a public phone box.

'Can't believe a man can drive through the roughest scrub and meanest roads all his life and come to the city to get bogged on the bloody bitumen,' he groaned. It was so ridiculous that we both burst out laughing.

'Anyway, it's just as well there's no damage done because tomorrow I'm trading it in for a working vehicle to drive home.'

There could never have been any awkwardness between patient and nurse in our case. We were friends who knew each other well and yet knew virtually nothing about each other. He dropped me at the hospital and confirmed the party for the following night.

It was to be held at the Northbridge home of the Sheils, the parents of John's mate David Sheil who worked on the property adjoining John's home, Inverway Station. David had urged John to make himself known to his family upon his arrival in Sydney. Until her dying day, Mrs Sheil talked about the strapping young stockman who came for a cup of tea and stayed for four months. From that very first contact until John left Sydney after his operation, the Sheil home provided a Sydney base for John and security for his car.

Within the comfortable homely environment, friends shed any familiar shackles of authority associated with hospital to unite for the last time before the inevitable farewells. Geoff and his wife Margaret were struggling to come to terms with what lay ahead of them. I played the piano, they sang a little, John produced a most impressive array of quality wines and the party began in earnest. Our caretaker host toasted his hosts, the Sheils, whose Queensland holiday was in full swing. So were we. As the wine flowed so did the doubts, the frustrations and fears. Friendship cemented the magic of the night and yet no-one lost sight of tomorrow and tomorrow and tomorrow.

Mr Sheil, a serious connoisseur and collector of wine, was astounded and dismayed upon his return to discover outrageously shiny protruders positioned throughout the dusty shelves of his sacred cellar. The bottles of Johnny Walker had been used as substitutes for missing prestigious vintage wines. However he, like his wife, had a rare capacity to make allowances for well-intentioned youth.

I was walking briskly down Victoria Street returning from Sunday Mass to go back on duty when I heard an unusual beep! beep! A tall figure in a tall hat manoeuvred his brand new Willy's Jeep alongside me. He was brimming over with excitement.

'Thanks for everything mate! I'm off now, I'm going home,' he said with his dazzling smile.

'Goodbye John Underwood. Look after yourself,' I waved.

The first postcard arrived five days later.

I think you're a bit of a darling. Love John.

Six months later his letters began: *Terry darling.* The intermittent letters became weekly letters. I thought it was important to evaluate our friendship. He reminded me that he had been to Sydney and insisted that I head north.

CHAPTER 2

A SPECIAL
CALLING

....

My restlessness was fuelled by cement and skyscrapers, congested channels of traffic and bodies banded together surging through the confines of narrow streets. There was no volume control button on the infernal sounds of the city. I yearned for someone earthy and rock solid. More and more the artificiality of urban living, the repetitious tracks, the pitfalls and pedestals were decidedly not for me. They would best be addressed by others. At the wonderful age of nineteen years, I knew myself too well. I wanted to marry a farmer and live as a wife and mother in the country.

My beginnings coincided with the conclusion of World War II. Beneath Monument Hill in Albury, the town on the NSW–Victoria border where I lived for the first ten years of my life, children played hopscotch in the streets and the horse-drawn milk cart clip-clopped past sleepy houses. My biggest challenge was to carry the enamel billy can containing freshly ladled milk back into the kitchen without spilling a drop.

Our spacious garden was a magnificent mixture of jonquils, tulips, roses, and masses of mixed flowers. The fruits of our overladen fig, cherry and peach trees were exchanged for scrumptious home-grown almonds from a neighbour. Out the back the best cubbyhouse in the world accommodated hours and hours of make-believe. Childhood magic effortlessly transformed the interior from hospital to florist shop to Indian tepee.

None of us ever ventured very far from home. There were always picnics on Sundays. Duck feeding at Yackandandah was my favourite outing and we usually passed gypsies wherever we travelled. The Murray River housed the Hume Weir and another familiar picnic location was Noriel Park. It was here that without warning a whirlpool claimed me when I was three years old. I submerged in helpless terror as it swirled and swished and sucked me around and under. Dad, a gentle, slightly built man, emitted superhuman strength as he hit the water to save me.

As a four year old I became big sister to brother Johnny. After his baptism we celebrated at a local cafe where I was allowed a whole Violet Crumble bar for myself. This indeed was a day like no other. Elder sisters Anne and Libby had a head start on us and seemingly forever after we younger two were addressed with the prefix 'little'. How could I know that for me this would last a lifetime?

It was always safe to ride to school on my tiny bike, but I had to pedal furiously to keep up with Anne and Libby. In the hottest of summers the nuns insisted on winter uniforms for our school visit to Wagga Wagga by steam train to wave at Queen Elizabeth II, visiting the rural city during her 1954 tour of Australia. I wondered if she noticed the fainting bodies falling like autumn leaves. On the return trip the sensibly dressed pupils from the public schools taunted:

'Catholics Catholics go to hell
While the publics ring the bell.'

There was in our world an eternal preoccupation with religious denomination.

On our way to Mass on a wet Sunday we would cover our mouths with handkerchiefs to avoid catching raindrops and breaking the required communion fast. The parish church, St Patrick's, was not only our Sunday place of worship, but the focal point of our lives. It was in this beautiful church adjoining our school, St Joseph's Ladies College, that we attended novenas, benedictions, retreats and sodality meetings. The smell of incense evoked mystery and reverence. So did the exquisitely perfumed rose petals that, as a little flower girl, I kissed and released to form a carpet for the celebrant leading the church procession. Our family always sat in the front pew so we wouldn't be distracted by anyone or anything. Mum and Dad silently prayed with closed eyes and moving lips and I wondered if I would ever be as devout as they. I had to wait for the communion queue to see who else was at Mass and what they were wearing.

Like religion, music was an integral part of our upbringing. Piano lessons commenced as soon as I turned five and I remember thinking that my wrinkled, bespectacled teacher was probably as old as Methuselah. She was kind and patient and sat me on several pillows so that I could comfortably reach the keys. The tiny scratch on middle C could only be seen by someone at my visual level and so Miss Perry was extremely impressed with my unerring recognition of this location key. With straightened back and a deep voice, she announced to my parents that I showed exceptional promise.

Whether it was a deep passion for the arts or misguided ambition, I experimented with almost every possible musical endeavour. The drum lessons were short-lived when the nuns discovered that the instructor concentrated on lessons from his knee rather than the appropriate stool. He was given immediate notice and shown one-way exit gates. May and June were two sisters who taught ballet and tap dancing respectively and with absolute joy I attended their classes. My transition from silent pirouettes and prolonged practice at the barre to the loud bouncing rhythm of toe tap, heel tap, shuffle shuffle was effortless.

Sister Thérèse, my namesake, was an excellent violin teacher. She encouraged daily practice after school in the music rooms before I walked home, proudly carrying my violin case and hoping that everyone would notice that I was a musician. Music was the food of my soul.

Apart from church events and school concerts, the other exciting outing was on Saturday afternoons to the picture theatre. This special treat was sometimes doubled with the purchase of a penny icecream and we competed to see whose icecream could last the longest. The black and white serial 'Spiderman' was so frightening and always managed to finish at the most gripping, nail-biting point and then we'd have to wait an endless week for the next series of events as good and evil continued to come to blows. Most of our entertainment came from serials on the home wireless. We waited patiently for each episode of 'Sparky and the Magic Piano', 'Biggles', 'Hop Harrigan', 'Yes What' and 'The Argonaut Club'.

It was a time when a glimpse of cleavage was not just provocative, but sinful. It was a time for Morning Offerings, prayers before lessons and meals and the family rosary at night. How often we were reminded that more things are wrought by prayer than this world dreams of and the family that prays together stays together.

Our faith involved much more than words. It was dogmatically applied to the business of day-to-day living and the purpose of our existence. We grew and learned in an environment based on deep love, hard work and consideration of others.

The missionary priests and nuns who carried the love of God to poverty-stricken overseas countries were always in need of financial support. My special cause became the Catholic Missions. Having collected cardboard cut-out circus figures from Cornflakes packets, I assembled a ready-made Big Top and charged a penny entry fee. Our garage became the venue for mini fetes and pantomimes. All the kids in the neighbourhood tried out for my production of Cinderella and the eventual performances enticed a huge crowd of mission supporters, namely parents and friends.

There were terrifying bushfires and irritating chilblains in this Riverina haven. There were Friday fish and chips nights in front of blazing log fires. Although the parish priest or nuns enjoyed family company whenever they visited, they preferred to have afternoon tea in privacy behind the closed doors of our lounge room. The indescribable smell of freshly raked, burning autumn leaves was almost addictive. We played with swap cards and silkworms in shoe boxes, fiddlesticks and jacks saved from Sunday roasts.

It was a beginning I wanted to maintain for my ending. I wanted to stay in Albury for the rest of my life.

My family returned to Sydney at the end of 1954. At the foot of a steep hill our old brick home nestled amongst a rambling split level garden, seemingly designed for Dad's tireless love of planting, pruning and weeding. Outside my bedroom window a winding creek played a constant murmur until heavy rainfall caused flash flooding and a deafening crescendo, and the base of our little white bridge became invisible. In contrast, from the top of the hill the blanket of smog over the distant city was frequently visible on my walk home from school. It seemed another world compared to the immediate surrounds of prolific gardens and natural bushland.

'A penny saved is a pound earned,' Mum reminded us. Wrapped in a warm dressing gown and carrying secateurs and a cleverly constructed rake, on many a winter's morning she would carefully select unmarked blooms from the higher branches. I stood beside her to collect as she plucked. Once inside Mum and I individually wrapped each camellia and magnolia in moist tissue paper. She then packaged them into large flat boxes and secured them with strong string before entrusting them to my sisters, who nursed their fragile cargo on the crowded city bound peak-hour trains. On their way to work Anne and Libby delivered these fresher than fresh blooms to a leading Sydney florist. We were always aware of the value of a shilling.

No-one was aware of my fretting for Albury. It was an emotional tangle which often overtook me at night. Seeking solace, I would climb our garden trees in order to be closer to the glorious sky, the one shared by country and city.

However, the resilience of youth gradually surfaced. My yearnings for yesterdays were replaced by a very real love for a beautiful city that pulsated with excitement. It commanded a response from its inhabitants. There were opportunities and experiences for adolescents and teenagers in particular that no small town could offer. The Elizabethan Theatre was then the city's cultural centre and we attended operas, musicals and ballets with luxurious regularity. Exposure to these performances enhanced my love and appreciation of the arts. To witness Margot Fonteyn and Joan Sutherland on stage was a thrill beyond description. I fell in and out of love with different musicals and wonder still how Mum tolerated the radiogram playing *The King And I* soundtrack repetitively for a fortnight, after which time I sang every word of every role with gay abandon. That was when Anne wistfully inquired if the record player was broken.

It was an era of trendsetters and followings, a time of changing cultures. Bodgies and widgies wearing luminous clothes affronted the blue-rinse set. Beatnik parties and beer gardens at the Newport Arms beckoned. If only I enjoyed the freedom to attend every gathering as zealously as some of my school friends. The Mouseketeers and Beatles took respective age groups by storm. When Col Joye finally appeared outside the Rex Hotel at Kings Cross, he penned his autograph on my arm. I was still proudly showing everyone the carefully preserved smudge a week later. Johnny O'Keefe was also everyone's hero, and following his concert I witnessed the performances of the Vienna Boys' Choir and visiting violinist Christian Ferras at the Sydney Town Hall. For as long as I could remember my love of music afforded equal appreciation of most operas, classical concertos and the rhythm and beat of good old rock and roll.

During my final year at school, most girls faced a choice between teaching, nursing or hairdressing, while the remainder of us enrolled for business courses. At the completion of my Leaving Certificate I turned seventeen. That was the day my application for general nursing training at St Vincent's Hospital was accepted. This heralded the beginning of the rest of my life.

I loved people, babies and the elderly in particular. Mum had only ever taken a break from nursing my grandmother who lived with us when I was able to relieve her. For a while it had been a toss up between teaching and nursing, but my future farmer husband and I would hopefully have beautifully healthy babies in some country cottage. Motherhood and teaching went hand in glove. To mould and guide my own little ones through life's journey would be not only the epitome of teaching, but would provide the most demanding challenge of all. Motherhood and teaching would be inevitable, I hoped. I therefore preferred to look for a different profession—that left nursing in neon lights. My adolescent energies were best directed toward helping the sick and dying. I thought I would make a good nurse because I cared about people and, moreover, I never did anything by halves.

On my first morning at St Vincent's, I walked briskly through the double doors of the room where trainees had been instructed to gather for inauguration into their preliminary training school. Further progress was impossible. The room was packed with a fairly mixed representation of blondes, brunettes and dark-haired women. Although we were all similar in age, shapes and sizes were many and varied. Everyone seemed to be talking at once. The almost palpable vibrancy and sense of anticipation were remarkable, simply because we were all strangers. That was to be short-lived.

A loud bell sliced through the babble and a single voice of authority requested everyone to take a seat. We sat upright and listened attentively to a petite sister with red hair and freckles. Her soft, shy, impish appearance conflicted with her words. There was no doubting her intention and I sensed that the discipline that had been a part of my family life would stand me in good stead.

After referring to the importance of personal appearances and impressions, she informed us that by the afternoon session we were to remove all jewellery, nail polish and any other artificial accessories. Our fingernails were to be short and clean. One or two chins lifted noticeably and I thought if there was a problem so early in the piece then it would probably be a good time for any fashion plate to make her escape.

'No faltering, distractions or second-rate performances will be tolerated,' another sister advised from centre stage. Although plump and smiling, the same suggestion of steel accompanied her message.

'From now on you are dealing with life and death, sickness and suffering, healing and recovery and you must honour your commitment with reliability and compassion. Above all, the dignity of human life is sacred. Hospital and nursing home rules are in place for a purpose and you are expected to uphold them at all times. Good nurses remain focused and dedicated. However, it is well to remember that there may be occasions when the burden seems too heavy and it is then, with help from others, you will find the strength to continue. Yours is a special calling and we welcome you all. You must be true to your hospital and true to yourselves. Any questions?'

The long-limbed, angular girl next to me had fidgeted constantly. Frowning, she leaned over and whispered, 'I'm not sure this is my scene.'

'Too soon to tell,' I whispered back. We had not even seen over the hospital, let alone met any patients. Little did we know that those experiences were well down the track and that we were just doing basic warm-ups. Nonetheless, I determined then and there to prove worthy to carry the lamp held aloft by Florence Nightingale and St Vincent's first matron, Sister Baptiste de Lacy, as a beckoning star to future generations.

The laundry cubicles were an urgent priority. Once we'd been shown how to attach white collar and cuffs to the blue and white check dresses, we tried on our new uniforms. All of a sudden everyone looked quite professional. There was only one problem. The wrap-around aprons were too long, especially on people of my diminutive five foot two and a quarter inch stature. Despite feeling I had donned a large white cotton ball gown, I secured my belt with its silver buckle and finally tucked my hair into the hygienic, white cap. It did not take me long to learn the tricks of the trade. A friendly group of nurses passing by stopped and laughed at my ankle-length apron. They showed me how to make the required adjustment. Unfortunately, later that very same day I was stopped by a senior sister who asked me to remove my belt and unwind my apron to its full length. New recruits were obviously vulnerable, but a good learner is a quick learner and all but two of our initial group measured up impressively.

Over morning tea weeks later, I chatted quietly with a small group of other trainees reflecting on our progress. It occurred to me then that the point of no return had well and truly been passed. With renewed resolve to care for the sick and injured, we learned and practised nursing techniques with increasing confidence. We took each other's temperatures, pulse rates and blood pressures. From books and charts, dummy patients and skeletons, we learned anatomy and physiology. Instruments were identified and trays for various medical and surgical procedures were set up over and over again. Inside laboratories, we examined diagnostic procedures and observed various healing processes, both physical and mental. It was so different from school classes, for questions and discussions were encouraged.

Bed making was no ordinary affair and the slightest imperfection resulted in the bed being stripped with the order to remake it correctly. I was amazed just how many types of beds there were to make, how many charts to keep, how many drugs to learn about and how all progress commenced in the pan room. New nurses were usually entrusted with 'bed pan alley', the flower room or foolproof dusting and polishing. I broke bed making records and scrubbed pans and toilets until the dimmest took on a new sparkle. At the compulsory invalid cookery classes, we exchanged news as we coddled eggs and whisked custards. It was all good for the soul, but the heart of a nurse beats for her patients. Of necessity we acquired patience.

Respect for seniority was an automatic unwritten rule. Upon entering or leaving a lift, juniors stood their ground until all those in authority preceded them. It was amazing to witness this orderly file of people moving about their business, individuals interconnected as they worked side by side to comfort, assist and heal others. I was forever aware of the privilege of belonging to such an auspicious, effective medical team.

Annie, Jill and Ros had all attended the same city convent school and so more or less spoke the same language. Anne and Colleen were as different as cheese and chalk, Flissy was like a pretty Dresden doll and Jasmyne was the drama queen of our core group. We all coped differently with the demands and expectations of our training. One of the most difficult struggles for each of us was to leave heartaches and problems behind when we finished a shift. Within the informal atmosphere of the downstairs nurses' pantry, emotions flowed freely. Over countless cups of coffee we laughed hysterically and cried uncontrollably. As predicted, many needed support while others provided it. To maintain equilibrium was essential.

We didn't earn much money, we worked broken shifts and attended ongoing lectures—and the nearby doctors' residence was out of bounds. Yet despite the odds, most of us managed to squeeze in a social life of sorts. Whenever we found a party, Ros and I were the last ones home.

CHAPTER 3

A RELUCTANT CHAPERONE

....

Together with my home values, the St Vincent's training laid the foundation stone for the remainder of my life. An extraordinary blend of toughness and softness was necessary to cope with our complicated and unpredictable world. It was also a time that established rock solid foundations for lifelong friendships.

My olive green Morris Oxford car, like an invincible army tank, painfully but purposefully conquered the steep hills between Darlinghurst and Pymble. Yet it was always good to return home on days off. Leaving behind the cramped, crowded structures of the inner city for the picturesque leafy suburbs was reviving. Although I loved nursing, I still dreamed about my cottage in the country.

As we finished the last decade of our nightly family recitation of the rosary, I mentioned casually that I had been invited to visit a friend in the Northern Territory.

'We don't know anyone way up there, do we?' questioned Dad.

'I thought you liked sunny Surfers forever,' commented Anne.

'Holidays again; lucky you,' stated Libby.

'How boring!' exclaimed sixteen-year-old brother Johnny.

'Where did you meet her?' inquired Mum.

My parents' reluctance to endorse a trip to see an ex-patient in an extremely remote part of our continent was not surprising. Just who was this young man for whom I was prepared to break hospital rules? How could I contemplate going out with someone from another world and another religion? I explained that he was the one whose regular letters arrived at home as well as the hospital. Of course my letters to him were no secret and the ensuing discussions became less intense.

The compromise came in an unexpected form. 'Terry, your brother must go too. It will be a lovely adventure for you both.'

Having just completed his Leaving Certificate, Johnny was looking forward to the sandhills of popular Bungan Beach, to catch a few waves and mingle with the crowd where it all happened. He took some persuading that the complimentary airline ticket was the very best thing that could possibly happen.

With numerous instructions and loving goodbyes, we boarded our first flight with a degree of anticipation and perturbation. The aerial views of the cluttered city teeming with activity seemed to reinforce the insignificance of the individual inhabitants. With surprising speed the sights beneath us changed to a widespread rural mosaic and later still to a multi-coloured arid landscape far below. It was an awesome view of our vast and diverse country. The adventure of a lifetime was under way.

From the door of the jet, the unexpected heat seemed like a vortex, intent on sucking us out of the protective, dim, cool corridor. Why hadn't the tarmac melted, I wondered. Even young eyes objected to the savage glare and we determined to purchase sunglasses at the earliest opportunity. During the long drive from the Alice Springs airport to the township, sunlight bounced from every red grain of dirt and rock. The incredibly fiery hues of the Red Centre pulsed hotly through the haze of heat. The stark beauty of the surroundings took us by surprise. At the motel the slow whirring of overhead fans and curtained rooms offered welcome relief. Sydney seemed grey and far removed.

At eight o'clock the following morning, we returned to the airport with a sense of familiarity. Endeavouring not to appear over anxious, we responded to the boarding call of the Connellan Airways pilot.

'Bob's the name. How're you going? Sit wherever you like,' he advised.

I was disappointed to discover that this would not be a direct flight to our destination. My present for John, a package of mixed chocolate blocks, already appeared shapeless and pulpy. As the small aircraft which carried more cargo than passengers staggered into the cloudless sky, I placed the package beneath my seat.

From Yuendumu we flew in a northerly direction. Thermals played constantly as we climbed, levelled out and yawed onwards. With evident concentration and satisfaction, the pilot was preoccupied with maps and instruments. From the cockpit he shouted loudly over the noisy engines.

'Lucky it's not too bumpy today.'

Johnny and I competed for a paler shade of grey. Eventually we landed at Hooker Creek.

The intense blast of hot air was almost a welcome alternative to the turbulent flight. Black eyes from black faces gazed at us in disbelief as though we hailed from another planet. Unable to comprehend the total desolation, we could well have been. The Aborigines chattered as they pointed in our direction. My newly purchased white crimplene suit with matching white stockings and shoes provided little protection from the devouring heat and the ferocious flies. With his suit sticking firmly to his sweating body, Johnny tried to smile.

'Help yourself to cool drinks,' called the pilot, waving in the general direction of an open shelter consisting of wooden posts supporting a roof made from dried branches and leaves. As we walked towards it, little black fingers clutched and plucked at my stockings from behind. Curious fixed stares from the grinning parents made my protests ineffective. We walked faster.

Hanging limply from the centre of the shelter on an old wire hook was a grubby hessian water bag. The odd drip of water seemed to evaporate before reaching the hard ground. Johnny unscrewed the cap and handed it to me.

'Thirsty?' he asked.

Thankfully I moistened my lips. It was his turn.

Feeling like the main attraction at a sideshow, I hurried back to the plane. Even our movements were out of context, for the native people either sat cross-legged or languidly strolled around. There was little conversation or shade as we stood beneath the wing during refuelling. It was too hot to talk and, besides, the smell of aviation fuel was sickening.

'All aboard,' announced our jolly pilot, 'next stop Inverway.'

The hour flight seemed interminable. Finally we began our descent and eventually, as one wing dipped, I managed to catch a glimpse of buildings amongst trees. As our wheels touched down on yet another dirt airstrip, I had a very real sense of being a long, long way from the rest of the world. Upon alighting I gazed around in disbelief. The welcoming committee consisted of a motionless giant windsock.

'Won't be long,' informed Bob as he unpacked boxes and a well-filled mail bag. 'It takes them a few minutes to drive here after they hear us fly over, you know.' How could I know that, or anything else relevant, I asked myself. The obvious was far from obvious to the city visitors. 'Are you the new governess, love?' he continued.

Beneath a cloud of billowing dust a familiar Willy's Jeep approached. As it slowed, red particles gravitated towards me with determination. It was as though someone had upturned a gigantic salt shaker filled with red dust all over me. John's huge smile of welcome radiated the only visible white. His blue shirt highlighted his eyes, bluer than the sky above. Suddenly I felt as though I was back in an air pocket, only it was my heart that was tumbling in free fall. It had been two whole years and now as he uncoiled he appeared much leaner and even longer than I remembered. I seemed to disappear in his bear hug welcome. The two Johns shook hands.

'Go0day.'

The pilot called, 'So long. See you in a fortnight.' The propeller blades turned with hesitation before spluttering into a spin. As the plane taxied, I relinquished my last contact with urban Australia. Within seconds the speck on the horizon was the only record of our journey.

Our suitcases looked almost new amongst the tyres and tools in the back of the Jeep. We drove through a wire gate onto a narrow strip which was in fact the wall of a dam. Our tyres straddled the entire width of the wall. As I looked down into the brown water surrounded by deeply cracked black soil, I was fearful of tipping down the bank. However, John was totally in control and we progressed without mishap. Suddenly an explosive cloud of white corellas raucously erupted from the tree tops, screeching and regrouping as they swooped in an arc of inspection. The sunlight played on their wing tips and I remarked on their beauty.

'Destructive bloody things,' John replied.

I glanced sideways at him. No longer the patient, he was now the man who worked and understood his country. Passing stockyards and stables, we eventually arrived at the homestead. Brilliantly coloured bougainvillea adorned the trellis above the front gate. Unusual and irregularly shaped stepping stones formed a winding pathway to the double glass doors. They were wide open and John led the way inside. Thankfully we followed. It was good to have finally arrived.

The attractive, simply furnished rooms that unfolded had been recently added to the original tin shed, John explained.

'I'll leave your gear here,' he announced as we reached the large open sleep-out verandahs. 'Out there is where we all sleep while it's so hot.' He signalled to the lawn area beyond, where there were three wire-based camp stretchers side by side. Johnny had been noticeably silent, but it was then that a small sigh escaped him.

Across the top of the piano were framed family portraits and John proudly introduced his four sisters and young brother, Reg, fifteen years his junior. A statement he'd made in hospital that 'they all bore the same brand' now took on a new meaning. A quick change into more sensible clothes was overdue, but wherever we went and whatever we did, flies in their hundreds faithfully followed. John called them friendly but we found them almost intolerable. In a black cloud they clung to our sweaty backs and when disturbed rose momentarily, before immediately resettling.

In the meantime John had prepared lunch: three plates filled with equal servings of thick slices of corned beef and beetroot surrounded by generous portions of bread.

'The old man and I share the cooking while Mum's in Perth settling the girls into boarding school. She was really crooked that she's missed out on getting to know you. Anyway, bet you've never tasted brisket as good as this. All home-grown,' he announced. 'Everything here is of course.'

When I poured the tea, he lifted his huge mug and laughed.

'Welcome to Inverway,' he said.

It was the middle of the Wet Season, but clouds refused to form even though temperatures soared daily well in excess of 105 degrees Fahrenheit. The seriousness of the drought was a reality. For the third year in a row the Wet had virtually been a non-event and John was concerned that it could even be a dry decade.

'In the bush, everything is cyclical,' he explained. 'Things tend to happen in decades. We just have to tough it out and do the best we can for our stock.'

There were no permanent watering points as rivers and creeks had long since dried up. Bores—drilled holes into the depths of the earth that were equipped with engines and pump jacks—meant that underground or bore water could be pumped into troughs and dams to water cattle. Although there were windmills on Inverway, the days were still and stifling. There was no wind and consequently no water. When John told us that older cattle can drink up to ten gallons a day, the repercussions of the water situation took on a whole new meaning. To think that we city folk had merely to turn a tap to access fresh clean water all year round was sobering.

Towards mid afternoon as I watched with fascination John repairing a well-used packsaddle in the saddle shed, we heard a vehicle pull up outside.

'That'll be the old man,' John advised.

The man who peered through the doorway was stocky, dark-haired and frowning. 'Gooday. Where's the other one?' he grunted.

I told him that Johnny was over at the homestead.

Reading my thoughts, John spoke as he tied the last stitch.

'The pressure is always on at times like this, and Dad's probably worried that your presence will interrupt my work. Don't worry, he doesn't know you like I do.'

We wandered out into the glare and heat.

My eyes were still adjusting to the luxury of endless horizons.

'You didn't tell me that you kept sheep,' I commented as I squinted across the shimmering distance at small white dots. He grinned.

'You're going to learn a lot about us, aren't you?'

Aborigines beside their shelters were silhouetted against the setting sun.

'You'll meet them tomorrow,' John promised. 'They live and work here.'

It was all so strange. There was so much space for so few people.

The pre-dinner ritual of a chilled beer after a lukewarm shower from the cold tap was strictly observed. Despite the heat which darkness had done little to dissipate, the combustion stove in the large, practical kitchen was the meeting place. When Johnny and I arrived, I couldn't stop smiling at John. He winked and said he still couldn't believe that we were together. For an altogether different reason I couldn't believe my eyes. Stretching upwards, I ran my hand across his upper forehead which, now grime free, was almost white compared to the rest of his weathered face. Then I looked across at Mr Underwood. His face was similar. Stock hats that shielded their upper foreheads had left their mark. Father and son were living proof that men never ventured outside without hats in this scorching, sundrenched land. I could not remember a beer ever tasting so good.

We were joined by a tall, thin man, Lee Graham, who announced that his claim to fame was as jockey and handyman. He and his brother Nick had previously spent years in John's stockcamp. Old Mark's entrance confirmed his occupation as horse trainer. With bowed legs, he walked as though still astride his mount, but reminded everyone that he too was general handyman when he wasn't handling horses. The conversation turned immediately to horses and racing.

During our delicious corned beef curry, a Mr Underwood special, the four locals discussed prospects for the mid-year racing circuit. They were extremely serious about breeding their own stockhorses and racehorses, breaking them in and selecting the 'most likely' for training, trialling and ultimately racing.

John's deep passion for horses and racing was a surprise. Mr Underwood fancied Audacity, while Mark put all his faith in Kingdom Come. With unprecedented conviction, John and Lee declared that Willie Win would prove unbeatable at every start. They explained that August signalled four consecutive race meetings, hundreds of miles apart, and depending on results, racehorses were kept on the circuit or returned home. The culture of the bush surfaced with unexpected clarity. The races were evidently not just the highlight of the year, but the only social events on the bush calendar. Every man and his dog made it their business to be there. When the racehorses were verbally 'given a spell', opinionated discussions continued about the associated rodeo and gymkhana events.

After dinner Johnny and I helped wash up as conversation returned to the drought. Johnny said goodnight then disappeared towards bed. Aware that I was having a much better time than he, I followed. I watched with amusement as he scrambled onto unbleached sheets covering a thin fibre mattress cloistered by a green mosquito net.

'Thanks for coming. 'Night.'

I returned to where John was awaiting me. Beneath an ancient bauhinia tree, we talked and laughed with the delicious realisation that we were still mates. As the splendid moonlight playfully traced mysterious patterns on the silent shrubs and lawns, he gathered me into his arms and kissed me.

It was still dark when the sound of the generator being started aroused the sleepy. Shortly afterwards the breakfast bell clamoured. It was already hot and the flies were everywhere. Over steak and eggs smothered with onion gravy, John and his father talked through the day's proposed programme. Collective energies were totally channelled into managing the station, reeling under the influence of another dry Wet.

An hour later John and we Sydneysiders climbed aboard the only spare vehicle. As we drove past their camp, the Aborigines waved. At the first gate, John pointed out the goat yard constructed from flattened forty-four gallon drums.

'There's your shearing shed,' he laughed. Pointing to the goat herd grazing in the distance, he identified the source of 'Kimberley mutton', fresh milk and home-made butter and cream.

We saw Inverway cattle for the first time. 'Hope it rains for you soon, you poor old dears,' John called out as we rattled past. Heads were down in search of feed and little calves clung to the shade and security of their mothers. As the sun rose the heat intensified and the deeply cracked soil offered little promise of any growth.

The battered, sturdy Jeep lurched across the drought-stricken land. It followed a track visible only to the concerned yet somehow contented stockman, anchored behind the vibrating steering wheel.

Hours later, the vehicle shuddered to a halt and feeling thoroughly shaken, we stepped down beside a parched creek bed.

With a broad grin of excitement John extended huge arms like the giant blades of a windmill and stated, 'See that country in front now? That's the headwaters of the Victoria River. When I get married I'm going to build my place there, my own cattle station.'

I saw only never ending horizons devoid of man-made interruptions.

'Poor bloody woman,' I muttered.

We devoured corned beef slabs trapped between thick, freshly baked chunks of bread in silent contemplation.

'Cup of tea?' John asked.

He tossed the tea-leaves into the bubbling water, picked up the boiling billy with his well-worn hat, then swung it around vigorously.

I repeated with greater conviction, 'Poor bloody woman.'

The vastness seemed impenetrable. As we departed, I compared our more predictable Sunday afternoon drives in Sydney, admiring manicured gardens and new homes. The variations were window shopping or buying an icecream, rather than the manipulation of a steep creek bank, the awkward opening of a heavy wooden gate, or checking a bore.

My thoughts were placed on hold as John, despite the noisy vibrating ride, proceeded to expand upon his future vision. It had always been part of the family plan and lease proposal that, when he married, he and his new wife would develop the eastern portion of Inverway. There was plenty of time to wonder about the poor bloody woman who would live at our lunch site forever after, because it took the rest of the day to return to the homestead.

After dinner, Mr Underwood wasted no time in telling us how, in 1950, he and his wife, Peg, had packed all their worldly possessions into a truck and with children John, Suzanne and Patricia departed Julia Creek in

Queensland and headed north. Tom Quilty, married to his sister Olive, was the pioneer cattleman who offered him and his young family a new life managing Bedford Downs in the Kimberley region of Western Australia.

'Actually it was Tom's brother Paddy who first took up Kimberley country in 1917, when he bought Bedford Downs in partnership with his father and brothers Tom and Reg. Paddy fell in love with the beautiful horses that Captain Bradshaw had imported from New Zealand and on this premise Paddy went on to buy Bradshaw and Coolibah Stations in the Northern Territory. When Paddy tragically died from appendicitis, these two properties were left to Tom. So Tom and Olive moved to Coolibah and Bradshaw, the hostile country with the devilishly crocodile infested rivers. It was said at the time to be the largest tract of land ever held by a single operator in Australia. That was the way it was. Today between us we still run a lot of country.'

'How much do you call a lot of country?' Johnny asked as we both braced for the reply.

Although relaxed, John's father fired up as he spoke of family commitment.

'Bradshaw and Coolibah were sold to purchase Springvale which is three hundred odd thousand acres. Inverway is one and a half million acres, Lansdowne is eight hundred thousand acres, Bedford is a little bigger and Ruby Plains is about a million acres. All up, we're talking in the vicinity of four and a half million acres. Tom and sons Rod, Basil and Mick are working the west and John and I are holding together the Territory side. Peg and Olive are good strong women, they've never skipped a beat. There's been some restless ones though, restless ones who have brought many a good man unstuck out here.'

Although Mr Underwood wasn't looking at me, I felt his obviously factual statement was a well-intentioned warning. My city background was considered a definite handicap by the toughened survivors in this lonely land.

John continued, 'In 1956 we left Bedford for Inverway. It doesn't seem nine years ago. Tomorrow, I'm going to give Uncle Tom a hand to shift some cattle, so you two can join me on a Cook's tour.'

He said this as though his uncle lived in the next suburb. I had a feeling that there was a long drive ahead.

It was strangely beautiful country even if largely inhospitable. Extensive open plains suddenly changed to timbered country with scattered cattle grazing pitifully or sheltering in any shade around a trough. The never ending dirt road leading us west was in fact the main road, the Buchanan Highway. It was stony and rough with numerous gullies and creek crossings slowing us almost to a standstill time and time again.

'The roads are as good as they get,' John shouted. 'After heavy rain they can be slow going or even closed in the Wet Season.'

It was increasingly difficult to believe that this was the Wet. Although John looked across to the horizon rather than up at the sky, he was aware of and familiar with the changing cloud formations.

'Today there are lots of clouds,' I commented. 'Are you hopeful?'

He shook his head. 'They've no chance of building up and getting together. I reckon we'll have to wait for the change in the moon. Trouble is, there's only two more moons until the Dry Season officially commences.'

The sight of circling kites and wedge-tailed eagles perched over the rotting corpses of perished cattle was distressing. I could sense the impact on the cattleman who, like his stock, was at the mercy of Mother Nature. Somehow he remained eternally optimistic.

We were now on the Duncan Highway having crossed into Western Australia quite without ceremony. Two hours later, the unexpected appearance of a picturesque spring surrounded by exotic palms called for a revival stop. Sam Hasluck, an old prospector, materalised from within his dwelling superimposed on the opposite hillside. He was pleased to have someone besides his goats to talk to and, like all people hard of hearing, roared his greeting. Over a welcome drink of tea, he proudly sifted through samples of his precious finds of gold and amethyst.

After driving for another hour the remnants of the old township of Halls Creek loomed like sentinels to an historical past. John explained that gold had lured many, proved the ruin of many more, but was influential in populating the Kimberley. We continued westward. Through the serpentine, dusty red hills we followed the incessantly winding road with dangerously narrow bends to the relocated former gold-mining town. There was an air of anticipation about John.

In 'new' Halls Creek we refuelled. Having passed the racecourse, general store, hotel, church, hospital, school and police station we had seen it all. John's friends Mopsy and John Storer who ran the general store were interested to meet the Sydney nurse they had heard so much about. The five of us were the only white people visible amongst hundreds of Aborigines who sat under shady trees or outside their houses.

Travelling along the Wyndham road, we eventually reached the Springvale Station turn-off. An hour later, we alighted beside an impressive stone slab fence, behind which nestled a freshly painted red and white homestead.

'Hello Auntie.' John greeted the woman who emerged to welcome us with affection and introduced Johnny and me. Her striking iris-coloured eyes twinkled and we felt instantly at home. The two Johns disappeared to the men's quarters and I was escorted to the guest bedroom, the Mauve Room. Auntie Olive pointed to the guest bathroom and suggested that I freshen up before dinner.

'The boys will be back from the yards with Tom directly,' she advised. 'I'll see you shortly, dear.'

Red dirt was ingrained in every crinkle and crevice and I was desperate for a shower. As I closed the bathroom door, I about turned to be confronted by an audience of bloated, watchful, shiny green frogs. They not only lined the skirting boards, but the biggest of all sat on the only cake of soap within sight. With bulging belly, protruding eyes and a lower throat that wobbled like semi-set jelly, number one frog seemed to be issuing a challenge. I soon discovered that frogs are not disturbed by hurtled toothbrushes or muttered threats of hist or shoo.

'Shake a leg and join us,' John urged, 'don't worry about your lipstick.'

The shower water threw the much detested creatures into ecstasy and the ensuing chorus of 'Grrumps' was deafening. If you are princes in disguise you can keep your castles, I retaliated. My shampoo finally did the trick of giving me the shower to myself, and feeling brand new I happily joined the others.

Uncle Tom Quilty had a craggy nose and bushy eyebrows and an irrepressible sense of humour. We were formally seated at the dinner table, when he scoffed a bowl of water.

'Out of pannikins are we, Olive?' he chuckled.

She explained that the seldom-used finger bowls always created confusion.

Winking and banging his pannikin on the laminex table, Uncle Tom called, 'Come on now, Olive, let's toast our visitors. John wants a beer and mine's a rum! What'll it be for you two from the big smoke—beer or rum?'

Later that evening Tom and Olive relived their days at Bradshaw and Coolibah Stations, highlighting the journey of Pat, Peg and their children to this great land of opportunity. Their sense of family was enormously strong. Back in Ward 3 John had proven a sound precursor.

'Together we Quiltys and Underwoods work this country and what's more we're survivors, aren't we John?' Uncle bellowed. His exploits with cattle were gripping. It was as though we were in the wild west. In fact we were. To be in the presence of this uninhibited, skilled bushman recounting his everyday feats was a real privilege. He talked about his chestnut gelding Bemi, the master camp horse in the country; Bemi, the smart horse, who worked cattle without a bridle. John reckoned he had an equally smart horse and the good-natured arguments flowed. A picture was beginning to emerge of the challenges of this largely unfenced, untamed country and those who responded to its call.

'How's my niece Betty Storman?' The question was unexpected. 'Remember her? You must know Betty, she lives in Sydney too.'

When John explained that she was married to Dr Bob McInerney, I was relieved to be able to answer that in fact I had recently seen them both at a hospital function and they appeared in fine form. Mrs McInerney often graced St Vincent's with her stylish outfits topped by sensational hats, and the nursing staff were all in awe of her honorary gynaecologist and obstetrician husband, whose early morning ward rounds were as predictable as the sunrise. Wearing an immaculate suit and leather gloves and every inch the smart city doctor, he would visit his patients after daily Mass. With a gracious slight bow, he would greet the most junior nurse as 'Sister'. However, if any problem arose due to inefficiency, no mercy was shown.

My thought pattern was suddenly interrupted by Uncle Tom bursting into verse:

There was excitement on the station,
When we got the information,
McInerney would be coming by aircraft.
He caused a great sensation,
When he gave a demonstration
How to draft.

The ringers thought he was a joke,
Who could only ride a poor old moke,
But he proved himself a ringer in disguise,
When he rode the station outlaw,
And beat an abo fighting south-paw,
He opened up their eyes.

When the bulls at night stampeded,
In no way was he impeded,
His horsemanship and courage did not fail;
What I relate is candid,
He held them single handed,
Till the other men turned up behind the tail.

And so on Uncle Tom declaimed animatedly till the whole exciting tale had been told.

Apparently Uncle Tom's poetic inclinations were almost as legendary as his cattle skills. His passionate recitation had transported us amongst the musterers and I could almost feel the pace of the chase. However I was having trouble believing that we were talking about the same suave Sydney doctor. That Dr McInerney was a relation as well as a ringer was absolutely astonishing.

Just as Auntie bid us goodnight and mine host called for a nightcap, a low growl of thunder rumbled through the night.

'Send her down, Hughie,' Uncle implored as the first hope of rain electrified the scene.

Another round and another toast, 'Live long and die happy! That's how to run your race, Johnny and Terry. Good to know you!'

The rain proved elusive. On our journey to visit Tom and Olive's youngest son Mick and his wife, Cherry, we saw more cattle carcasses lying amongst ant beds and patchy grasses. Clumps of spinifex offered the only real green tinge. On our arrival at Ruby Plains Station, Mick, who closely resembled his father in features and stature, proudly showed us his recently broken horses in the house yards. John and Mick were obviously close mates as well as cousins. At the homestead, Cherry's table was laden with home-cooked goodies. For the first time the flies that hounded us were beaten by her white lace doilies. There was so much attention to detail and we had just started to relax when 'bogey time' was announced. As she directed me to the bathroom, Cherry explained that 'bogey' was the Aborigines' word for bath or clean up.

'Sorry about this,' smiled Cherry apologetically, 'the station bore is u.s. and we all have to share this one tub of water.'

At least no frogs, I thought, until I went to the toilet where frogs that dwarfed all others lurked in waiting.

From behind the curtained partition, I heard Johnny ask what u.s. meant. In unison Cherry answered, 'unserviceable' as Mick stated emphatically, 'up to shit!' We would be confronted with this terminology and its implications over and over again. There certainly were no automatic city services out here. When something broke down, people simply had to fix it themselves.

In the wee small hours the two cousins surprisingly donned their hats. They had been conferring in the corner while Cherry and I chatted rather aimlessly. Johnny had already retired. Hats at midnight; I was intrigued. Then Mick produced his revolver. The cousins started target shooting through the dining room louvres, challenging each other's reflexes and accuracy. A startled Johnny appeared and wide-eyed absorbed the extraordinary spectacle.

On our return journey to Inverway, we pulled up abruptly to inspect a massive snake that John had run over and killed. As he held up the lethal king brown and identified its poison glands and other attributes, we were joined by a lone traveller who introduced himself as the Lord

Mayor of Halls Creek. It appeared that George Appelbee was a good friend of John as well as Shire President.

'Nice going, Underwood,' was his farewell as he winked at me. I was not sure if the reference was to the limp reptile or someone from Sydney.

As we drove through the hills and into the vastness, John divulged the number of holdings in the area owned by the British family, the Vesteys. Since the turn of the century they had purchased an almost unbroken chain of cattle stations from Flora Valley in Western Australia right across the Northern Territory to the Katherine area. Apparently the original inhabitants of Inverway, the Farquharson brothers, had sold to the Leahy brothers on the understanding that the property never be sold to Vesteys.

'We at Inverway, being in the middle of predominantly Vestey owned country and furthermore being not for sale, became very much in the way,' John explained.

John supported the spirit and stance of the three pioneering brothers, Archie, Harry and Hughie. They were nephews of the legendary explorer and drover, Nat Buchanan, and they named their laboriously constructed stockyards after him. Mount Farquharson, also on John's end of Inverway, was a well-known landmark on maps and charts. These were men who left an imprint and legacy which acknowledged and upheld private ownership. The significant involvement and investments of the Vestey empire in northern Australia were unquestionable and invaluable. However, there will undoubtedly remain the pride of the private operator who, in saluting the giants, doggedly determines that 'they can't own the whole bloody country'.

John's father was pleased to see us and told us to call him Pat. This gesture was a sign of real progress. Having keenly absorbed news of the relatives and their drought status, he reinforced emphatically, 'We'll all survive these bad times, even though it gets pretty disheartening. Last night the moon looked wet. I think there's a change in the weather.'

When food rations were collected by the Aborigines the following evening, they giggled and displayed a shy interest in 'that girl belonga John and him brother too'. I found it difficult to understand what they said. Extended families lived together with what appeared to be at least one dog for every adult. Despite the seemingly ramshackle living conditions, they exuded contentment and well being.

All too soon it was almost tomorrow. John's mother would be arriving on the aeroplane on which we would depart.

Following the completion of the evening meal and clearing of the kitchen, John patted the canvas he had spread on the lawn. 'Come and talk,' he invited. Optimistically he'd flung his wireless aerial up across the overhead clothes line. Radio reception was a luxury, he had explained to me while in hospital, and tonight proved to be no exception. His portable wireless played loud static interrupted by occasional bursts of music.

His father called out that a man was trying to get to sleep. Now with the power plant turned off for the night, the silence was acute. The eerie howl of a lone dingo breaking the stillness was chilling. As we walked away from the homestead the darkness enveloped us. His big rough hand grasped mine reassuringly. I felt minute walking beside this resolute young giant. Quite suddenly the wooden rails of the stockyards loomed and he guided me to a huge ironwood post lying on the ground. There we sat in silence for a long time. Overhead the glorious star-studded skies provided an unimaginable vision of wondrous beauty. How infinitesimal we were! The power of the man and his land touched my soul.

As we exchanged greetings at the airstrip, I noted that the facial features of Mrs Underwood and her son were carved with uncanny similarity. Her impressions of me were likewise absorbed in a glance as we departed all too quickly. I experienced a physical and emotional wrench as we became airborne and the aeroplane wheels clunked into the undercarriage.

I could still feel John's goodbye kiss. I thought about that poor bloody woman he would one day marry and bring to the middle of nowhere. Deep inside I tried to contemplate the full implications of the ambitious yet gut-driven passion of one young cattleman. As we ascended into a frowning sky, I realised that the privilege I'd been given of being a passive observer was no qualification or enticement for living in such a primitive, untamed and ever-demanding country.

It was hellishly hot and we were fully loaded. For hours our small aeroplane lurched through lumpy skies, surrounded by escalating giant woolly thunderheads. Johnny and I watched in fascinated horror as vivid lightning danced wildly through the increasing blackness. It illuminated silver wing tips as it teased and tantalised and terrified. It was an enormous relief to eventually arrive at the safety of our Darwin motel.

All through the long night we witnessed the breathtaking, electrifying fireworks as tropical skies accommodated tropical storms. When heavy rain finally pelted on roof tops, my heart cried out for the parched country and its people we had left behind.

CHAPTER 4

THE KEY

··

Without any need for embellishment, Johnny's and my adventures were largely accepted with some astonishment by our family and friends. However, we found it absolutely impossible to adequately describe the wide open spaces that constitute the vast inland of our great continent. Perhaps when Johnny's photographs were developed, those images would give additional muscle to our verbal account. My brother's favourite story was describing the thick clouds of sticky flies and how it would have been impossible to stick a pin between them. I had lost count of the number I swallowed, especially when I laughed out loud! At the time, John's revelation that they were even more prevalent after rain and a green pick seemed unbelievable.

It was good to be home and back on familiar ground. But strangely, that very familiarity was tempered by an emptiness. I couldn't wait to resume my correspondence with John, though it would always be a poor second-best to being with him.

Our ongoing weekly letters, each like a diary, often covered both sides of twelve pages or more. Sometimes John wrote from beneath a mosquito net in the midday sun in order to escape those persistent flies. He wrote before breakfast and last thing at night before falling exhausted into his swag beside the stockcamp fire. Depending on his activities and ability to 'post' his letters, he penned thoughts three times a day or three times a week. Similarly, my letters evolved over days and events, thoughts and feelings. We shared a new bond which distance could no longer distort and which time could only strengthen.

> *Terry Darling,*
>
> *I remember telling you on that first night in Ward 3 that I had never fallen seriously for any girl and then I turn around and fall for you. God knows why. He must have arranged it. How are you, my little nurse?*
>
> *The annual rainfall total is 625 points, which is the lowest ever recorded here. No wonder things are so bad.*
>
> *We've just come in from the stockcamp and we're going out again tonight. I'm holding up the ship, but I'm going to write a decent letter to you because I owe you a letter and mainly because for the next two months I won't be within fifty miles of the station and will have to rely on visits from Mum and Dad to convey my correspondence, so prepare yourself for some scattered, outdated letters.*
>
> *I'm starting bullock mustering. Have 1500 stores to get together, so I'll be properly busy. Our horses will only be fit for work for these couple of months. The rest of the year they'll be flat out keeping alive.*
>
> *Just been working out price comparisons between Katherine and Wyndham meatworks—both clearing about thirty-seven pounds a head. Losses are heavier to Katherine though.*
>
> *Yesterday was driving along a road about 30 mph dodging the ruts when a centre bolt on the front spring broke and the front wheel slipped back. Result was the wheel locked and I couldn't steer or rather turn it one way. This I didn't know of course. Was in timbered country on a narrow road. Next minute a big tree approached in front of me and the truck was drawn to it like a magnet. Couldn't turn away. Anyway the tree had no intention of shifting and I sideswiped it on the driver's side. The Jeep has a*

*facelift now, one dented mudguard, one out of shape cabin, one
dented door that won't close, and the side of the body is mutilated.
Also one driver whose head was about 6 inches from the tree as it
passed was very frightened, but counted his blessings because things
could have been worse—much worse.*

*You asked me what a ringer is. He's a stockman, more so a
bushie. One of those blokes that even if he was dressed up in a
tuxedo you could still pick him for a bushie.*

*I'm waiting for you patiently enough, but conscious of every day
passing and every new day being one day closer to our meeting
again.*

Think of all the writing paper we'll save when we are married!
Well, I'm not here mate. Bye Darling.
All my love
John
p.s. I still reckon you wear too much eye shade.

Through his letters I met his mates—Tony Clark from Wave Hill,
Graham Fulcher and others. Whenever John planned to muster an unfenced
boundary area, he gave notice to the relevant neighbouring station. Their
stockcamp would subsequently join forces with John and his Aboriginal
stockmen to muster together and return the right cattle to the rightful
owners. He wrote to me about those musters, the brandings, the company,
and the after dinner music called a corroboree.

John always maintained that on his return from our meeting in Sydney,
he had declared to one and all that marrying his Sydney nurse was only
a matter of when. He talked and wrote about our future together as
naturally and assuredly as he approached life in general. John simply
never considered marrying any other woman.

My letters described hospital life, news of the nurses whom John had
met and family activities. Unlike some school friends, Johnny had escaped
conscription for Vietnam and was studying medicine at Sydney University.
John always sent his regards to my parents and 'all about', even though
he had not yet met them.

We two people, so far apart and from such different backgrounds, had
forged an inexplicable need of each other, and yet in our mutual recognition

of this proceeded independently to pursue personal goals and objectives. I never lost sight of the fact that to love the man and love his land were two different things. But the longing, controlled as it was, permeated everything.

It was not there yesterday. It moved when I swallowed, and I knew with certainty that the lump was on my thyroid gland. With racing thoughts and deep concern I joined the queue in the Casualty department waiting to be seen by the resident doctor on duty.

Sitting amongst the injured and ill made me decidedly uncomfortable. I was only familiar with an administration role, but was now an involuntary observer. I was the patient.

Sirens constantly wailed as another ambulance pulled up to deliver another accident victim. The entrance to casualty was directly opposite our senior nurses' home, Notre Dame, and the sound of sirens was background noise in our sleep. I watched sisters bustling from doctor to doctor and patient to patient. It was organised chaos at its best.

All around me the wounded and maimed were assessed, treated and observed; transferred to emergency theatres, intensive care, or the appropriate wards. There was a hurt and hopelessness particularly amongst young people in this part of the big city. Desperation to escape the world, and ultimately themselves, left them dependent on sources of evil and destruction. Drug overdoses were common.

Suddenly the dreaded loud buzzing sounds indicating an emergency blurted through the sounds of humanity. Someone somewhere was probably suffering cardiac arrest or haemorrhage.

The short, roly-poly figure shuffling through the doorway was oblivious to the alarm, which ceased as abruptly as it had started. Wearing her trademark tennis shade and tennis shoes, Bea Miles was as familiar to Sydneysiders as their giant coat-hanger bridge. No doubt she had once again arrived by taxi. Her agility defied her generous weight when in the midst of traffic congestion she repeatedly transferred from cab to cab, avoiding pursuit and ignoring the tariff. With no fixed address, particular destination or agenda, Bea Miles was an honorary citizen of Sydney.

Even as my eyes followed her passage, I was called. After an initial consultation I was on my way to the Outpatients area for a radioactive iodine uptake test to determine whether my lump was a foreign growth.

Thankfully the result elimininated cancer. However, I had suffered a haemorrhage into a cyst and the possibility of a further haemorrhage causing respiratory obstruction could not be ignored.

How could I possibly undergo surgery six weeks before my final examinations? Already my colleagues and I had spent countless hours and countless weeks huddled over text books and empty coffee mugs. With near unadulterated terror, we revised and reviewed knowledge and skills as we determined to pass and pass well. The pressure created by our mentor, Sister Paulina, was not only recognised, but cultivated and maintained.

Mum and Dad agreed with the doctor. Surgery was necessary and despite the proximity of my finals I knew I had no option.

I had really enjoyed my term in the operating theatres. However all of a sudden it was me on the trolley. With the premedication injection taking effect, I was wheeled through the doors into the anaesthetic bay. I knew that I was in the hands of the best medical experts in the land. Another injection and then there was nothing.

The gentle voice of my highly esteemed surgeon, Dr Noel Newton, was unmistakable.

'It went very well, Terry. Say a few words for me, please.'

My whispered thank you seemed an understatement. My vocal cords were intact and the operation had been successful. I had no sooner closed my eyes with incredible relief than the sister in charge handed me a telegram.

> *Kingdom Come won the Cup. Hope you're O.K.*
> *Love John*

We were all madly excited when our nursing friend, Flissy, and Dr Ross Unwin announced their engagement. I was thrilled to be selected as one of her bridesmaids. We celebrated the news with an impromptu party.

Who would be next to wear an engagement ring, we wondered. Most of us had regular escorts, most of us had suffered cracked if not broken hearts, most of us were admitting nothing.

'What about you and that gorgeous hunk who broke his back to meet you?' Ros asked.

'We're still writing,' I smiled.

That really was stating the obvious. They all mentally acknowledged the distinctive bulging airmail envelopes regularly lodged in my letter box in the lobby. Quite spontaneously they gave three cheers for patient and nurse, simply because no-one could have imagined a courtship by correspondence that lasted for years and years and years.

A letter had arrived that very morning.

> *Dear Terry,*
>
> *Last mail day I struck pay dirt, received two letters from you. Reason for the big silence, well there is about 1650 of them and they're all in the form of steers. Luckily they're sold and will be out of my hands by Easter.*
>
> *Am writing this on a water canteen in the car lights, it's about eight o'clock at night. We're watching cattle and I can hear the two blokes on night watch riding around them singing at the tops of their voices.*
>
> *Lucky to get the cattle away and sold at a good price so early in the piece, because they will be flat out living through the year. Thank heavens for good rain in Queensland and on the Barkly Tableland making store markets so high.*
>
> *I've been flat to the boards from 2.30 am until 8 pm every day for three weeks now. Things being so dry makes it hard and also having horse trouble, no grass and they're clearing out all the time. Our present horse plant is just about buggered. I deliver on Thursday and I can then give all the horses a holiday.*
>
> *Since I last wrote I went to Katherine with Dad and had a wicked trip in and out with trouble both ways. To top everything off, we*

tried to execute ourselves. Had the car jacked up, fixing broken U-bolts and the b. thing fell off the jack. We both got caught underneath. Spring fell across Dad's neck and strangled him.
I wriggled out somehow and jacked the car off Dad and pulled him out. He was unconscious for about fifteen minutes. Then he was quiet for a while and then he started screaming blue murder. Had the portable wireless in the car and contacted Camfield Station and they sent someone out. Dad was O.K. by then, only a headache. Such is life, but I nearly lost a father and you nearly lost me.

Been thinking about you all the time. Yesterday we had a big mob of cattle on hand and there was a little roan dog-bitten calf who had given up hope of finding his mother. I felt sorry for him, knowing the dingoes would eat him—naturally thought of you and your special love for animals. All of a sudden he found his mother and I swear that calf laughed. Reckon you would have been pleased too. I know I was.

Good luck with your exams. Cheers for this week.
All my love
John

My hospitalisation proved a minor hiccup in my study programme and nursing routines. Sister Bernice, the Mother Rectress, and Sister Paulina, the senior sister in the Tutorial Department, imparted good luck wishes to each of us sitting for the October final examinations. We were well prepared, both practically and theoretically.

Even though my general nursing training would continue for another three months, I had already applied to commence Midwifery at another Sydney hospital as soon as I finished at St Vincent's. I was intent on preparing for the reality of life in the remote Outback.

Meanwhile, my duties at the newly opened psychiatric Caritas Centre introduced me to a world of grey and confusion that affected people from every walk of life. These disturbed people led me into their wilderness in order that I might help them through as painlessly as possible.

I observed group therapy, electro-convulsive therapy and the results of medications including LSD. Within the labyrinths of minds, doors marked closed were forced open. With the removal of dusty cobwebs, monstrous hallucinations and unpredictable responses surfaced. I had to acquire new personal strengths and use every possible resource to manage these bruised souls on the brink of emotional drowning.

As always, John's letters were refreshing and enlightening.

> *My darling Terry,*
>
> *I'm droving, taking the cows over to Wave Hill to meet the next drover there. There is too much time to think and to make matters worse the cows have been rushing. They've taken the yards two nights in a row, so as a result I'm not getting much shut-eye.*
>
> *Back home. Today I had horse Terry in the yard. Pulled her shoes off, bombed her and bushed her out into the big paddock for a well-earned holiday. She is a bit poor and terribly hungry. She is a beautiful mare, not a real oil painting because her head is common and her ears too big, but everything about her suggests power and endurance. Both of these she has ample of. She is a good mustering mare but hasn't much savvy in handling a beast—but she is very quiet and a real Darling. I speak to the mare in the same tone I talk to you.*
>
> *Cyclone Dolly is a few hundred miles out to sea, so am praying that it makes a bee-line for Inverway and stops here for a fortnight. Hope you said those ten Hail Marys or ten Masses or whatever you were going to do to make it rain. I can feel it, I know it's going to rain this month.*
>
> *Now Monday morning. Blew like hell last night but only a few drops of rain. Dolly is a long way off according to the wireless, but she must be a beauty. It's overcast this morning but the clouds are high.*
>
> *Monday night. Guess what? It's been raining all afternoon, only sprinkling and hasn't done any good. But if it keeps up all night . . .*
>
> *Tuesday morning. Guess what? Three inches of rain overnight. Guess what? Dad's bed was in water when he woke up this morning. Guess what? The dam wall is close up gone under as water is running around the edge and washing the bank away. It is terrific rain and is still raining, but I hope the floodwater has reached its highest level. Cows are standing up to their udders in water and*

*calves are in about eighteen inches of water. However it's dropped
about 6 inches in the last couple of hours. There won't be any plane
today.*

*Yeh mate, it's a long time since we were together. But I've given
up thinking how long since . . . I just think how long till . . . Too
bloody long. Either way you put it.*

Love John

Finally our long-held dreams were realised and John was on his way
to Sydney for a week's holiday. A phone call from Newcastle advised that
he was ahead of schedule and would pick me up at the hospital that
evening as we were to dine with the Sheils—his unfailing friends and
supporters from Northbridge—at a prestigious sailing club. In his
excitement and scurry for Sydney, John hung up without my full response.
My immediate dilemma was that my ever reliable all-weather coat was
hardly suitable for the proposed venue and there certainly wasn't time to
head home for a change of clothes. Although nursing colleague Liz was
two sizes bigger than I, she insisted that her pretty floral dress with lacy
frills be adjusted for Cinderella. With no alternative, I slowly turned as
she adjusted the hem with straight pins, as no safety pins were on hand,
advising me to remember that they were there. With every movement
bringing a fresh prick, there was little chance of forgetting. John could
not work out what was different about me as with great difficulty I
negotiated chairs and tables and toilets with a fixed grimace of delight
belying acute discomfort. The most difficult navigating ever performed in
my limited experience of sailing was of secondary consequence. My
captain, the ringer, had returned.

John's presence in our family home impacted on each member. Mum
and Dad absorbed his irrepressible humour, thoughtfulness and generosity
with growing interest and our religious disharmony was the only possible
cause for any concern. Johnny was pleased to see his former host, tour
guide and, as he strongly suspected, future brother-in-law again. Anne
and her husband John and young family travelled down from Newcastle
for a weekend reunion. Libby too returned and our Pymble home was
filled with curiosity, queues for the bathroom and lots of laughter.

John's mannerisms were different to ours and his expressions reflected an unfamiliar background and culture.

Even my limited experience with men of the inland had illustrated their reluctance to debate or engage in lengthy discussions, unless a rum derivative was in use. They were men of few words, men of action, who worked long hard days all year round. They were independent and often loners, never in need of conversation for the sake of it. I had listened in puzzled concentration to phrases rather than sentences, hyphenated by nods, sighs and grunts. To me it was strange, but it was their way. When a problem arose or someone needed 'sorting out', then a push or shove was more effective and certainly more available than a telephone call or a bunch of flowers.

John did not like telephones or jostling crowds and city traffic bothered him. I understood these things. This huge man was like a beacon, as undeniably beckoning as he was irresistible.

It was a broken darkness until heavy clouds racing across the full moon accumulated and obliterated all light. On the little white bridge that crossed our garden stream, we too were invisible. All the written words and all the thoughts concertinaed into speech. John's proposal was as predictable as my response. As warm raindrops fell, we returned to the empty lounge room. Everyone had retired. Seconds before sleep finally descended, the faraway sounds of a city bound train intruded into the mystique of the night.

John returned to his people in the Northern Territory and I ascended the stage amongst forty-five other graduate nurses. Our carefully shaped veils were in place and with unspeakable pride we welcomed parents and family to our graduation ceremony. After various musical recitals, Sister Bernice, the formidable yet serene Mother Superior, presented our badges and certificates. By candlelight we recited the nurses' pledge with charged sincerity and emotion. We had lost and won battles. In forging through turmoil and calm, we had survived by giving of ourselves. Our sense of achievement was as bonding as our memories.

Ten days later, the same nurses celebrated unofficially at the Alhouette Restaurant. Those engaged to doctors compared notes and most others were finalising overseas travel arrangements. When I mentioned that I would no longer be joining them, they were shocked. I tried to explain that the challenges of marrying and coping with life in the middle of nowhere were monumental enough and I could not risk returning from Europe unsettled. Moreover, obstetrics training would hopefully have practical application for me sooner rather than later.

My friends were even more concerned when they heard of the lifestyle I would be embracing. How was a city nurse going to transform herself into a capable, productive country woman, living four hundred miles from the nearest shops, Europe or no Europe?

'No television!' Colleen gasped.

'No house,' I replied. I reminded them that John and I intended moving immediately to the eastern end of Inverway to fulfil his lifelong dream of developing his own property from scratch. He always referred to it as the headwaters of the Victoria River country.

'Knowing you, it will all work out, but for goodness sake—home-made soap, as well as bread and butter! It sounds like Noah's Ark,' stated Annie.

'Well, quite frankly I think you'll go crazy without television, family and friends,' worried Jill. 'Ring me once a month so I know you're all right.'

'There's no phone either,' I sighed almost apologetically. I was relieved when the spotlight was turned on another in the group.

Although we were aware that Victor Chang, one of the St Vincent's resident medical officers whom we all knew well, had slipped through Ros's fingers, no-one was prepared for her bombshell.

'I'm going to join the Franciscan Missionaries of Mary,' she announced. Everyone moved closer. She wasn't joking. Ros was my fun-loving party partner of the last four years. She was the most outgoing and outrageous of our group. I could only think that the Almighty calls the best as we ordered more drinks to celebrate this most unexpected announcement. It was a momentous gathering, for our next reunion, if there was to be one, was in the lap of God.

To witness the birth of a baby proved the most humbling and stirring experience of my twenty-two years. During my twelve months at the Royal North Shore Hospital Maternity Wing, I delivered twenty-seven babies and witnessed more than one hundred births. I loved working in the nurseries and became adept at 'topping and tailing' the babies as well as the alternate full sponge bath. Efficient and constant handling of these tiny ones did not detract from my constant wonder and affection for each baby. I longed for my own babies, although when John talked about at least six children I suggested we keep our numbers non-specific. It was enough that we both hoped for healthy babies.

The world of the maternity wing was mostly dominated by love and joy. However, I grieved with the mother who bore her infant only to be confronted by tragedy. The rawness of human emotions unravelled all around me.

In between studying the mechanisms of labour, I wrote to my man.

> *Dear John,*
>
> *So we are back to talking by pen. The newspaper today shows rain in your area. As your depressing and worrying Dry Season draws to a close, I hope the desperately needed early storms come your way.*
>
> *My weekend at Newcastle was, as always, wonderful. Anne and John are relaxed and well and their daughters all want to be our flower girls. Remember Mum's sister, Auntie Mary, with the carrot coloured hair? She has already bought three hats for our wedding and can't choose between them! She is so flamboyant and enthusiastic and supportive.*
>
> *Our night at the opera was one of those occasions of pure magic. I think even you would enjoy Puccini's* Madam Butterfly. *The love and hope that change to despair and ultimate tragedy tear me apart every time. Butterfly never stops believing that her adored American naval husband, Pinkerton, will return as promised in the blessed season when the robin builds his nest. In Japan the robin has built his nest three times and she wonders if he builds it less often in that*

other faraway land. Despite the growing fears of her maid, Suzuki,
she maintains her vigil beside the little son who has yet to meet his
foreign father. Her affirmation of unshakable faith and love as she
sings 'One Fine Day' is heart-rending. Butterfly believes her beloved
will return to his tiny little wife, his sweet-scented flower as he called
her. Both the words and the music bring tears to my eyes.

I know you prefer happy endings, John, and how fortunate you
and I are. Our future is up to us. You won my heart a long time
ago, probably before either of us was fully aware of it.

It is as though my life was a big corridor at the end of which was
a huge door—and a lock to which there was no key. I have found
the key, John, for I have found you.

I don't know what lies ahead in this new country, for your way of
life is still a little foreign. Yet at your side I shall and can do
anything.

Yours forever,
Love
Terry

At the Kimberley Hotel in Halls Creek, Mrs Beryl Macguire was delighted
to be hosting the engagement party of the most eligible bachelor in the
country, John Underwood, and his city fiancee. She looked forward to
telling the young lady how, in bygone days, John and his mates, without
warning or apology, would uproot her palm trees whenever a point needed
to be proven. What a relief to know that there was change afoot.

CHAPTER 5

'I WILL'

....

In many ways our engagement party simulated a wedding reception. The guests travelled from far and wide to inspect the soon to be Mrs Underwood junior and to celebrate with John and his family. The women I met looked as though they had been born where they stood. They were healthy and strong, salt of the earth women who reflected an unquestionable ease and affinity with their environment. Their curiosity was thinly disguised and although everyone was friendly enough, conversations revolved around things of no relevance to me. They compared correspondence school reports, the number of eggs the ducks and chooks were laying—and the season. It was always the season and the rain or lack of it that controlled everything they did.

When we were on our own, John handed me his engagement present. The necklace was made from aspro sachets joined together by equal-size silver safety pins. I loved his imagination and ingenuity. 'One day I'll replace it with the real thing,' he promised as he pinned it around my neck.

Another favourite present was equally unusual. Kyber was a huge black labrador and he sensed my love of dogs on our first meeting at Inverway.

His owners were Roy and Margaret Harvey from the Wave Hill Police Station. During Roy's prolonged absence with bush work, Margaret sought female companionship with the Underwood women. The Harveys' support and friendship weren't surprising, however their wonderful engagement present was totally unexpected.

'Kyber is yours, Terry. We'll mind him until you're married and then you'll have a friend waiting for you when you arrive to live here.'

I was touched beyond words.

'What a flash party,' John said as he kissed his mother in gratitude. She had planned every last detail to perfection. John's sister, Patricia, now called Trish, had returned from her Karitane nursing training in Perth with boxes of beautiful fresh flowers. Jim Tough, who was to be our groomsman, read telegrams from my family, Sydney friends and a few locals who couldn't make it. After cutting the heart-shaped cakes, one pink and the other blue, we danced and laughed and mingled with the folk who lived by the sun and for whom no challenge was too great. All the while I marvelled at their numbers and the distances they had travelled. They had little time or opportunity to congregate in this immense country, and it became increasingly obvious that when they did they certainly crammed into every moment the fun of being together. It was almost time to get up when we went to bed.

Back at the station, I watched the stockcamp preparations. John organised the packing of everyone's gear, cooking utensils and food rations for a fortnight into pairs of pack bags. He selected packsaddles for packhorses and mules; small packsaddles for mules and larger ones for horses. Des Leahy, the horse tailer, then took charge of these reliable beasts of burden. Although he looked young, he knew his job well.

Riding alongside a hundred-odd horses, Des Leahy (his given name) and another blackfella started in the lead. Their cross-country journey to the main camp site at Mucca Waterhole would take two days. Next day, much to Peg's consternation, I climbed aboard John's stockcamp vehicle to share the sixty mile drive from Inverway to Mucca. It was unfenced country that adjoined the Vestey property, Wave Hill Station. Notice had already been given to the Wave Hill manager, Tom Fisher, and therefore it was no surprise to be joined by their stockcamp the following day. They had come to attend the Inverway muster.

Old Duncan, the camp cook, performed the seemingly impossible every morning at three o'clock by preparing breakfast by torchlight. 'Proper early,' he called it. Although he looked awkward holding the torch in his mouth, he seemed completely at ease. I couldn't take my eyes off the little old man as he scurried around, pouring and mixing, kneading his dough and finally igniting the first flames which greedily devoured the wood.

Des Leahy and an offsider had already left to locate the hobbled horses by the unmistakable sound of the Condamine bells worn around the necks of those horses known to graze further out. While we waited in the growing light of dawn, John explained that horses, like people, have different aptitudes and worked according to their categories. Packhorses and mules, generally strong and placid, carried balanced packsaddles filled with stockcamp gear. Musterers rode stockhorses to muster the mob. Night horses were kept for night watch when several stockmen rode around the mob, singing loudly to keep themselves awake and their cattle settled; man and horse intent on keeping the mob together, ever aware of the threat of the cattle being spooked and rushing uncontrollably. The bronco horses were ridden by stockmen swinging head ropes to capture beasts for branding. John ensured that each horse took its turn, and that none were overworked or overlooked.

From a distance I watched Des Leahy catch the horses. He approached in a stooped position in order to remove the hobbles on a horse's forelegs. Attaching the hobbles to the horse's neck strap, Des Leahy then directed his charges back to the camp. Once they were 'on camp', the stockmen selected the horses they required for the day's operation. As they tucked into a hearty breakfast, never knowing their lunch hour (as it was dependent on the morning muster), Des Leahy and his offsider placed bridles on the required horses and tied them up close by to await their riders. To them all, it was just a natural sequence of events. To me, it was sheer magic. John's mates from Wave Hill were as competent as he. I continued to watch mesmerised as Sabu Sing, Tony Clark and Lynny Hayes saddled their horses, then rode off into what was the unknown to me and to them the 'beyond'.

While Duncan cleaned, baked bread and damper, and generally fussed around his 'kitchen', he talked to himself non-stop and to me occasionally.

'Oh Chri', I cook em plenty tucker, they proper hungry dis mob. Proper good fella, dat John.'

Duncan's affection for and loyalty to John were shared by all the stockmen. I sensed their powerful bond, an invisible cord of respect and instinct and co-ordination between each other, and between man and beast as night and day merged and the stockwork continued. Out here there were no boundaries, no limitations. There was a purity of purpose about the existence that was quite haunting.

Every day while Duncan prepared tucker, Des Leahy organised the horses for 'dinner camp'. It was often when the sun was at its highest and hottest that the musterers would pull up at the new makeshift camp site where we three awaited them. As everyone lunched on corned beef, damper and golden syrup, the bellowing of the cattle being held nearby indicated that it had been a reasonable morning's muster considering the distance covered. Over large pannikins of scalding billy tea, John and his mates asked how the holiday girl was faring. With instructions for the afternoon in place, they all changed horses and rode off to implement the afternoon's muster back to the main camp at Mucca.

The best part of the day was the return of all twenty stockmen around sundown to the main campsite—the power base, the board room of the bush. Around the evening camp fire, the humorous yarns and tales of endurance were absorbed by one city girl with a new sense of life beyond the bright lights of the city.

There was so much to see. Before the mustered cattle were yarded, men on horseback cut out or separated the Wave Hill cattle. It was thrilling to watch a good stockman on a good horse working a beast out of a mob. Once the mob was yarded I sat on the top rail of the stockyard, gazing through the billowing dust at a stockman on a bronco horse lassoing a beast, then dragging it up to the bronco panel where skilled stockmen leg-roped the cleanskin and pulled it to the ground ready for branding and castrating. This continued until the last beast was branded. At the end of the week's muster, Tony, Sabu and Lynny walked their cattle home. It was twenty miles to their first stop at McDonnell, and from there they walked their mob back to Wave Hill Station.

When John departed to construct a fence line, he left me at the station to give Peg, his mother, a hand. The harder he worked, the happier he was. Having previously pegged the line, he was unfazed by the country where the bedrock was close to the surface.

Jack Kelly, an author from Canberra, was at Inverway collating information on his soon to be published study of the northern beef industry. Pat, John's father, offered to escort him to the southern neighbouring property, Birundudu, and invited me to share the outing with them. It was an opportunity to see another part of the never ending Inverway. The only available vehicle was the old red Bedford truck. Waving goodbye to Peg, John's sister Trish and Margaret Harvey, I climbed aboard. As he started the noisy motor, Pat called out that we should be back for supper.

Once again, it was a barely discernible road. Due to Pat's expertise as a bush driver, we eventually arrived at an old tin hut occupied by the Beebe brothers, Jack and Noel. They were like Dr Jekyll and Mr Hyde. Jack was overweight and animated and Noel was like a beanpole, long and thin and expressionless. With typical response to rare and unexpected company, they had a round of rum. And another. There were no spare pannikins so they used empty fruit tins to drink from instead. Jack had no trouble in gathering his information. As the level in the bottle dropped, so did the sun. Later rather than sooner Pat declared that the time had come to make a mile, otherwise the girls at home might worry about us.

'You drive, Terry, we're a bit too relaxed,' I was instructed.

Never having driven a truck in my life, I was reluctant. However there was only one Terry in that hut and I never drank rum.

That old red Bedford seemed to gather speed of its own accord. In the middle of the night we tore through thick scrubby bushes with brittle branches poking through the window and brushing against my cheek. As we rattled past gnarled tree trunks, I grappled with the wandering wheel. My two cheery passengers shouted boisterously, 'Atta girl! You got it! Hang on to her! You little beauty!' as for two long hours we swayed and thundered through the night. That good old truck must have known its own way home.

Next morning, I overheard Pat telling Peg that John's girl might be all right after all. It was almost a relief to return to the safety of city roads and traffic lights. In the space of six short months, I would be back permanently.

However my life had already changed, even before my address did. I had been introduced to another world in which the simplicity of detail and complexity of the workload stirred me. Above all, the harshness of the land and the productivity of its inhabitants overwhelmed me. It was a land of intrigue and soon it would be my home.

Continuing my night nursing shift, I meticulously planned every aspect of our wedding in consultation with Mum and Dad. Married friends provided advice as they shared my excitement. They were resigned to my madness. Although I had returned to Pymble after my graduation, I was fully aware now that my days at home were numbered. I cherished my time there as never before. Mum and Dad spoke of missing me terribly, but also of looking forward to having another son-in-law called John.

Just as I had committed myself to leaving the known for the unknown, so too did John accept the implications of marrying a Catholic. Although he met the priest and agreed that our children be raised as Catholics, there was neither consideration nor expectation that John change his religion. By whatever name his religion was called, it was impressive. John really believed that all mankind were his brothers and treated them accordingly.

Side by side we would live in the middle of nowhere and side by side we would marry in the Catholic church. Over a quarter of a century earlier my parents had been married in St Mary's Cathedral and now John and I were to follow in their footsteps. After five years of letter writing, our profound love led us to God's altar. During our exchange of vows, I prayed for the endurance that our love promised. 'I will' was offered with unfathomable faith, trust and love.

While we were signing the register a shabbily clothed, wizened old man carrying a hessian sack of scrawny kittens meandered through the wooden pews. 'Want to buy?' he badgered our guests before shuffling off through the side door. The pathos of this intrusion touched everyone.

Just as we were about to leave the altar, John, at top volume, reminded our best man David Sheil to tip the priest. The congregation sat down again as we all waited while David fumbled in his unfamiliar tuxedo pockets. Finally the mighty organ again reverberated forth, family and friends stood once more and we walked down the aisle together as husband and wife.

The reception was a wondrous mix of bush and city guests. John's mother and sisters Trish, Marion and Anna represented his family and I was supported by my entire family. The Underwood women, shy at first, noticeably relaxed as everyone warmly embraced my new family. Swanny, the grader driver, danced with Auntie Eileen from Bellevue Hill. My brother-in-law, John Ell, proved an effective and popular master of ceremonies despite forgetting his carefully compiled notes. Julie, an old school friend and Cathy from St Vincent's were my beautiful bridesmaids who thoroughly enjoyed the jubilant celebration. The Carlton Rex Hotel had never held such a gathering and every detail of that evening remained indelibly imprinted on two minds and hearts.

The flight to Melbourne to board our honeymoon liner, the *Angelina Lauro*, allowed the fruition of another long-held dream. It was spectacular to sail through the amazing Heads and be greeted by the beautiful harbour cherished by all Sydneysiders. It was also ironic that this arrival was in fact my farewell to Sydney. John found the confines of the ship restrictive and consequently relished the tour of the productive farming country surrounding Auckland, our first port of call. Other honeymooners surfaced as we sailed onwards to Noumea where schoolgirl French proved mildly helpful. On board, professional entertainment was appealing to many; however Mr and Mrs John Underwood were still overwhelmed by the wonder and thrill of their new togetherness, twenty-four hours a day. Our voyage continued into uncharted waters.

A fortnight later our wedding gifts were packed carefully into six tea chests and loaded onto the red Bedford truck. Goodbyes were difficult, but were always going to be so. I did not know when I would next see my family and friends. However, I knew with unfailing conviction that John and I were meant for each other.

Although we had been travelling for five days, it was still more than two hundred miles to Inverway. Heavy rain ahead prevented further progress and we were grateful for accommodation with Brian and Fay Crowson at

Montijinni Station. Helping wherever possible, I admired Fay's ability to do at least three things at once as she attended her young band of sons, infant daughter and a multitude of station duties. That night as John and I lay in bed discussing our possible departure, we heard our host and hostess murmuring the rosary. Suddenly Pymble was far far away and in that instant I missed my family terribly.

Our delay reinforced the fact that planning ahead in the bush was always subject to the vagaries of nature. Nobody could afford to mind because everything else was secondary to the life-giving rain. Three days later John's cousin, Basil Quilty, picked us up in the light aircraft shared by the Underwoods and Quiltys and flew us to Inverway. We would collect the Bedford and all our worldly goods later.

Just as John had survived his compulsory pre-marriage instructions in Catholicism, I had survived Peg's pre-engagement inquisition. I had answered in the affirmative to all her questions. Yes, I could cook, mend, dressmake, knit, crochet, do needlework and tapestry, garden and book keep. Household duties as such seemed of less consequence to me than the business of starting our station from nothing. However, I had told John ages ago that I could live with him anywhere and I was ready to prove it.

All of a sudden John was no longer beside me. After only one night at Inverway, he had gone on ahead to set up our camp. Hoping to be useful in the laundry, I approached Peg to offer my services.

'Nail polish, eh?' she said as she turned away. I was more determined than ever to prove my capabilities.

The laundry was a very serious affair. Some articles were soaked, others starched and I lost count of the sheets that were wrung by hand. The men's working clothes in the boiling copper were poked and prodded with a long wooden stick and eventually rinsed, ready to hang.

There was a method and a pattern to everything and a surprising preoccupation with detail. I was shown how to peg out the washing. The socks went side by side, as did the shirts, the underwear, the jeans and the handkerchiefs. I felt inadequate and unqualified. There was nothing romantic anymore about that clothes line beneath which John and I had gazed at the stars.

I knew that the heavy irons heated on the wood stove in the kitchen were changed over regularly. Surely I could handle the ironing without any trouble? It was all about timing and with an iron the right temperature I claimed sweet victory over the repetitive wrinkles and creases.

I wasn't really surprised when John's mother said that I was too young to call her Peg. Everyone called her Mrs Underwood. When she invited me to call her Mum, I was speechless. I sensed already how much John would be missed at Inverway and his mother's efforts to embrace her new daughter-in-law were appreciated. However, that was when I missed my mother most of all and realised that the elongated road ahead of me stretched endlessly.

Kathleen and Murray, the two Aboriginal girls who worked in the house, padded barefoot across concrete floors. Kathleen's big grin was a fixture and she giggled uncontrollably every now and again. Murray remained serious and ever wary of the vigilance of the Missus. Together they swept and polished, weeded and raked.

That afternoon I wrote letters home telling of our arrival. Then it was shower time and a change of clothes for dinner. Ceremony reigned at the evening meal. The Aboriginal girls carried gleaming silver dishes to the table. At the head Pat carved the meat and on his right John's mother served the vegetables. I wondered what John was eating in his solitary camp beneath the stars. When the last plate was filled and passed on, we removed our linen serviettes from shiny silver serviette rings and started eating. The evening meal was certainly an occasion. The formality of the setting was counterbalanced by the jovial and often rowdy accounts of the day's activities. I listened attentively. There was so much to absorb and learn. I did not know where to start. Things were different now because I was there to stay. I had a new family.

'Got any tips for the new place yet?' Pat asked searchingly.

'Of course,' I replied, then added rather lamely, 'When do you think I'll be going to join John?'

Three weeks later the Harveys delivered Kyber just as I was stacking my suitcase into the station vehicle. He remembered me and we became instantly inseparable. After a quick smoko, we said goodbye to Roy and

Margaret. Soon we were driving through the gate near the goat yard and heading east. My parents-in-law were delivering me to their son. The caravan in tow was to be our additional shelter, although I could not imagine John fitting through the door. At least it would provide a reassuring touch to the photographs sent home. At Laura Bore gate we left the last fence line before reaching the country that would be home to John and me.

Away from the station complex, the great width and depth of the mighty country overwhelmed me all over again. It was almost as though I was seeing everything for the first time. My sense of arrival was more real than any sense of belonging. Rains had generated green pick and I listened attentively to Pat as he explained the need for follow up rains to keep the grass growing.

Sweeping black soil plains opened out to lightly timbered country until we slowed before a sudden steep drop which was called the jump up. After cautious negotiation, we journeyed on through silvery grey shrubs, native grasses and trees. It was rough and stony and progress was slow. There were irregular red croppy hills and in the distance I saw faraway bluish mauve hills shimmering as they interrupted the ever changing landscape.

We were driving through scrub when four adult camels burst through the bushes in front of us. Unwittingly we gave chase. Strung out in a line, they kept to the road and there was no way to pass them. If we accelerated slightly, they matched the pace. Their dust-coated spit flicked back onto the windscreen as they galloped along with swaying humps and heaving sides.

'Not so long ago we used to work the buggers,' Pat commented just as the sandy coloured, ancient quadrupeds slewed away to our left. He explained they had been used as beasts of burden, carrying loaded packsaddles before the days of packhorses and motor vehicles.

Upon our arrival John's face lit up. His relief to see us spoke volumes.

'You must have known I'd do such a good job as a carpenter that the caravan wouldn't be necessary,' he laughed.

To everyone's amazement the caravan was no longer attached to the car. Somewhere between where we stood and the last gate fifty miles back, the tow bar had let us down. We all agreed the caravan could stay where it was until morning.

The wood pile before me was stacked high and not far from it was my stove, an open fire. A blackened camp oven rested to one side.

'Welcome to your kitchen, little wife. Thought I'd cook dinner on your first night. We'll have eggs with my stew if you've brought any with you. I knocked up some johnny cakes too just to impress you. Why don't you set the table?' And he pointed to the dining room.

I was impressed all right, but tomorrow that would be me stirring the cooking pot.

'It's a good bough shed, John,' commented Pat, pushing against the posts. Aha, I recognised this design from the Hooker Creek airport cafe where Johnny and I had sheltered briefly on our way to Inverway three years ago. However, my newly constructed dining room was far more endearing. The rickety old wooden table in the centre was more secure than it looked.

'To your left is the master bedroom,' John directed. He lifted the tent flap to reveal two familiar camp stretchers now pushed together. We looked at each other and understood that our beginnings had begun.

CHAPTER 6

RIVEREN

....

From my first day at our bough shed I became fully aware of the magnitude of our undertaking. There was not a coil of wire let alone a fence, no herd of cattle, no buildings. From basic beginnings it was ours to develop. There were just the two of us.

John had always known that he would call this place Riveren. As he had declared to Johnny and me three years ago, this land was at the headwaters of the Victoria River, the biggest river in the Northern Territory, the historic river that meanders five hundred miles to the Timor Sea.

Every year the blackfellas in John's stockcamp would ask, 'When we bin musta that ribren country next time, Muluga?' as they pointed towards the eastern end of Inverway. White fellas similarly referred to it as the river end of Inverway, even though it was really the river beginning.

I remember when I first heard the story and thought how lyrical Riverend sounded. Being a stickler for grammar and pronunciation, I naturally inserted the missing 'd'. However, when I understood the origin of Riveren, I thought it was perfect. There could never be a 'd'. Riveren sounded right because it was right.

Once the caravan was recovered, it was positioned opposite the tent, thereby becoming an extra wall that also served as a wind break. John's parents wished us luck and said they would see us in a few weeks time when we travelled to Inverway to collect our mail and stores.

My bathroom and toilet were separate structures and that was not so much a luxury as a necessity. A rubber hose was draped across the tin wall of one enclosed structure making it the bathroom. It was the three sheets of galvanised iron surrounding the hole in the ground that bothered me. My innate city sense of privacy was stubborn and I asked for a fourth sheet. With a roar of laughter, John dismissed my request for a door. 'Who on earth is going to see you out here?' he asked.

Mum had taught me well that 'what can't be cured must be endured' and I was about to prove it in a whole new way. Though huge steel trusses—a thoughtful, practical wedding gift from John's friends in Wyndham—lay on the ground three hundred yards to our east, I knew it would be some time before our first official station building, denoting privacy and protection from the elements, would be erected. In the meantime, I would just have to make do.

In the kitchen area, the old kerosene fridge was protected from the elements by additional sheets of iron. This most important piece of furniture was filled from top to bottom with meat which John had slaughtered a few days earlier. Picking up an entire tail, I asked my knowledgeable husband how on earth I should cook it. Pointing to a large slab of yellow fat, I then asked him what that was for. The rump and roast on the second shelf looked quite different to those displayed in the butcher's window at Pymble. However, my multi-skilled husband had all the answers and the first of a lifetime of lessons commenced right there and then.

On previous occasions I had accompanied John when he organised the meat supply for the station. It was called 'getting a killer'. Out on the run, John, with rifle in hand, would climb a tree to await the small mob of cattle being driven towards him by the stockmen. When the unsuspecting cattle were underneath him, John would shoot the appropriate beast.

He was an excellent butcher, even though it wasn't his favourite job on the station. I had watched John and an offsider carefully remove the hide that would later be treated and made into ropes and hobbles. Each section of the beast was also carefully dissected and handled. My understanding of anatomy and physiology assisted in identifying the various organs and cuts of meat and I scored reasonably well whenever John quizzed me. When all the meat had been placed on thick leafy branches in the back of the open tray vehicle, the killer was delivered to the station butcher shop.

Not only did we not have a station butcher shop, but I was John's only offsider!

'You need to know the most important things first. Always keep your butcher knives sharp,' he advised, as with alarming speed he demonstrated how to use a steel. Holding the steel in one hand, he ran the knife swiftly and repeatedly across it. This flicking, rasping action looked a lot more difficult than shaking down a thermometer, which was something John found hard to do.

He took the long tail, cut it between the joints and handed me the segments of bone. Into the camp oven they went and as I added water, I smiled with satisfaction. The fire was the right heat and stage one of my first oxtail stew was under way. John showed me how to slowly melt or render the slab of greasy kidney fat. Before it set, I poured it into an empty flour drum. It was my cooking fat as well as dripping for cakes and biscuits.

John's mother had demonstrated setting the hops mixture for bread making, using potato or beer as a starter. She warned me that hops were temperamental and did not like extremes of temperature. With no fear of failure I mixed the flour and hops and lukewarm water, working my dough just as I had practised in the Inverway kitchen. With the rounded loaf in its first stage of preparation, I returned it to the silver bread tub. As though it was filled with golden eggs, I carefully wrapped it in canvas and then in an old grey blanket before carrying it to the most distant corner of our bedroom tent, away from direct heat, flies and dust. Apparently the dough was equally temperamental and had to be kept at a certain temperature or it would not rise.

Several hours later, I pushed down the marginally expanded dough, hopeful that the second rising would make up for the first. Not so. Eventually I tipped the sluggish dough onto my canvas sheet, kneaded it, divided it, then shaped the individual loaves before placing them in the camp oven to cook. The end result was even more abysmal. Despite my best efforts and optimism, my inaugural bread making was a complete flop.

There was no point in wiping down the table every hour of every day. The persistent dust left a permanent red film over everything. Like chalk dust, it was finely grained but I could taste it and smell it. It was through my hair, under my fingernails, in my ears and between my toes. John wasn't even aware of it. It was a far cry from Moree or Mudgee, those country towns about which I had so often dreamt. I thought about Mum and Dad enjoying their morning tea on the back patio surrounded by camellias and azaleas, droning bees and warbling magpies. As I raked the ground of my first home, I tried to picture the crowds at Sydney's Central Railway Station being propelled into the already packed train carriages.

Kyber loved his new home without boundaries or restrictions. When cawing black crows stalked the camp fire area, he hunted them with deep woofs of displeasure. His equally shiny black coat absorbed the heat like blotting paper and his pink tongue lolled as he panted noisily. With one eye always on me, he rested regal head on huge paws, waiting and watching. Twenty-four hours a day Kyber was my shadow.

We lived by the sun. When day turned to night we went to bed. Breakfast always beat sunrise. As the first golden rays splintered across the pink and mauve and blue-smudged sky, we had already started work. I carted water in an old drum to heat over the camp fire for washing the enamel plates and pannikins. The same water source was used to wash our clothes, and it was surprising what a scrubbing brush and elbow grease could achieve. Our camp site deliberately adjoined the bore chosen as our station water supply or house bore. Although the drillers had had to persevere to a depth of three hundred feet, the water was both plentiful and incredibly soft. At Inverway the bore water containing lime was quite hard and the Underwood girls usually rinsed their hair in rainwater.

Without any warning, innumerable black stink bugs invaded our camp. For a whole week these horrid creatures lodged everywhere. They congregated inside billy cans, water bags, bedclothes and boxes. When I disturbed them they emitted a foul odour, giving credence to their name. I swept them up by the thousands and every night they increased their advances. I couldn't imagine their place in creation and wondered if St Francis of Assisi himself could love such vile insects.

John taught me many things. I learned about the native grasses; the perennial Mitchell grasses and the annual Flinders grasses. Although the annual average rainfall was approximately eighteen inches, John explained that it was how and when the rain fell that was all-important. Early storms that generated the first green pick needed follow up rain to keep the grass growing. If it rained in November and not again until February, the green grass died. Steady soaking rains were needed to fill the cracks in the black soil, as well as the creeks and billabongs. There were few green Christmases as the first months of the calendar year usually brought the heavier falls. Although I had witnessed the wrath and ferocity of the tropical Wet Season storms, I had not experienced the full rainy season from October until April. With the approach of the Dry Season, I looked forward to seeing the seasonal transformation of the landscape with cloudless skies and cooler weather.

There was so much to learn. Between John and Mother Nature I had the best teachers in the world.

We were well practised in letter writing and my epistles continued to family and friends. We kept diaries and in our station or work diary John recorded not just our daily activities, but the quantity and description of any materials used. From day one his work ethic was evident and the accountability that would govern our lives commenced in our camp that gradually blossomed into a station on the banks of Camel Creek.

Sometimes we went for long walks at the end of the day. Along the dry creek bed, John identified trees and stones. When he said the creek flooded in big rain, it was hard to imagine. I glimpsed sand goannas rustling leaves as they scuttled past. There were wallaby droppings amongst the unmistakable tracks of a dingo pack. Brilliant bright green bush budgerigars twittered and swooped overhead almost too swiftly to be seen.

It was a country teeming with surprises and yet I had seen very few cattle. There was no floor plan for Riveren and I sensed all over again the magnitude of our challenge. How would we achieve our objectives? Progress seemed interminably slow. However, John had the vision and I had determination and faith. We were certainly not frightened of hard work and were resigned to the fact that any progress would be step by step, day by day. How often we reminded ourselves that Riveren, like Rome, would not be built in a day.

My bread continued to resemble a burnt offering. I faithfully followed the recipe, the instructions and the tips. As he attempted to get his teeth through a particularly rocky chunk, John looked at me and said, 'Not bad; not good either. Things can only improve.'

He might have loved me eternally, but his honesty never faltered.

The fortnightly mail plane was due at Inverway. I thought this eagerly awaited day would never arrive. We planned an early departure, as I was looking forward to 'posting' my letters in the canvas mail bag as well as receiving some. We secured the tent flap before we left. On the previous afternoon an unruly willy willy had whisked through our camp, leaving choking dirt and debris as a reminder of its brief visit. It churned red dust into a giant icecream cone, twirling and whistling as it spun on its tail. I followed the path of the spiralling dust storm gathering in intensity as it skimmed across the horizon. When it was no longer visible, I commenced the massive clean up operation.

The old red Bedford growled in objection as John shifted down another gear. The jump up seemed steeper than ever and the truck laboured as it gradually inched forwards and upwards. I cheered when we levelled out at last and the excitement of an outing was shared by man, woman and dog. Just as we picked up some pace, the truck started to wobble, then wobble violently as it swerved towards the turpentine scrub. John pulled up with a degree of difficulty. He swore when he saw the flat tyre. I walked off to find rocks to chock the wheels, John located the weighty kangaroo jack and the confounded business of changing a tyre began. When we finally drove up to the station homestead four hours later, we discovered that the mail plane had already been and gone.

John's mother always opened the mail bag and sorted the contents. The small pile for us contained two letters postmarked Pymble and the *Racetrack* magazine addressed to John. After lunch, my husband and his parents moved into the office for business discussions and I read my letters for the third time.

Feeling a little despondent and quite redundant, I took Kyber for a swim in the dam. Upon our return, I asked if I could send a telegram to

my parents as they would not receive my letters for another fortnight.
There were no telephones in these outlying isolated areas and all the
stations were dependent on the Royal Flying Doctor base in Wyndham
for all their communications other than mail. Telegrams could be sent
and received at set times on weekdays and Saturday mornings. I had seen
the two-pitched whistle on hand in case of an out of hours emergency.
Every weekday morning there was a medical session and at midday the
airwaves were up for grabs for a whole hour. The hectic galah session, as
it was known, allowed station people to exchange news, discuss boundary
musters with neighbours, organise the borrowing or return of goods, or
advise travel arrangements between stations.

I found the radio language very strange. To speak into the microphone
one had to press a button, repeat each phrase at least twice and at the
end of the message say 'over'. Above all, everything was so public. As one
who was used to the pristine privacy of a suburban doctor's rooms, I
hoped that I would never have to consult a doctor over the radio. Everyone
sounded so proficient as they spoke using the phonetic alphabet, repeating
words and phrases so that the operator in Wyndham could decipher the
message above the intermittent but noisy bursts of static. There seemed
to be standard, frequently used sayings like, 'all OK, all OK', 'roger, roger',
and 'over and out'.

Inverway's call sign was SZ or Sierra Zulu. It was stupid to feel nervous.
With stammered perseverance, I continued. Eventually I managed to make
myself heard as well as understood as I sent a telegram to let Mum and
Dad know that all was well.

Our supplies came from the Inverway store. Its supplies came from
Perth by ship twice a year. When the ship reached Wyndham, the large
silver seatainer destined for Inverway was loaded onto the fuel truck,
alongside forty-four gallon drums of diesel, machine oils and other
requirements. I looked at the dozens of tins lining dozens of shelves.
There were tinned fruits and vegetables, tinned butter and tinned cheese
for special occasions, tinned fruit cakes and tinned meats for emergencies.
There were sacks of flour and sacks of rice. Amongst mops and brooms
were furniture polish and Silvo, clothes pegs and starch powder.

Pat had prepared a bag of his home-grown potatoes, onions and
pumpkins for us. I carried the boxes of stores set aside for Riveren out

to the truck, while John loaded the cement mixer and other tools that we needed to borrow. Our last stop was at the Aboriginal camp where Alan was waiting. This young lad had completed his education in Perth and was coming to Riveren to be John's other offsider.

One of those who belong not entirely to either the Aboriginal or the white man's world, his quietness verged on sullenness. Since time eternal white men had sought the comforts of Aboriginal women and the offspring of these relationships often existed in a sort of 'no-man's land'. The birth of a light-coloured baby usually created havoc in the camps. Many of these children were fostered or absorbed into station families.

John had told me the story of his mate Sabu Sing, the ringer from Wave Hill. His father was a Chinese station cook and his Aboriginal mother already had a mob of piccaninnies. Tom Fisher, manager of Wave Hll, had fostered little Sabu from a very early age. John was adamant that Sabu was not just a top horseman and bushman, but was unique in that he was equally respected and accepted by all peoples.

It was another slow journey home. As we approached Buchanan Springs, a rare permanent water source, we were confronted by an arresting vision. A flock of large birds was moving before us like performers in some pagan ritual. Even as we watched, others glided in to land. With outstretched wings, they extended their legs forward and downward like the undercarriage of a plane. In hushed silence, we looked in amazement at their pale grey plumage, long dark legs and long straight bills. Almost as though they wore scarves, bright red bands swathed their heads which dipped and lifted and arched at an increasing tempo. Initially the wing flapping was gentle and slow, then it accelerated vigorously until the birds were actually lifted up into the air. They rose excitedly and glided down, over and over again, leaping and pirouetting like a well-rehearsed ballet troupe. Their elaborate display was breathtakingly beautiful. From dress circle seats in an Outback opera house, we had unexpectedly been entertained by the ballet dancers of the bush.

Alan was almost as happy to have arrived as we were to return. Dropping his swag under an old snappy gum, he joined John to discuss the job ahead. After rib bones, steak and luxurious fresh vegetables, we were all ready for bed. Alan said goodnight. John disappeared into our tent. As I cleaned my teeth by the firelight, I saw again the mesmerising movements of the beautiful grey birds. Minutes later, in the land where the brolgas dance, we slipped intertwined into the world of dreams.

Selecting a suitable red stony ridge, John had already pegged out the shed, the post holes were dug and the gravel was in place for the cement work. From the camp site the silhouette of the shed gradually changed. I knew that sheds symbolised the pivotal point of a station to a man; however, this shed was to accommodate more than tools for repairs and maintenance. When the first corner room was eventually completed, we moved into our second home with a sense of real progress.

I was glad our nights in the tent were behind us, for as the months rushed by, the coldness surprised me. Our proximity to the Tanami Desert guaranteed low temperatures at night. The Dry Season heralded the transformation of green grasses to straw coloured natural hay, and the chilling easterly winds whistled around and sometimes through us day and night. John was equally surprised by rain falling every month. My first Dry was atypical in that sense.

There was another, thrilling reason I was glad to have a 'proper' roof over our heads. We both adored children and were overjoyed to be expecting our first baby. When the news reached Inverway, Peg was quick to recommend the Halls Creek hospital from personal experience. However, during my midwifery training, I had witnessed unexpected outcomes and complex problems during labour and delivery. There was no reason for me to take any risk by relying on local hospitals offering limited facilities. John supported my decision to have our baby in Sydney and we both agreed that this would be the only reason for such an extended separation. On the day that I wrote to my family of this additional dream come true, I also wrote to Dr Bob McInerney, Tom Quilty's ringer in disguise and esteemed obstetrician, to make the booking for my confinement.

By now our small plant of horses had been walked down from Inverway. Towards the end of the Dry, these horses started to look wasted and ill. John's complaints of nausea were worrying because he and I had always boasted cast-iron constitutions. Most of my potted plants had long since shrivelled beyond revival. Interestingly, I remained free from any symptoms.

Perhaps that could be attributed to the fact that I mainly drank boiled water in the form of tea and coffee. The abundant supply of super-soft water that had been so influential in choosing the location of our future homestead had been classified as 'fair'. It had been a reasonable expectation that with increased use of the bore the water quality would improve. The water warranted retesting.

Meanwhile, the building materials for our homestead had arrived, and from Bundaberg in Queensland carpenters followed to take up residence in the second corner room of the shed. Even though I had graduated to cooking on a wood stove with an oven, my bread battle continued. These men proved good sports as well as skilled tradesmen.

'Good exercise for the teeth, love,' they chuckled as they dunked their crusts in rich thick gravy.

I resorted to damper as a back-up. For one who was a perfectionist, I was a little low in self-esteem.

Within three weeks the basic structure of the prefabricated homestead had been erected. Built three feet above ground level, it was designed for the tropics with every possible wall space being substituted with windows. I barely had time to absorb the significance of four walls and a roof, front door and back door, before I was Sydney bound. I had lived at Riveren for just ten months and was not looking forward to leaving my new husband and new home.

'Don't be lonely,' John and I farewelled each other. 'See you when we are three.'

CHAPTER 7

A LITTLE RINGER

....

I had never felt more isolated. Beyond the front gate at Pymble were countless masses of unknown faces intent on individual agendas. In the past I had automatically taken my place in the crush. Now I was affronted by the city's concrete jungle and claustrophobic crowds. I had become an outsider. No longer a gregarious creature seeking the comforts of the herd, my thoughts strayed to the spaces and solitude of my home in the sun. From afar, I tried to imagine what John was doing.

Dr Bob McInerney was pleased to see me. As he combed his hair in the large mirror on the back of his door, I found it difficult to reconcile this impeccable professional with the ringer who had single-handedly mustered the rogue piker bullocks back to Springvale Station. He was extremely interested in family news from the Kimberley and knowledgeably discussed the seasons and markets. Finally he examined me; confirmed that bub was coming along nicely and that I should continue weekly visits until my estimated date of confinement. His only additional instructions were to enjoy being back in town. However, for me the ensuing weeks dragged endlessly.

Mum, on the other hand, was thrilled to have her youngest daughter back and we chatted as we shared the household chores. Over many cups of tea we looked through old family albums as Mum relived my babyhood and other favourite memories. We lingered over an old photograph of the two of us with prams. Mum was taking baby Johnny for his daily walk and alongside I stood proudly with my doll's pram. It contained my much loved baby, a velvet soft golden cocker spaniel puppy called Rusty. How clearly I recalled my inconsolable sobbing after he died from distemper.

Mum hugged me. 'Always remember Terry that your children are on loan from God. Treasure each moment for the years pass so quickly.'

The nurses' luncheon reunion was organised with lightning speed. My old friends were all anxiously awaiting my first-hand information and photographs. They demanded every conceivable detail. What did I wear? What did I cook? How was John? Was I lonely? What did I do all day?

It was so good to cuddle their babies and observe the changes that motherhood had engraved. My friends in their familiar urban patterns were as happy as larks, comparing the progress of their infants and toddlers, weekend outings and community activities.

Anne's delight to see me again was disguised by her mock disappointment. 'I was hoping for a cake of your home-made soap, Terry.'

In promising not to forget next time, I obliged their curiosity by describing how it was made.

'I take a large quantity of fat from the killer and render it in a huge cauldron over an open fire, then add caustic soda and resin,' I told them. 'I make sure the mixture is boiled before I pour it into flat tins to set and then later I cut it into slabs.' I explained that even though everyone living on the station used the soap—visiting carpenters too—one preparation lasted a long time.

Then, of course, they wanted to know what a killer was. It seemed I could talk all afternoon and still barely scratch the surface of their questions.

In promising to write, they all copied down my address as care of Inverway Station, via Wyndham. No exaggeration was necessary to highlight the excitement and anticipation that preceded mail day once a fortnight. It was difficult for them to understand that fortnightly mail to Inverway did not guarantee fortnightly mail to me. Sometimes the mail would accumulate for a month or longer until a vehicle travelled between Inverway and Riveren for whatever reason. As I plunged into the importance of the written word in our lives, namely rainfall records, capital improvements book and diaries, I sensed a loss of interest. How could they relate to those things? I now lived in a different world.

'How often do you go shopping?' worried ever-practical Flissy.

It was a simple answer. 'We don't.' I explained the bulk order system from Perth. The bottom line was that, apart from those goods, what we didn't grow or make ourselves, we went without.

Final reminiscing was reserved for our common foundations. We were all immensely proud that our St Vincent's Hospital was continuing to lead the way in its commitment to excellence and groundbreaking surgery. During our training the nation's first coronary bypass had been done there, and now Dr Harry Windsor had performed Australia's first heart transplant at St Vincent's.

As they each departed to settle their children and prepare the evening meal for husbands, I longed for a telephone connection to Riveren. Just to say hello to John would have been wonderful, but of course there was no telephone his end. We were back to weekly letter writing.

There was no mistaking the first labour pains. Having the inside information of my midwifery experiences would give me a rails run, I reasoned. However, I'd completely underestimated the intensity, force and impact of contractions. Dr McInerney arrived at the Mater Hospital just in time. He smiled his reassurance and encouragement. Delivery was imminent and within minutes he announced, 'Oh, good girl, well done Terry, it's a little ringer!'

Our baby son was exquisitely beautiful and I was completely overwhelmed by the realisation that this new life was the product of our love. As I held and touched the little baby who had journeyed safely from the protection within me to commence his life with us I ached with joy, relief and love.

My heart and mind and soul were flooded with a new sense of fulfilment. It was as though I had waited all my life for this moment. I longed for the one to whom he bore such an undeniable resemblance. He was a miniature John. As I gently kissed our precious baby, I whispered, 'Little baby son, you don't know how much you are loved.'

In anticipation of my loneliness in missing John, visitors came in droves. I was thoroughly spoilt as people and flowers competed for space in my hospital room. As the physical and emotional changes following childbirth evolved, I understood fully at last all the things I had learned from text books. In the classroom of life, personal experience is the most perfect tutor of all.

Although Mum telephoned the Halls Creek Store immediately with the good news, no-one could contact Inverway on the two-way radio. Either Pat and Peg did not have their radio switched on that Saturday afternoon or they could not hear 'Sierra Zulu' being called repeatedly.

I was bitterly disappointed that John did not know about the safe arrival of our tiny golden-haired bundle until the Monday telegram session. That was when the whole country found out too. I murmured all this to my baby boy, whose perfectly shaped lips made silent sucking sounds against his tiny fist. On the other hand John, who had always lived within the communication limitations imposed by geographic isolation, experienced only immense relief and total happiness when he eventually discovered that he was a father.

To celebrate the safe arrival of his son and heir, John remained at Inverway overnight. Beneath those incredible outback skies, Pat and Peg, together with old Mark and Lee, gave John a hand to wet his baby's head.

The identification card with birth details and discharge weight was a treasured souvenir from the hospital. On the back, words of reassurance were printed: 'Take this with you on your regular visits to your baby clinic.' Motherly instinct would have to suffice for me. Our baby would progress without the traditional infrastructure and community network that many new urban mothers depended upon. The very knowledge that the back-up system existed was for them a comfort.

In preparation for motherhood in isolation, I visited the baby clinic at St Ives, not far from my parents' home in Pymble. I also purchased a heavy, somewhat cumbersome set of Karitane baby scales so that I could record weights and monitor my baby's progress. Remoteness would not be allowed to interfere with my new role of motherhood and there was nothing more vital to me than the well being and progress of our beautiful baby son.

The hand-crocheted lace bonnet and booties worn by John at his christening had been carefully preserved by his mother. It surely could have been baby John all over again as the Pymble priest baptised little blue-eyed Martin John. He was indeed the littlest angel in our midst and I was impatient to introduce him to his father.

Our return journey had been organised to enable us to meet up with Peg and John's sister, Suzanne, in Perth, and then we would all travel home together. It was hardly a short cut, rather a rare opportunity to shop for major purchases in person.

The flight from Sydney to Perth with a brand new baby was of considerable duration. However, it reinforced the marvels of aviation as our huge jet effortlessly traversed our great Australian continent from east to west. We were as one. Baby Martin nestled snugly into me as he dreamt the unknown dreams of the newborn.

Perth appeared a gentle city, without the intense pressure larger cities imposed on their citizens. The first Underwood grandson was welcomed at the airport by his adoring grandmother and aunt and instantly became a source of pride and affection to the immediate family and family connections.

At a large retail store, Peg and I selected a simple bedroom suite, dining room buffet and cot. The luxury item was a bedside reading lamp. These purchases would be transported by ship to Wyndham, and then make the long road journey to Inverway and later still to Riveren. It was another step forward.

Our flight from south to north covered an impressive distance. Even from the awesome altitude, the vastness was alluring. It reached up to me as it stretched across our land. At Broome and Derby, we gasped in the sweltering heat as the oppressive coastal humidity embraced us. It was a restless overnight stay, necessitated by the schedule of connecting flights.

Towering, dark, menacing thunderheads next morning ensured a turbulent flight in a smaller aircraft to Halls Creek.

There was no-one at the airport on our arrival. It had not seriously occurred to me that John would not meet us. It had never occurred to him to do so. His commitment to the job was absolute. He was attending a muster at Kirkimbie Station.

Once again the family shared aircraft came to the rescue. Three days later baby Martin, mother and grandmother were flown south-east to meet Daddy and Grandad at Inverway.

After a welcoming lunch we returned in haste to Riveren, bathed in emotional fulfilment. Martin settled well. With great excitement, I absorbed the many changes that had occurred during my long absence of two months. Inside our homestead, the restful Hans Heysen landscape, Mick and Cherry Quilty's wedding gift, was not only unpacked but hanging on the lounge room wall. John had thoughtfully hung our two other pictures and a mirror to enhance my return to a real home. The only problem was that I would need a ladder to access those images at eye level.

Outside, the high tank erected above the bore to store water was the sole remnant of our original camp site. John had sent water samples away for analysis and the results were anxiously awaited. John's two offsiders, Alan and the new boy, Aaron, were digging trenches for French drains and septics. They used crowbars and shovels and worked well as a team. The wiring of the 32-volt electricity cables had been laid and power finally connected. It was thrilling to press a switch and have a light respond. At night after our generator was stopped, the attached battery cells gave sufficient light until morning.

John had built the goat yard to the same design as the one at Inverway. Its inhabitants Billy, Nanny and twins were on free range until the house fence was erected. Of greater importance, though, was the House Paddock fence. Fencing pickets were driven into hard stony ground that in places threatened total resistance. Gradually, wire fence lines with four barbs stretched further out across the landscape.

John had an agenda to build practical, long-lasting improvements. His efficiency was absolute and his philosophy was echoed in his favourite song by Ned Miller, 'Do What You Do Do Well'. He commenced construction of our main station stockyards using railway line and sleepers instead of the more commonly used wooden posts and lancewood rails. Days and weeks of constant welding left his eyes bloodshot and weary.

Our homestead was both basic and luxurious. Not only did I have electricity and running water, I had a new kerosene refrigerator and a gas stove. I had insisted on gauzed windows, despite advice that their presence made it hotter. Of paramount importance to me was the screening of flies, mosquitoes and all other insects. Perhaps most important of all was our own Traeger radio transceiver in the corner of the dining room. We were at last in touch with our immediate world and had access to the outside world too through the Royal Flying Doctor Service. Our allocated call sign was SUM or Sierra Uniform Mike.

Fortunately, both three thousand gallon rainwater tanks were full. Due to our water crisis, the horses and goats and the few cuttings that had survived were given rainwater. The goats made short work of the frangipani trees we planted, and further gardening was reluctantly postponed until the house fence was in place and the bore water problem resolved.

As daily temperatures soared, the scorching sun relentlessly baked the earth. Towards midday, as the heat intensified, the zincanneal walls of our homestead creaked in objection. In accompaniment the rooftop groaned as the tin tried to reject the blasting red rays. Overhead the blinding fireball enticed wisps of clouds to play together until they accumulated to form mountainous cumulonimbus clouds. During the build up, the blistering dry heat was challenged by a new humidity, warning that the long-awaited rains were not far away. We sweated often and slept little. At night, damp pillowslips were common. John and I bumped into each other in the hallway on our frequent visits to the refrigerator for cold water. Little Martin drank thirstily too. Through the wet sheet draped across his cot, the airflow from the mantle fan helped to keep him cool.

John had driven to Inverway to collect a contractor and some fresh meat. That afternoon Martin and I were startled by ferocious, growling thunder and rising winds, which quickly whipped into a frenzy bringing the glorious smell of rain. Through the closed window we looked out at the distant horizons and the rapidly approaching curtain of blackness. It was rent by brilliant and irregular jagged sheets of lightning. As the first raindrops splattered, they individually marked the red dusty ground until they quickly intensified to bombard the rooftop and turn dust into mud. The torrential downpour was deafening. The house shuddered and I held my little boy to reassure him as the storm raged all around us. Mother Nature's performance could not have been accommodated on any man-made stage. This spectacular drama unfolded before us in the amphitheatre of creation. Hours later as the downpour reduced to a drizzle, the choir of frogs erupted as they celebrated water from the sky. The final players were millions upon millions of flying ants, which somehow negotiated the fine gauze and lay dying on my floor. They shed their filmy wings in a final act of surrender.

'Sierra Zulu, Sierra Zulu to Sierra Uniform Mike.'

Now more familiar with radio techniques, I answered John's call and advised that I had just measured three inches of rain. His astonishment was genuine as not a single drop had fallen at Inverway, the skies were clear and it was only in my direction that a faraway band of cloud was visible. It was my turn to be astonished. From within the storm it seemed certain that the rain was widespread.

'I reckon your rain just fell in the rain gauge so I'm leaving now. Expect me in a few hours and look forward to fresh chops for dinner. Over and out.'

Eight miles to the west of the homestead the rain-drenched road bogged his vehicle. Carrying an entire nanny goat carcass across his shoulders, John walked through heavy, sticky mud and running creeks towards home. The contractor followed. A muddy, weary John showered while I prepared dinner and we celebrated our reunion and the beautiful rain, hoping for follow-up rains in the immediate future.

Escalating temperatures and resultant rains highlighted the workings of the land. Encouraged by the hot sun and intermittent drenching showers, fresh green pick protruded through the dampened soils. As our baby chuckled and grew so did the grasses, and our station slowly but surely expanded.

The following months provided a great learning curve for me. There were too few guidelines, and from mistakes I learned the hard way. Baby time was prime time. The days of being single had faded into oblivion. Even the days before Martin's arrival seemed of little consequence. I simply could not imagine life before motherhood. I became an instant expert juggler with feeding and cleaning, washing and record keeping. The cooking was something else again. My bread was becoming edible, and I cooked scones, buns, cakes, biscuits and all the cuts of a killer in the appropriate form. Corned beef had become our traditional lunch and every day I made junkets and custards, both boiled and baked, from goats' milk. All these activities I pursued vigorously against a backdrop of love revolving around my big man and our baby infant, both so alike, both such indispensable parts of me, that my spirits soared with the joyful realisation.

Upon their arrival Mum and Dad were amazed by the growth of their little grandson and impressed with our set-up. It was wonderful to have parental understanding and much-needed support. Martin too loved the extra arms and attention and we worked and walked and talked together. It was such a special time.

For as long as I had known them, my parents had worked selflessly and tirelessly for the well being of their children. Their shedding of the pressures and tensions of years while at Riveren was almost visible. They enjoyed the pure air and wide open spaces with never ending wonder. For the first time they fully understood my contentment.

As the days turned into weeks, Dad recounted with renewed enthusiasm his jackerooing experiences at Booligal in New South Wales and Augathella in Queensland. The Riveren atmosphere seemed to revive nostalgic memories of his own battles with floods and drought, good times and bad times. Though I'd grown up in urban Australia, Dad's empathy with the land had always been apparent. Perhaps I'd inherited my love of the Outback from him.

An overnight visit by John's parents allowed Martin's grandparents their first real time together. The men were happy to start and finish with Paddington, the suburb where Dad had grown up and where the Underwood family founder had held a hundred acre grant. Dad puffed his pipe contentedly as Pat yarned about Underwood family history, and our laughing chubby baby was passed from knee to knee. Looking at Martin, I wondered if his descendants would one day recall our beginnings at Riveren. It was peculiar yet meaningful to establish and fuse past into present in the middle of nowhere.

The marriage of John's second sister Trish to Johnny Westaway was destined for May at Inverway. Apart from Trish almost exchanging vows with David, whom the minister mistook for his twin Johnny, the wedding proceeded without mishap and with much merriment. However, Martin had a cold that was not improving and having farewelled Mum and Dad, I was anxious to leave behind the crowded homestead and gonging meal bells for our quieter but equally efficient Riveren routine.

Martin remained unwell and subsequently unsettled. He fretted in the bouncinette so I nursed him as I performed routine daily tasks. His sleep was fitful and broken. When his symptoms continued to multiply, I called in to the medical session on the radio. After a routine consultation, Dr Tony Noonan suggested an immediate evacuation. I packed hurriedly, John fuelled the vehicle and drove us to Inverway. Within hours Martin and I were airborne in the Royal Flying Doctor aircraft.

On reaching Wyndham, Martin was admitted to hospital. There were many words spoken, words without meaning or resolution. There was no indication of a specific diagnosis or prognosis. Dr Noonan and the other doctor mentioned a probable blood disorder. I struggled as though trapped in a fog. Motherhood had created a mantle of love and protection that completely obliterated my nursing knowledge and experience. The only thing I knew was that whatever was wrong must be fixed and I emphatically stated my desire to take Martin to the best doctor in the country. They recommended that my husband join me and that Melbourne be our destination.

At the Royal Flying Doctor radio base, I met the people whom I knew only by voice. The director, Everett Bardwell, and his assistant Belle could not do enough for me. They had John on radio standby and he and I exchanged the words necessary to ensure his flight to Wyndham the following day. From a public telephone box, I informed Mum of my predicament. Even though the Country Women's Association dwelling in the vicinity of the hospital was comfortable, sleep eluded me.

The news that available seats on the commercial flight south were doubtful added to my confusion. I rang home. Mum rang Dr McInerney and the plea for help passed through various channels all around Australia.

As we boarded the aircraft at Wyndham, Dr Noonan handed me an envelope for the doctor at the elected hospital in Melbourne. He warned

Baby Terry Augustus with elder sisters Anne (right) and Libby (left).

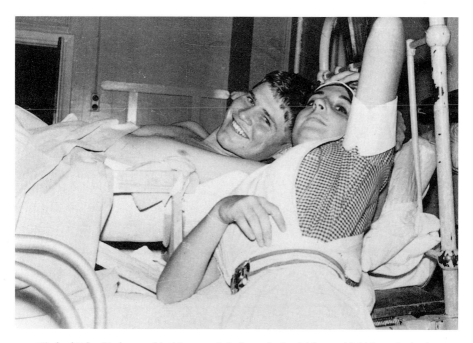

Big bad John Underwood in his extended plaster bed, which engulfed his entire body but not his spirit, and second-year nurse Terry Augustus on night duty in Ward 3 at St Vincent's Hospital, Darlinghurst, New South Wales, in February 1963.

Terry and John's wedding reception at the Carlton Rex Hotel, Sydney, on 6 January 1968. Terry's parents, Frank and Bess Augustus (left) and John's mother, Peg Underwood (right).

The three pioneering Farquharson brothers Archie, Harry and Hughie, pictured here with an unknown mate. They were nephews of legendary explorer and Boss Drover Nat Buchanan, who had formed Wave Hill Station in 1883. In 1894 the Farquharson brothers took up Inverway Station.

Inverway homestead in 1957. Just seven years earlier, the last of the Farquharson brothers, Archie, had died here, at the age of 89. John's father took over the station in 1956, and it has since been divided into three Underwood-owned properties, including Riveren.

John's mate Tony Clark in the Wave Hill stockcamp at Catfish Waterhole in 1960; typical of the way it was.

Terry with faithful shadow Kyber at her Riveren beginnings – the camp fire stove, the bough shed living area and the tent master bedroom – in the middle of nowhere.

John and Terry with Kyber and
Ratsy beside the newly constructed
first homestead, against a backdrop
of never ending horizons.

Terry with first baby, Martin

The young Riveren family: Terry and John, proud and loving parents
of Marie and Patrick, just twelve months apart in age.

Above left: Becky, Marie, Michael and Patrick working diligently at their lessons in the Riveren schoolroom in February 1979. Correspondence lessons and Katherine School of the Air were a way of life for eighteen years.

Above right: Barefooted bush kids: Becky, Michael, Marie (holding Cuddles' paws) and Patrick, in 1981. Later, John went missing while flying this plane. When the search party spotted the tangled wreckage, grief turned to hope when a leg was seen moving in the gaping cockpit. Miraculously, John had survived.

Pope John Paul II, the most travelled Pope in history, aboard an RAAF Boeing 707 flying from Alice Springs to Darwin on 29 February 1986. He is holding photos of Becky and the two other Katherine School of the Air children, Jacqui and Angus, who were chosen to speak to Pope John Paul II on the aircraft radio during his Australian visit. Becky's question to him was last: 'Holy Father, what is the hardest thing about being the Pope?'
(Photo courtesy Northern Territory Library)

that Martin might find travelling difficult and that I might wish to reconsider options upon arrival in Perth.

It seemed an automatic action to remove and read the letter from the unsealed envelope. It requested the receiving doctor to perform blood tests unavailable due to limited facilities in Wyndham to confirm suspected leukaemia. The signature blurred as I handed the letter to John.

'What does this mean?' he pleaded.

'Our baby is going to die,' I sobbed.

Martin deteriorated dramatically throughout the long flight. His pallor and stillness protested against further disturbance and I was fearful of the next long journey. It seemed that the decision had been made for us in a way. We were driven to the Princess Margaret Children's Hospital in Perth, where a paediatrician met us. Martin was taken from us and we waited for the news. It was not long in coming.

'I am sorry to tell you that your baby son has acute myeloid leukaemia.'

There was no disbelief, just total devastation.

We were accommodated at the hospital. The following day as I sat beside my baby's cot, I watched the approach of the medical team on ward rounds. At each bed the doctor in charge quietly discussed the case and treatment with assistants, medical students and nursing staff. As they bypassed us, I understood the nods and looks of concern and sympathy. Our story would be discussed beyond my hearing.

Despite the kindness and support of the staff, I welcomed the doctor's suggestion that we look after Martin away from the hospital environment. Within a week we had moved into a self-contained motel unit, and embarked upon a semblance of family life. As the illness irrevocably and insidiously progressed, we cared for our baby boy with heavy hearts and infinite love. There were no tears left.

Every moment was meaningful. All attempts from family and friends to distract and assist us were rejected. Mum's offer to be there just to help in any possible way was likewise refused with gratitude. I was adamant that Martin be remembered as our healthy, laughing, gurgling infant. John's old Perth-based friends, Judy and Peter Monger, were the only ones who came and went without notice or fuss, whether to deliver a home-cooked meal or to take John for a break.

The two-week remission period brought wonderful comfort simply because Martin felt better. Baby laughter lightened our burden. There was no thought or plan beyond the immediate moment. Day in and day out, we walked long distances along the streets of Perth, carrying in turn our baby son. It was always just the three of us. As the world sped by, our lives were placed on hold.

Martin was in my arms when he stopped breathing. The angels had claimed one of their own. We were always going to lose the battle, but could never have been prepared for the final separation. Mum and Anne arrived from Sydney and Peg flew down from Inverway to stand beside us in our grief. With breaking hearts, we obeyed that which had been decreed by divinity: 'Goodbye Martin darling.'

He was nine months and nine days old. The two of us drove from Perth to Riveren to try to pick up the pieces.

CHAPTER 8

THE OUTBACK RADIO CRACKLED

....

She was twelve weeks old, black and madly affectionate. Although the space on my lap was filled by a wriggling, licking, labrador puppy, the space in my heart was agonisingly empty. Our sorrow was as unremitting as the miles that stretched ahead.

Five days later we pulled up at our blue homestead door. As we walked inside, the awareness that nothing would ever be the same was reinforced all over again. I crumpled as I stood beside the empty cot, touched baby clothes and picked up baby toys. Our sense of loss was overwhelming. John held me tightly and we knew fresh beginnings must be made. We were home.

Silent grieving became synonymous with silent living. The steadfastness of the land was somehow reassuring. The vastness and the isolation were strangely comforting. As through our love we gave each other fortitude, the compelling castled hills seemed to emanate power and additional strength. It was my total surrender to Riveren and all that it encompassed that assisted my healing. I knew with certainty that people, however well meaning, would create additional pressures and friction. If there was such an entity as salvation, it went by the name of solitude, and it stalked and surrounded me like a friendly phantom.

Gentle, gigantic Kyber's woofs of delight at seeing us again had doubled when I presented the squirming Perth puppy. They romped and roamed, yet always remained faithful shadows to me.

Our mail had accumulated over the many weeks away. Many friends had struggled for words with which to comfort us, others simply penned prayers and love for little Martin and his parents. Others wrote: 'What can we say?' We were deeply grateful for so many expressions of support and heartache. With memories so fresh and so permanent, I carefully tied the thick stack of letters and cards with blue ribbon and lovingly placed them in the large hat box which stored the hundreds of air mail letters John and I had exchanged over a five-year period.

During our absence Pat and Peg had handled our station mail. When the eagerly awaited and vitally important analysis of our bore water arrived, everyone's worst fears were confirmed. The soft water in such abundant supply contained an excessive amount of fluoride. There was no possibility of filtering or removing the chemical.

By this stage the foundations of our new station were permanent, the rainwater tanks were low and the Wet was months away. Our water situation was critical. The report read that the Riveren Station bore water was condemned for stock, agriculture and human consumption. Moreover, we were in Perth.

Pat had acted instantly. He telegrammed Water Resources in Darwin for urgent assistance. Within weeks the specialists arrived to organise the replacement bore. Drilling was a very expensive exercise. If water wasn't forthcoming, reimbursement of costs was possible providing the bore site had been selected by a government employed hydrogeologist. Pat escorted the specialist across our roads, sketchy in places and non-existent in others, and remained with him at Riveren until the new site was finally identified. Pat then organised the drilling rig to start work as soon as possible. We were extremely thankful for his invaluable assistance. To locate good water was like discovering gold, even though the quantity at the new site was restricted.

Now that we were back, our immediate priority was to equip the new bore and relocate the high tank. The two-inch polythene pipe used to carry the water to the homestead had to be laid in a shallow trench. Using the tractor borrowed from Inverway to break through the rock hard ground, the process was an absolute nightmare. Having etched the line, we attached a ripper to the tractor to tear the ground. The final and most effective tools were picks and shovels, wielded with unlimited elbow grease.

Thankfully there was so much to do. There was still so much to understand. I was still discovering John's never ending diversity of skills and my transition from city to bush continued at grassroots level. Gradually, I was learning to see what I was looking at. My favourite images were of rich red ochre hills jutting above a patchwork of greens and browns, all of which contrasted boldly against brilliantly clear azure skies. These sights held less appeal for John. He recognised beautiful country as that which supported cattle. He recognised and was grateful for the opportunity of a lifetime, one afforded to so few. Together we would develop this place, incorporating all he had learned over the years to make it the very best, subject to available resources.

They seemed to arrive from nowhere. The rat plague was of the worst dimensions imaginable. Hundreds of thousands of huge, furry, ravenous rats infiltrated the country. They devoured every blade of grass, ringbarked trees and covered the earth like a gruesome, grey, lumpy, feral carpet. Whenever John drove home after dark, his tyres crushed them in their hundreds. For them there was no escape. They were side by side, shoulder to shoulder, an army of predators intent on their survival and our destruction. Only food and the other goods stored inside forty-four gallon drums were spared. Blankets, clothing and shoes were chewed. The rats were disgusting and frightening. Their destruction was horrific.

At Inverway, Pat awoke to find two rats gnawing his toes. John's young brother, Reg, was the right age to issue a personal challenge. He rigged up an ingenious but simple trap by attaching a piece of fat to the end of a board which he balanced strategically on the edge of a forty-four gallon drum. As the voracious rats approached the bait, the board tipped inwards and threw them into the barrel. One particular night, Reg counted rat number three hundred and twenty-seven as it dropped into oblivion.

Kyber was also on a mission. The playful black pup copied him constantly. Together they hunted the rats. 'Watch!' he seemed to command.

He pounced, crunched and dropped the revolting rodent. The pup became an instant expert killer too. Her pedigree name, Beauty, was immediately forgotten. Instead we called her Ratsy.

I don't know why our disposal of rats reminded me of Bonfire Night in Albury. Instead of tom thumbs and double bungers, catherine wheels and skyrockets, we had rats. There was no flickering firelight playing on excited faces. There was just the stench of crunched bodies burning in our well-fuelled inferno.

In my sleep I saw watchful beady eyes backed by long bristly whiskers twitching like antennae. I hoped their fearful cunning and desperate bid for survival would be threatened by the superior cunning of two glossy-coated, untiring dogs. Kyber and Ratsy sniffed and chased and pounced as they won another round. But still the dreaded, mangy rats came.

The destruction and desolation struck at our already aching hearts. A blackness had descended upon us and our country. Although rejuvenation was inevitable, I prayed that it might be soon.

Inadvertently, somewhere along the way, I had adopted the fastidious attitude of other bush women. Chores that would be weekly in the city, I undertook at least daily, as with obsessive determination I scrubbed and swept, mopped and cleaned. There was no lawn to break the dirt surrounding the house, so the floors were impossible to keep clean. Despite my constant efforts the enemy remained victorious. Fine dust was firmly ingrained in everything. Nevertheless, I cleaned onwards and upwards: walls, windows and ceilings. Outside the laundry door, my copper boiled non-stop as grease and stubborn stains were gradually dislodged from our work clothes. Peg's introduction could be proclaimed an unqualified success.

Even though radio reception was unpredictable, the background noise was companionable as I attacked the floors with a vengeance. Sometimes the reception improved marginally at night when Radio Australia and occasionally the Australian Broadcasting Corporation broadcast from Perth the world news in fits and starts. One evening, we picked up the news quite clearly. To hear local news at all was rare. To hear news from so close to home made the news itself seem unbelievable. However, the limited information about a small aircraft fatality at Montijinni Station could not be ignored. Both the pilot and passenger had been killed, but no names were available. We worried and we wondered. Several days later the Bush Telegraph, or galah session, relayed that it was Brian Crowson and his nephew who had perished in the Cessna 150. Our hearts went out to Fay and her brood of young children who had so captivated and impressed me during our stay at Montijinni on our way to Inverway following our honeymoon. The uncertainty of tomorrow had been proven one more time.

The onset of the cat plague suggested that the rats had been located by the bush Pied Piper. The feline thousands were less threatening to us personally as their battlefields did not extend to drawers, cupboards and all things inside and sacred. However, my nursing instincts surfaced yet again and with Dettol and scrubbing brush, I scoured and cleaned until my hands were raw.

When the owl plague followed the cat plague, I wished that John, mustering at Inverway, was beside me. The moonlight reflected on the silver rooftops of the homestead and shed and throughout the long nights owls would dive into the roofs with a weird pinging sound. Their suicides were sad and eerie.

Every Saturday was store day and every second Saturday was mail day at Inverway. Every day was the same at Riveren. As we remained dependent on Inverway for everything, we always arrived there with a long list of requirements.

Following afternoon smoko, all the Aborigines wandered out from their humpies and camps. Men, women and children squatted outside the store shed, laughing and talking excitedly as Missus 'opened up'. The men shopped first. They bought luxury items including tinned fruit cake, cream biscuits, tinned apricots, hair oil and torch batteries. Men and women of all ages reminded the Missus about nikki nikki. These four squares of stick tobacco were their most precious allocation and possession. I had seen them suck and chew on the rough uncut plug, allow it to stew, then suck some more and spit out the excess brown juices as they accumulated. I had also seen half-chewed tobacco stuck behind ears and John said it was often rolled in ashes before being chewed again. From my corner of the store where I was chief stacker and packer, I wondered why they loved this dreadful looking stuff so much.

The women kept their money securely knotted in colourful scarves which were thrust deep within their pendulous bosoms. 'Might be somewhere,' they reckoned, while rummaging to retrieve the 'wallet'. Untying the knotted corner was even more complicated and time-consuming. However, it was all performed with lots of giggles and apologies. I wondered if I would ever learn enough of their dialect to freely follow their conversations.

As I returned to the homestead, an old grey-haired lubra slowly approached me on bowed, spindly legs. It was Minnie. With tears coursing down her cheeks, she told me in her pidgin English that old Duncan might be coming back soon on the doctor's plane. Like her lovable camp cook husband, she baked delicious bread and pastry. Duncan was being treated at the East Arm Leprosarium and apparently his prognosis was good.

Others did not fare so well. The age-old rampant diseases of tuberculosis and leprosy remained active among the Aborigines and the diagnosis, treatment and follow-up checks provided ongoing challenges to Outback medical teams.

Leprosy, that dreadfully misunderstood disease, was legally notifiable. There were stories of policemen in the pursuit of their duties hunting leprosy suspects. Getting wind of this, some of the sufferers would go bush or into hiding until the doctor's plane or policeman's motor car departed. Dr John Hargreaves was not only a great pillar in the treatment and management of leprosy, but a champion in the cause of winning the trust of the patients and their families. Vital early detection was often prohibited by the very real fear of hospitalisation. An early symptom was elevated red patches on the skin. However, sometimes the disease progressed until deadened nerve endings resulted in the sufferer receiving knocks and burns from camp fires. Aborigines sometimes presented their charred extremities as the first warning of leprosy.

The Aboriginal families referred to me as 'dat shista belonga John'. We were friends from the start because they all loved John and also because they respected medical knowledge and often sought my advice. The routine station medical chest at Inverway contained an assortment of basic drugs, medicines and bandages. Each bottle and jar was numbered as well as labelled. At the conclusion of an on-air medical consultation, the doctor could order the drug of choice by indicating the number. I listened while the doctor on the radio, repeating each phrase twice, responded to my sister-in-law Trish's medical call about an Aboriginal child with an infected wound. 'From the refrigerator, select number 23 and give one teaspoonful of the yellow mixture every six hours for ten days. If the inflammation and pain do not subside within thirty-six hours or so, please let me know, over.'

Aerial medical services periodically visited Inverway, where a large population of Aborigines continued to work and live with their extended families. Everyone was entitled to routine vaccinations and health checks, particularly babies and all the old-age pensioners. Runny noses, colds and ear infections were common. The supply of liniment for scabies and lice was on permanent order. My initial dismay at the living conditions in the blacks' camp was shared by many others, including the visiting doctors and sisters. The solutions were less obvious. Help was welcome. Interference was not.

Our first visitor outside of family came to stay. Colleen, my old nursing friend, came to me in my time of terrible emptiness. I was no longer conscious of the continual glare and long hours of unbroken sunlight until Colleen started wearing sunglasses indoors. I explained that curtains were not high on the list of station priorities. There were bores to equip, troughs to install, fence lines to clear and fences to erect. Everyone was looking forward to the well-deserved break promised by the annual Halls Creek race meeting.

With uncontained excitement the preparations for the races were fine-tuned. At Inverway we joined the convoy of vehicles slowly heading west. The race and sports horses had been sent ahead and now two days later the owners, punters and families followed. Past the recognised landmark, the China Wall, the procession slowed to thread its way through the sinuous, tortuous hills towards Halls Creek.

John organised the erection of what appeared to be a tent city on the outskirts of town. We set up camp with all the other station people who pooled not only tents, but supplies and resources. Colleen and I, city-trained nurses, had always practised strict economical use of medical supplies. However, even we were impressed by the conversion of white flour-bag calico linings into tea towels. Everything had a use and a purpose.

The men congregated to exchange information on cattle conditions and meatworks prices for their turnoff, commonly four to five-year-old bullocks. The women chopped great quantities of beef and vegetables in preparation for an enormous stew to feed everyone. All the while, whispered words about specially made ballgowns drifted deliberately like the swirling smoke from the crackling camp fire. Dress details were to be a surprise. Preparations for the outing of the year were certainly taken seriously.

At the calcutta that night I showed Colleen the large room where our engagement party had been held. The hotel was crowded and foaming jugs of beer were being passed in all directions. The demand and flow seemed less to do with thirst than the festivity of friendship. The air of anticipation gathered momentum as horses in the feature races were auctioned. John explained to Colleen that he always bought his own horses for loyalty and luck.

We had barely closed our eyes when it was time to leave for track work. Before daybreak we arrived at the makeshift stables to chat with Mark and Lee, the Inverway trainers, and say hello to Willie Win and Kingdom Come. In nearby stalls the Springvale horses looked impressive. Live Long and Die Happy had been named after Uncle Tom Quilty's favourite toast to mankind. From the buzz of activity at the stables, it seemed everyone in the country raced horses, not just to make up numbers but more so because it was an integral part of their lifestyle. Although the sense of fair play was an unwritten law of the bush, no-one was there to come second.

The Inverway colours of white stars on a black background were easily visible, apart from which the first race of the day was a three horse affair.

There were no starting stalls or race commentary. However, it all seemed to work and the crowd cheered in a frenzy as two horses galloped stride for stride past the finishing post in a cloud of thick, choking dust. The remaining five races were equally thrilling.

Not long after the last race distant shouts of 'head 'em up!' echoed through the dust as coins were tossed high into the air. The light was fading as the swelling crowd pressed forward to take a turn at two-up. Across the other side of the track, the aptly named Father Heaven, from Balgo Mission, was celebrating Mass. There were about fifty blackfellas and a dozen whitefellas at the open air ceremony. Mothers suckled infants, dogs scratched and bit fleas and children played on the side while voices murmured in praise of the Lord. There was an indefinable unity in the joining of prayer. The evening star ascended to witness the final blessing. It was play time for some and togetherness time for all.

John had always proclaimed that winners could laugh and the losers could please themselves. It proved a grand party at the Halls Creek Race Ball. John was president of the historically accurate but somewhat grandly titled Kimberley Goldfields Amateur Jockey Club, which had organised the meeting. He had earlier arranged the display of trophies and placed prize cheques in appropriate envelopes. The presentation speeches were enthusiastically received by a relaxed, cheery gathering. Good old Willie Win had won again and I was delighted when my president husband presented me with the race trophy. The green enamel gas iron complete with collapsible ironing board would be very useful.

As the Belle of the Ball dance loomed, there was a flurry and a scramble for the ladies room. Everyone queued for the single mirror to check that hairsets were in place and to apply fresh lipstick. Many wore long satin gloves. It seemed there was little interest in second placings in these stakes as well.

Since his back operation, John had wisely withdrawn from the rodeo events which took place the following day. John had loved competing and he and his cousin Mick Quilty had also proven to be a very effective and competitive pick-up team. When the rodeo chute gate opened to discharge the bucking horse doing everything possible to dislodge its rider, the pick-up men would position themselves in readiness for the whistle, indicating the rider had made time. Then thundering hooves doubled in number as the pick-up man now alongside the bucking horse, reached out, grabbed the rider and deposited him safely on the ground. The other horseman in the pick-up team would gallop quickly to secure the riderless horse by grabbing its flying halter shank and would then escort it back to the yard. It demanded split-second timing as well as horsemanship skills.

Now it was John's turn to assess the skills of others. He was judge of all the various events over the two days of rodeo and sports that alternated with the two race days. John stood inside the arena, carrying stockwhip in one hand and scoresheet in the other. If a rider stayed mounted with one hand high in the air and spurring all the while for ten seconds, the timekeeper's whistle signalled that he had reached 'time' and John would allocate a score. If the bronco rider 'bit the dust', John would raise his whip and the rider was 'cracked off'. The scores were often influenced by the draw of the horse or bull. A feisty beast, if mastered, could help draw a high score. If the beast sprinted around the ring without the anticipated bucking, the judge granted the competitor a re-ride.

Colleen and I were absolutely fascinated. Everyone wanted to have a go and as the burning sun reached its zenith, there was only increased activity. Galloping hooves and gusty easterlies guaranteed thick dust all day long. Undeterred we sat on the top wooden rails of the rodeo ring amongst the other spectators who yakkied and yelled cheers of encouragement when someone rode well. They groaned dramatically if anyone fell, or worse still was trampled or kicked by the rampaging beast. This day of fun and competition had serious undertones too. Each rider wanted to be the winner. It all looked fraught with danger to us and we were surprised that there were not more injuries. The tough, hard-working inhabitants of the inland were fearless. Whenever they collided with the ground, they picked themselves up and shook themselves down as though they'd fallen onto a sand pit. They knew and respected their horses and their fellow competitors. This was their day.

Many of the predominantly Aboriginal audience were also successful participants. 'Any colour as long as it is red' could have been their motto, as in newly purchased town finery they contributed to their favourite time of year. Most of them wore bright red Akubras. Their shiny red or purple satin cowboy shirts were separated from stiff new jeans by wide leather belts with shiny big silver buckles. Gold engravings adorned these buckles, featuring bucking bronco riders, bullock heads or snaking lasso ropes. They wore multicoloured, casually knotted bandannas around their necks. Brightest of all were the flashing teeth as grins and laughter became one.

That night the laughter of the unknown attractive Rodeo Queen tinkled through the decorated hall. Amongst the pleasantly weary crowd we met John's mate Ken Warriner who had started his jackerooing experiences at Springvale Station under the guidance of none other than the master himself, Tom Quilty. A recent widower, Ken and his two young sons had returned from central Australia to manage a Kimberley cattle station. As the two old mates picked up exactly where they had left off years earlier, it was apparent that this country, combined with fate, proved a harsh taskmaster and those who survived often wore deep and invisible scars.

The meeting over, we farewelled Colleen, my flood of tears my best attempt at gratitude. She had never intruded, but had been there for me. By the time we returned to Riveren, I felt as though we had been away for a month.

Although our advice had been to avoid mating Ratsy during her first season and despite my every effort to comply, Kyber proved the conqueror. I had let her outside for a quick run. Minutes later I discovered the attached lovers and my shouts of disapproval proved little deterrent and far too late anyway.

The following morning, however, the absence of Ratsy's husband was puzzling. I looked far and wide before I discovered my big black dog staggering backwards in a strange circular fashion. He looked vacant and very ill. John helped me bring him home. Even as I stroked and talked to him, he slipped into a coma. There was nothing we could do. I stayed beside him for hours and quite helplessly watched Kyber die from what I suspected was a brain haemorrhage. My good friend and wonderful companion would be the first of many much loved animals that we sadly buried beside our homestead.

Very few people stumbled over us on our remote, isolated, slowly expanding station complex. Very few, if any, outside of family knew of our existence. One night John brought Harry Selmes in from the camp to meet me. Harry said little. It was only after the cards were reshuffled for the umpteenth time that we heard about his youth at an exclusive Sydney boarding school. Harry and John were both accomplished card players, as indeed were most of the bushies with whom I'd come in contact. Harry lived alone as a full-time brumby shooter. Camped by water holes (on this occasion Mucca Waterhole), he shot feral animals as they came in to water from the edge of the desert. My sentimental regret was quickly quashed. In this environment, sentiment and sustainability were strangers. Over many years, those users of grasses and water were reduced by ten thousand head by Harry's rifle alone.

Meanwhile, John's latest project would possibly entice more visitors to Riveren. He had been busy clearing an area for our airstrip. It would be preferable to have it close to the homestead; however, the closest suitable ground surface for our all-weather strip was three kilometres away. Having welded together a huge structure to drag the surface, John worked on the Riveren aerodrome for many hours. The boundaries would be identified by marker drums painted white.

The first pilot to use our airstrip was Gary Maxtead, who pioneered aerial mustering in a fixed-wing aircraft. He responded to John's invitation by flying in without notice on one of the many days I was alone without a vehicle. Consequently he had to walk the three kilometres to the homestead. When John eventually arrived home that night, he suggested to Gary that he demonstrate his mustering techniques in conjunction with the current Riveren muster. I suspected that Gary's infectious enthusiasm and the ensuing aerial mustering results would not only hasten the purchase of our own plane, but also John's implementation of a new kind of efficiency—controlling cattle from the sky.

In fact, plans were already under discussion to purchase an aircraft for Inverway and Riveren. The plane shared between the Quilty and Underwood properties was no longer servicing our needs. Within a few months, a green and white Cessna 175 with VH-KIM painted across its wings was purchased, delivered and parked at Riveren until such time as John learned to fly it. I sensed aerial mustering would quickly follow.

As Ratsy's belly swelled, our baby grew within me. The world was filled with hope and promise. It was dreadfully difficult leaving John for another Sydney confinement, yet there was never consideration of an alternative. Even before losing our baby son, I would never have left anything to chance.

'See you in six or eight weeks,' I murmured to John, as I climbed aboard the plane that would take me from Inverway to Wave Hill—just one of many stages in my journey to Sydney.

The city swallowed me in its daily humdrum of activities. As the power brokers plotted, the intensity and pace of Sydney overwhelmed me once again. However, I respected those who thrived, or at the very least survived, within the machinations of this man-made madness. I missed my evocative country which was truly more about soil, grasses and livestock than about people.

At Riveren the radio air waves crackled.

'W.B.Q. to S.U.M. Whiskey Bravo Quebec to Sierra Uniform Mike. Do you read John? Do you read? Over.'

'Sierra Uniform Mike to Whiskey Bravo Quebec. Reading you loud and clear. Go ahead. Over.'

'W.B.Q. to S.U.M. Congratulations mate. You have a baby daughter. Both well. Over.'

Our new darling bundle was a gift from God when we needed her most. With her blonde curls and blue eyes, baby Marie Thérèse was straight from heaven.

Incredibly, on the same third day of the third month of the year 1970, mare Terry had a filly foal naturally called Marie. Even more incredibly Ratsy delivered her litter of puppies on that day too.

Mum returned to Riveren with baby Marie and me. John met us at Inverway and we hurried home to celebrate the safe arrival of our precious little girl; celebrations that would last a lifetime.

CHAPTER 9

OUR OWN STOCKCAMP

....

J ohn adored our Marie Thérèse junior. The tiny little girl almost fitted into the roughened, hard-working palm of his hand. She looked inquisitively at her Daddy and sensed her world was complete.

John's welcome home present for me was almost finished and he asked me to avoid the shed until he gave the all clear. The mountain of chores that required my attention curbed my curiosity in any case. As the final fingers of golden sunlight traced their cathedral-like columns across the golden land, Mum, Marie and I strolled back to the homestead from the goats' yard having completed one of the last tasks of the day—counting and locking up the herd of fourteen. Along our bedroom wall stood newly painted, handmade book-shelves. John was stacking my beloved books as I entered.

'Welcome home, darling,' he grinned.

John epitomised innovation, balanced with practicality and thoughtfulness.

I was grateful for Mum's company and delighted she would be with us for eight whole weeks. While she loved nothing better than being with family and lending a helping hand, Mum had some trouble becoming accustomed to western time. It was so far behind eastern time. As the Wyndham Royal Flying Doctor base remained the pivotal point of our communications, our clock was set to western time and in sync with Inverway. Mum found the breakfast bell at 3.30 am a little daunting, whereas next door at Wave Hill Station, the clock hands pointed to a far more civilised 5 am. Our eastern neighbours had always operated on central time and conducted their on-air communications through Darwin. John and I were not particularly fussed either way, because we continued to live and work by the sun. Our completion of breakfast coincided with piccaninny daylight.

Another mustering season was about to begin. John had managed to employ some old Riveren hands and some new recruits in Halls Creek. The stopover at Inverway on the return to Riveren in order to replenish stores afforded everyone a happy reunion. The Aborigines' all seemed to be related to each other, and aunties, uncles, cousins, brothers and sisters and grandparents sat comfortably on the gravelly ground to excitedly exchange news.

Although they had tribal or skin names, I could not work out connections by the names they called themselves on an everyday basis. Sheila and Jimmy Jamtin were back and so was Freddy Menzies. Henry and Nora McHale and Henry's brother Frankie were all pleased to see me. Peter Gordon and Poppy Barangari returned with Eric and Alison Smith. Banjo Wallaby and Mosquito told John they might come out for a job by and by. Dreamer was another who did not use a surname.

Within viewing and walking distance of our homestead, the newly constructed humpies were soon fully occupied with adults, children and a various assortment of dogs. The families were pleased with their two and three bedroom corrugated iron buildings. Outside the additional ablution block, which incorporated laundry facilities, John had installed a home-made hot water system. My old wood stove from the shed had been moved to the communal humpy kitchen, but it remained a permanent ornament. The camp fire was not only the Aborigines' preferred cooking place, it was where they gathered at every opportunity. The ovens of choice were holes in the ground and temperature control was achieved by the removal or addition of hot coals.

Meanwhile we were playing host to another visitor. Eileen Steenson was an accomplished pilot who had clocked up many of her flying hours in the treacherous New Guinea skies. This in-house instructor was pint-sized but most particular. Upon her arrival, her fluffy little dog wearing a pale pink bow had been smuggled into her room, despite my protestations that our backyard was of adequate dimensions for all animals, large and small. However, John's flying lessons had to be executed with a minimum of fuss, so I ignored the dog basket and its occupant on its daily transfer from bedroom to vehicle to cockpit.

At the conclusion of another lesson John sat studiously gazing into the techniques of flying text book. Without warning Eileen descended and removed the insert.

'Mr Underwood,' she admonished, 'you'll never pass your examinations if you continue to read *Racetrack* instead of studying your theory.'

Although John's endeavours were genuine and only mildly diverted by Eileen's hand slaps, administered for any slight error, the outside distractions were constant. His offsiders regularly sought advice from the Boss and the most effective method of imparting knowledge was by example. John and Eileen and I conferred and all agreed that John needed concentrated experience well clear of station activities. After weeks of flying around Riveren, the Cessna transporting pilot, trainee pilot and fluffy dog departed for Kununurra.

In John's absence, I assumed the role of manager with a degree of confidence. I had acquired a sound overview of general station activities and had been reminded often enough that it was all a matter of commonsense anyway. It was often not that simple. The blackfellas were not used to working alongside a woman and usually responded to my directions and suggestions by saying, 'Might be, Missus. What does Boss reckon?'

My reassurances that 'John reckons same' worked wonders.

Although I did not expect regular telegrams from John, I always tuned in to the sessions in case there were any messages. Forever conscious that he was practising short field take-offs and landings, stalls, cross wind and forced landings, I hoped and prayed that the lessons would progress smoothly. I did not doubt John's ability to be the best at whatever he did, it was just that I worried about all things mechanical. I was by now well versed in radio techniques and etiquette, knew the phonetic alphabet by heart and managed to decipher most words through the roar of static and interference. I recognised voices from faces I had never seen. Mum, on the other hand, found it extremely difficult to follow the thread of any conversation. I often interpreted so she was aware of the day-to-day happenings in the lives of the isolated, independent people who worked this land of unending horizons and limited communications.

In the process, we heard some unexpected conversations. The manager and his wife from Nicholson Station were on leave and in their absence the handyman was behind the microphone ordering engine parts. Everett, the radio base director, managed to copy the list of goods required, however the signature remained a puzzle.

'Is it G Golf, R Romeo, E Echo, A Alpha, S Sierra, E Echo? Over,' he queried.

'Roger, roger. Over," was the reply.

'All OK, all OK. However, I'm sorry, I still do not have the surname. Would you spell please? Over.'

'The name is Gun. I spell, G for Jesus, U for onion, N for pneumonia. Over.'

We laughed as, just to be sure, that great Outback character, old Grease Gun, repeated it all again.

Upon his return home, John commenced grading roads and clearing proposed fence lines with the grader borrowed from Inverway. Amongst a million other duties, I was rearing three kiddy goats whose appetites were insatiable. The rapid tapping of little hooves as they climbed the homestead steps was echoed by a desperate chorus of bleating through the kitchen door, signalling that it was time to fill their bottles yet again. Nanny, Bambi and Dearie had each given birth to twins and each had also rejected her weaker twin.

The other Riveren babies were fairly well. Our gorgeous daughter with curly blonde hair was growing quickly and loved to play and crawl beside Ratsy's seven puppies, six black and one gold. As Ratsy was not much more than a pup herself, she often led her babies astray. Their idyllic existence of drinking and sleeping left our days problem free. However, the dissemination of energy occurred after dark. We were usually not long in bed when the yapping commenced. It might have been a starter's signal, for it was followed by the sounds of the race and chase. One canine mother tore around the house with puppies in hot pursuit. I could sense John's exasperation as they fled past our windows for the third time. Excited little yelps blended with huffs and puffs as round four was completed. His roars of objection were usually ineffective.

The curse of the bush was bung eyes. Sticky bush flies made a bee-line for eyes and they only had to linger a second to leave their legacy. First they sucked moisture from the eye, then the bite which followed caused the whole eye area to become grossly swollen. Sometimes the eye became invisible and remained so for several days. I had seen miserable Aboriginal children with two bung eyes. They were virtually blind until the swelling subsided. The best prevention was a fly veil and Mum sewed by hand fly veils galore. She wore one herself while pegging out the washing. The pop-over head cover, made from mosquito netting, was light and cool with an elastic base which fitted comfortably around the neck. Marie never objected to wearing her miniature version. Just as we all placed hats on heads when going outdoors, Marie's fly veil was popped over her head before her hat. Respect for the fierce long hours of sunlight as well as persistent flies commenced on day one.

Like a learned elder or wise old witch doctor, John knew many bush remedies. His anti-swelling trick usually worked. If the fly struck, it was simply a matter of spitting on your finger then rubbing saliva into the corner of the eye.

Although we were officially in the Katherine Parish, the priest from Kununurra arrived to introduce himself. Father Willis was tall and young with big feet and a big smile. He carried a portable Mass kit and a guitar wherever he travelled. His spiritual beliefs drove his commitment and for him, like us, distance was not a deterrent. With the intention of two visits to Riveren a year, he promised to become one of our few regulars.

It was he who baptised Marie at Inverway. Brother-in-law Joe was thrilled to be godfather to our little girl and Mum was stand-in godmother for my sister Anne.

Mum had been feeling the ongoing heat and decided to return to Sydney. On our early morning trip to Inverway to connect with the mail plane, we incurred yet another flat tyre. Fortunately we were ahead of schedule and decided to make it an occasion and have a last cup of tea together. There are many essential requirements permanently stowed in station vehicles, including spare tyres, water, matches and a tucker box. Since my first early impressions and reservations, I had developed a real love of billy tea. There was no tea in the world to compete with it and there was no way to adequately describe the unique flavour. We all agreed that it was particularly thirst quenching on the hottest of hot days.

From our plateau position on the unmarked boundary of Inverway and Riveren, we could see in all directions the variations in landscape. Black soil plains were covered by Mitchell and feathertop grasses, stirring lazily in the playful breeze. Gently undulating country broken by watercourses stretched as far as the eye could see. On the flat red laterite country there was no shortage of stunted eucalyptus trees, turpentine and wattle scrub. Marie was slurping happily on her rosehip syrup, while Mum and I savoured the spectacular view.

'This is actually the watershed for the whole district,' John informed us as he poured from the billy. 'It's about thirteen hundred feet above sea level where east meets west, and from this same plateau the water runs off in all directions. To the east the water runs into the Victoria River. Water runs west into Sturt Creek and its tributaries. They eventually run south into inland Australia where some four hundred kilometres later they empty out into Lake Gregory.'

John pointed as he continued. 'The Stirling and Negri Rivers also originate here and run north into the Ord. It's a pity you're not staying longer, Bess, so that we could take you to Nongra Lake, south of the Inverway homestead. It's right up on top of the plateau with its own watershed of about six hundred square kilometres.'

I had heard about this incredible lake and looked forward to seeing it for myself one day. With a deep sense of wonderment, I contemplated this significant place; this land whose mystique and power bewitched and beguiled the unsuspecting. Suddenly John called for action. We put out the fire before completing the remaining twenty kilometres to Inverway.

As Mum boarded the mail plane, I thanked her again for being the best mother in the whole world. She was utterly selfless and always had been. As a mother she understood how it was for me, inwardly aching and ever conscious of the gap in our hearts, gradually adjusting and stumbling still.

John and the ringers had no sooner left for the stockcamp than Pat and Peg arrived with Auntie Olive for an unexpected visit. I could not persuade them to venture out to the camp to see John. Understandably, their interest centred on Marie. Sipping sweet sherry, they keenly observed my progress. I was less ignorant perhaps than the bride who had come to Riveren several years before, but had a long way to go to match their experience. Had they known my secret they might have acknowledged me as a good breeder. That was a desirable attribute in female cattle and many an Outback dweller had been known, on occasions, to compare people with cattle. However, John would be the first to know that we were to be blessed with another baby.

Janey, a pretty young Aboriginal girl, had remained behind when everyone else left for the stockcamp. She told me her 'lations' from Halls Creek were planning to visit and she intended returning to town with them. We never could fathom how these messages penetrated the Outback. My family visitors had departed and I was about to follow my baby to bed when I heard strange noises at the door. Fear was foreign to me in this vastness where only the fearless survive. Nevertheless, I was puzzled by the unknown sounds. I opened the door to discover Janey shaking and crying and stammering.

'Dat debil debil might get me,' she cried, 'I'm properly scared.'

There was no doubting her terror and verbal reassurance was a waste of time. I settled her in one of our verandah beds and she slept soundly all night.

There were long periods when Marie and I were the sole occupants of the growing homestead complex. I talked to her all day long and she responded with baby prattle. However, my constant gnawing concern was what would happen to her should something happen to me. Recent scars were raw scars, and I was conscious of the dangers of being over protective. However, the isolation was acute when there were just the two of us. What if I suffered a stroke or a heart attack or more realistically a snake bite, I worried. My little girl was only out of my sight in the early mornings when I milked the goats while she was still asleep. I performed this duty in record time.

Once I opened their yard gate, the goats commenced their day long feed. Our newly completed house fence proved effective until the day that an unlatched gate found the whole herd wasting no time in devouring a new menu. Beneath the clothes line, Billy was swallowing the tea towel while Nanny chewed the leg of my jeans. The others were munching on newly planted shrubs. The nonchalance and bemusement with which they responded to my shouts and whacks were infuriating. At length I had them on the right side of the fence. I never tired, however, of watching the kiddy goats buck and gambol and play.

Despite my vigilance and concern, Marie became ill. Her vomiting and diarrhoea were severe. Aware of the dangers of dehydration, particularly in view of our remoteness, I was on full alert. Several days elapsed during which she improved considerably only to have a serious recurrence. Thankfully, Dr Tony Noonan in Wyndham received my on-air medical consultation, and with immediate understanding organised an evacuation to assess, treat and observe our little one.

I could hardly have made a dispassionate return to the children's ward of Wyndham hospital and was glad of Tony's warmth, understanding and reassurance. My doctor's bright eyes were both kind and inquisitive and he had a razor-sharp mind. You could tell in an instant that he loved the profession that he honoured. Once Marie's medication was changed from that prescribed over the radio, she improved noticeably. It was nevertheless almost impossible to extract me from her side. The outbreak of gastro-enteritis was far reaching and I dreaded a relapse. Every hospital bed was filled and Aboriginal babies were the predominant patients.

Tony's chirpy wife, Liz, insisted that I stay with them. Although it was last thing at night before I left the hospital, it was wonderful to have new friends and a town home as well. The Noonans and I had much in common and they effortlessly yet deliberately absorbed me into their busy family activities. Tony in particular was fascinated by Riveren and our challenges. My invitation for them to experience first hand our way of life was heartfelt and open-ended.

To my absolute joy and relief, Marie was discharged from hospital at last. Tony, together with Father Murray, the Wyndham parish priest, was off to the Halls Creek races and kindly included two extra passengers so Marie and I could meet John there. Marie was well and settled. Throughout our journey, the two intelligent and experienced men talked through many subjects pertaining to life in the North. The subject to which we all returned again and again was the plight of the Aborigines. From three different perspectives we exchanged encounters and concerns. Tony's patient who displayed no evident abnormalities or physical illness was dying. The bone had been pointed at him and there was no white man's weapon to break the power of that forceful conviction.

Father and I shared other concerns. Dedicated people on the missions provided support and education directed towards self-determination for large numbers of Aborigines and their efforts were constantly being thwarted by the welfare system and decision makers from down south. There were no obvious simple solutions for these complex problems.

John was beside himself with excitement. His two favourite girls were back and it was his favourite time of the year. He escorted Father and Tony straight to the bar.

'Thanks for everything, drinks on me.'

Father suggested that some race tips might be handy as the starters in the first were being led into the saddling enclosure.

John's tips paid off as the Inverway horses won three of the six races, including the Ladies' Bracelet. Father and Tony blended into the excited throng of punters and spectators. Mother and daughter were greeted warmly by the collective Underwood clan, while others, previously just voices from the radio, milled around to introduce themselves and express relief that Marie was well again. John ran his own race from stables to the bookies' stand, from the secretary's office to the bar then back to his two favourite girls. Marie was happy to play in the familiar warm red dirt, but despite the exhilarated crowd and top racing programme, I couldn't wait to return home.

A week later John and his offsiders left the homestead at first light to equip the new bore at Hut Creek. Goldie and her five black brothers had all gone to new families and there was a waiting list for Ratsy's next litter. The number of Marie's playmates had rapidly decreased. Only Ratsy and one big floppy pup called Kyber remained.

One little girl, one dog and one pup rolled in the warm dust as I folded the washing. In the south-west a dark cloud spread right across the sky. Even as I watched, it moved closer.

'Oh thank goodness, an early storm,' I announced to those who were too busy to listen. Carrying Marie in one arm and the washing basket in the other, I returned indoors. Having closed the windows on two sides of the house I continued to fold and stack the chocolate brown bath towels. Suddenly our world of stillness and silence was shattered. Wild dust-filled winds tried to take us with them. I ignored Marie's howls of terror as I rushed from window to window. It was as though we had lost our walls. I swallowed dust even though my mouth was closed. The house seemed to be all windows! At last the final window was secured, yet still the dust continued to swirl. Holding Marie I tried to make soothing sounds above the shriek of the ferocious dust storm. With gritty eyes we looked at the redness whirling around us. The sounds were deafening, the blurred images unnerving. The dust infiltrated every orifice and tasted more like gravel. It seemed an eternity before the hesitant sound of raindrops on the roof terminated the fury of the attack. Believing that at least outside would be cleansed, I had no sooner whispered 'hurray', than the drops stopped. It was over.

The difficult clean-up began. Every article in every cupboard was discoloured and laden with dust. The copper boiled, the wringer groaned and the second bucket of dirt from the floor was emptied. That night John's surprise was genuine. From a distance they had observed an apparent storm heading for the homestead and were hopeful that decent rains had fallen. It was the best part of a fortnight before law and order were established in my limited linen cupboard and throughout the household.

Our departure for Perth signalled the impending arrival of our baby and the continuation of John's flying career. There was much preparation and to leave home was to leave enormous responsibilities with the nominated caretaker, in this case my sister Libby and her man Sandy, who had been in the North all year. This was not just house minding. It was about keeping livestock watered and monitoring other complex aspects of our station.

Family members constituted perfect caretakers because they knew Riveren, our system of management and reliably upheld our expectations. Regular holidays were by no means a consideration at a time when expanding our new property remained the priority. In later years we forfeited holidays, rather than risk a repeated disaster after one such unforgettable experience. The day after our departure the recommended caretakers left for town and intermittenly called back to discharge their responsibilities as they saw fit. The disappointment of returning to a neglected Riveren negated any holiday bloom. It was always easier to stay home.

John's flying experiences extended from Riveren to Kununurra and now to Perth. At Jandicot Airport, he obtained his restricted pilot's licence. In the former city of heartache, we celebrated John's success with a night out on the town.

We flew on to Sydney where the staff of the Mater Maternity Hospital welcomed their most distant patient of twelve months earlier. Having witnessed foals, heifer and bull calves dropping with the frequency of flakes in a snow storm, John's reaction to witnessing my delivery was somewhat of a surprise.

'Women are funny cattle,' he later commented. 'I reckon you'll be right on your own next time.'

My mother and father brought glorious home-grown flowers with a card reading: 'Congratulations Patrick John junior on your choice of parents.' He was a tiny, beautiful baby. His little sister wanted to hold him forever.

Back home, busy productive days merged into weeks and months. The old Blitz truck carted fencing materials over long distances as we gradually developed further out. It also carted many loads of river sand to mix with the red soil around the house in preparation for the long-awaited lawn. In order to remain in touch and to educate our babies that there was a world beyond our homestead gate, we would sometimes share John's outings to check fences, waterholes or the condition of our small herd of cattle. To ride in the Blitz was to ride in the devil's own chariot. With two little ones and bottles perched on the left side of my lap, I used hessian bags to cover and protect my other leg from the scalding air. The heat from the motor blasted up around the gear-stick column on the floor, heating the cabin and making it akin to the fire keeper's den in an old steam train engine. Marie and Patrick loved any outing and John's sweaty face was one big grin with the excitement of having his family on board.

Shorthorn was the common breed of cattle in this country. While the established pastoral families planned their herd improvements, John and I continued to acquire cattle and build basic infrastructures. Throughout the extreme drought years of the previous decade, many of the waterholes along the bed of the Victoria River had dried up, causing many cattle to perish. The survivors had become our nucleus herd.

Uncle Tom Quilty had imported Zebu or Brahman-cross bulls from North Queensland in 1954, and had observed a welcome hardiness in these cattle. The progeny of the new bloodline proved better able to walk extraordinarily long distances. The real improvement in the Quilty cattle was evident as they undertook the seventeen-day trek over rough stony country to the Wyndham meatworks. In urging his sons and brother-in-law at Inverway to purchase this new breed, Tom had pledged his intention to ultimately breed the most suitable beast of all. He would call it 'T.Q.' for top quality.

The Underwood men had been keen to follow Tom's lead, and Pat had bought Brahman-cross bulls too in the early 1960s. From those earliest beginnings at Riveren John also used Brahman bulls over our Shorthorn breeders.

Any of our cattle suitable for turnoff were walked to Inverway. Stock inspectors employed by the government were responsible for issuing movement permits and it was the nature of their job to make regular visits to the properties in their area. 'Stocky' Gavin McDonald arrived to view our developments and was instantly given a handful of lawn runners and requested to plant as he talked. Good natured and agreeable though he was, he admitted losing count of the hours he spent beside us on hands and knees covering the green tufts and patting down the dirt. Our anticipation was matched by our elation. At last we had water suitable for a garden. We dug by hand deep holes for our saplings. In the bottom of each hole we added charcoal and manure before planting the poinciana and rain trees. Lastly we built tree guards to deter hungry goats.

John's pilot's licence was becoming something of a saga. His last cross-country flight required to complete his unrestricted pilot's licence was from Darwin to Riveren. John had been in Darwin for a week and in anticipation of his return I prepared a special dinner, found an old bottle of dried-out nail polish and stuck rollers in my hair. I picked fresh bush flowers and set the table with great care. It was on the fourth evening of repeated preparations that the long-awaited sound of an approaching aeroplane brought whoops of joy as I gathered my little ones and dashed to the vehicle.

John's unavoidable delay, due to a combination of deferred business appointments and inclement weather, did little to dampen his enthusiasm in returning home on this all important flight. His Riveren landing clinched his unrestricted private pilot's licence at long last.

It was with excitement and a great sense of humility that one month later we awaited the sound of another aircraft. That Dr Tony Noonan and family were arriving from Wyndham by charter plane was a great pledge of friendship.

Like every Riveren occasion, it was a matter of simple pleasures bringing the most joy. We fished at Mucca and explored Battle Hole Creek. Marie and Patrick became less cautious of all the new faces as the days passed. On their last evening, Tony and I sat up late playing cards. As Tony shuffled the deck, he asked me if I had read his unsealed letter when I'd boarded the plane from Wyndham to Perth three years ago. Silently I nodded. It was the one and only time he referred to our first born. I understood Tony's way and was grateful for his compassion.

Tony Clark was now overseer at Wave Hill and his unexpected visit unfortunately did not coincide with John's rare presence at the homestead. The friendship of these two was unique and their bond intangible. I had observed them together in the stockcamp or solving the world's problems at race meetings. They laughed and argued or just nodded and smiled, at ease with each other and their lot. Even as an observer I found their mateship enriching. Tony's wife Sue and I still hadn't met. As I stirred the custard after changing nappies, Tony and I pledged our determination to organise a get-together some day somehow.

Tony relayed news of their brandings. He also told me how he and station manager Ralph Hayes, upon discovering a mob of perishing cattle and with no men on hand to relocate them, had gone to the blackfella walkout mob at Wattie Creek. This was the Wave Hill strike by the Gurindji people against Vesteys initiated several years earlier. Tony and Ralph often visited their friend Vincent Lingiari, one of the leaders of the walkout who had previously been in Ralph's stockcamp. Eni Mulloo, as they called him affectionately, told his sons Victor, Peter and Harry and 'nuther fella Algie to go help Ralp and Dorney shift em cattle'.

The strike by the Aborigines for equal pay continued on and off for years. It changed the composition of stockcamps on many cattle stations and was the beginning of the Aboriginal Land Rights Movement. Eventually the Vestey country around Wattie Creek was surrendered and granted to the Gurindji people. In subsequent years that place called Daguragu was leased back to others, including Vesteys in the years of drought.

There existed a respect and friendship between these men who worked the cattle and country side by side. I told Tony that I witnessed that bond constantly between John and his team.

'Tell the big fella I'll catch him at Negri Races,' Tony called as he drove away. Weeks and months were of no consequence in terms of social interaction in this land beyond time.

Brisk easterlies were dominant on the evening that the goats did not return. Their pattern had always before been utterly predictable as every evening they assembled in their yard and waited for me to close the gate.

There was no vehicle at the homestead, just Dreamer, one of the blackfellas, my little ones and me. I asked Dreamer to catch a horse and ride out to track the missing herd. Darkness quickly followed twilight, postponing the search until next morning. When John returned from Inverway, he and Dreamer followed the tracks for nine kilometres. Dingoes had split the herd into adults and kids. The pitiful bleats of terror and blood-stained rips told the story. Dreamer rode home behind those that appeared unmarked. The kids, injured nannies and billies were placed on the back of the vehicle and driven home.

Ever susceptible to shock, too many died. I was distraught. Furthermore, the wild dogs had now tasted goat and would be back.

Marie mothered the orphaned kids. Along with the two 'Pat-twicks'— her brown-eyed baby brother and Patrick Jamtin—her favourite doll, Mimi, the pup and the kids were fed mud pies and Sunshine milk rock cakes. They all played together happily, catching grasshoppers and moths or dressing up, engrossed for hours in the wonderful world of make-believe.

Unbelievably, it was time to depart for our third Christmas at Inverway. Heavy hard rainfall, particularly in our neck of the woods, quickly transformed dry creeks into swiftly flowing torrents. This we experienced first hand as we set off early on Christmas eve. As we crossed Revolver Creek, the water level was rising. Although the rain ahead appeared to be lessening, we arrived at Buchanan Springs to find the raging waters spilling over the banks.

'Don't worry, we'll try and get home,' John stated firmly as he turned the vehicle around with a degree of difficulty. It was boggy and slippery. The little ones were both asleep. It seemed the rougher the ride, the better they slept. As we returned towards Revolver Crossing, we saw from afar that it too was now in flood. The width of racing waters which had developed in so short a time was unbelievable and quite terrifying. I bit my lip hard.

'Buchanans will drop before this,' John advised as once again we turned around to slip and slide in the opposite direction. Several hours later the flood waters gradually dropped below the sticks positioned by John to monitor the water level. Much later still, we arrived at Inverway to the relief of everyone who by now were concerned for our safety.

Santa managed to brave the storms and visit the happy family gathering. The heat and flies and flooded crossings were forgotten as excited children emptied bulging pillowslips used for Christmas stockings. Around the freshly cut and decorated tree, adults exchanged gifts—leather belts crafted by Pat and new clothing made by Peg and her daughters. This was third year lucky for me as the books I had ordered from Sydney as gifts for everyone actually arrived on time. As the extended family happily sat down to a delicious roast turkey dinner, a sudden growl of thunder realised shouts of encouragement, intensifying the elation of another bush Christmas.

On Boxing Day, the traditional sports and races were held. Apparently, in earlier times, old Sam Thomas, the bookmaker from Halls Creek, had fielded at the popular annual Inverway Races held on this day. Despite the heat we all participated in every possible event. There was no need for a bookie to spur us on. As Marie and Patrick played in the dirt beneath a shady bloodwood tree, their parents joined foot races and horse events according to ability. Like everything else I had witnessed, the application of individuals was beyond reproach. In work and play it was unquestionably a matter of 'give all of yourself all of the time'. As the years unfolded, this philosophy would prove the survival and salvation of some, yet ironically cause the destruction and loss of others.

We were thrilled to be approaching the birth of another baby, and I was delighted that I could take Marie and Patrick with me to Sydney to spend some time with their grandparents, affectionately known as Nanna and Gran Gran. At home, the children witnessed their father building, erecting and creating every station improvement. As we approached the Sydney Harbour Bridge, Patrick asked in a very matter-of-fact little voice, 'When did Gran Gran build this?'

On our first morning in the city I headed to a local shopping centre. Our dear family friend Ronnie Mullan gasped in delight at our unexpected encounter. She gazed affectionately at the two little ones in the stroller and then with astonishment at my basket full of infant shoes of graduated sizes. 'Why on earth are you buying all these, Terry darling?' was her first of many questions. It was difficult for city people to comprehend that I was buying so much in advance as shopping was non-existent at home.

It was just as well we had complied with the requirements of the airlines, which demanded that pregnant women fly no later than four weeks before their estimated delivery date. My dash to the Mater Maternity Hospital was three and a half weeks early. As baby Michael John was born, Dr McInerney announced with uncontained delight, 'Another little ringer! My goodness, you'll soon have your own stockcamp at Riveren.'

I was initially alarmed when my beautiful baby was rushed to a humidicrib where he remained for several days. It was frustrating to look but not to hold the little one who from first glimpse was the image of John. However, our impatience was tempered by relief that our son was in the best possible medical environment. At the end of the week he was cleared by the paediatrician who, at the insistence of my obstetrician, had examined each of my babies before discharge and the long journey home. Dr McInerney knew not only the need for my total reassurance and peace of mind, but understood our isolation from follow-up medical services.

With another of God's masterpieces in my arms, Riveren abounded with baby prattle, love and laughter. Our family and team, a seemingly insignificant number of people, were growing and expanding in every dimension. We were conscious even then of our significant responsibilities and contributions not just to Riveren, but to the world beyond our boundaries too.

CHAPTER 10

SCHOOL OF
THE AIR

....

The miracles of creation surrounded us. Our three children, like steps and stairs in age and size, loved the earth and soil. Their closeness and contribution merged as with great care they helped me transplant gum tree saplings from Paperbark Waterhole. The little boys tirelessly carted the sand they spread over the lawn. They loved noisily driving their toy trucks through the freshly and optimistically established garden. Every day I carried drums of water to trees beyond the homestead. They seemed reluctant to grow and, although still alive, had not undertaken the growth spurt so evident in our children.

As she repositioned her pram load of wriggling plump puppies and co-operative dolls, Marie fiddled and fussed. She was a born organiser and mothered her baby brothers too. Ratsy had delivered her second litter with yet another single golden baby amongst four black puppies. The children wanted to keep them all, or at the very least keep Pretty One. When Ratsy's eyes like liquid chocolate engaged mine, I could not ignore her silent plea. One male pup would stay to care for his devoted mother.

Marie was no taller than the motherless calves that were brought home for us to rear. Those that had not sucked the invaluable first milk, colostrum, were more difficult to save. John had just pulled up outside the front gate and there was the usual scramble to meet him. For something so young and new, this latest arrival made deafening sounds. Fear and hunger created a kicking, struggling mass of hooves and hide and wide eyes. Marie, Patrick and Michael were fearless. I prepared a bottle of Denkavite, a dried milk preparation and handed it to Marie. We all held the little calf while its mouth was prised open to insert the hard rubbery teat. As the warm milk trickled down its throat, it jerked and thrashed in objection. Infinite patience was required to coax these huge babies to take nourishment and teach them the difference between a natural mother and the milk and love offered by the adoptive family. Patience was no stranger to any of us.

Later that day, John called us outside.

'Surprise everyone!'

Beside a young rain tree stretched the slippery dip he had finished. It was much taller than the tree and there was no bend towards the bottom to break the landing. I wondered if it was for John or his offspring. Without any handrails either, it nevertheless instantly beckoned all three children. Marie and Patrick climbed like monkeys and whooshed with a rush downwards to the sandy soil where little Michael sat watching with envy. I carried him to the nearby swing that John had previously made. Beneath snowy blond fringe, his blue eyes shone with excitement as we swung to and fro, watching the exhilaration of two sturdy blond children enjoying their new toy.

We continued to make more practical, but no less eagerly awaited improvements to Riveren. The construction of our cold room was another sign of progress. It was wonderful to have the facility to hang a complete killer and store the large tub of salted meat. This would be cured and progressively cooked as corned beef. John installed shelves onto which I stacked various grocery items, dried fruits, icing sugar and the flour drum of rendered fat. The time that elapsed between our foodstuffs leaving Perth by ship and arriving at Riveren by road usually resulted in weevil-infested flour.

'They haven't eaten much,' John would comment as I sieved the flour for a sponge cake a third time.

At least we could eat fresh vegetables. Plots beside humpy and homestead had been prepared simultaneously by the Aboriginal women and me. The most time-consuming part had been breaking through the ground surface. It was hard but satisfying work digging, filtering stones and mixing manure and sand. We planted seedling beds of lettuce and tomatoes first. Cabbage, carrots and beetroot went straight into laboriously shaped garden beds. Climbing beans were planted beneath a wire mesh trellis. We watered every morning and evening and waited and watched for the first sign of green to sprout through the wrinkled soil. Surprisingly, watermelons and pumpkins appeared early and their vines rapidly infiltrated the surrounding area. When the male and female flowers appeared on the pumpkin vines, it became a competition to see who hand-fertilised the most female flowers each morning.

'We got three fella today,' announced Elizabeth proudly. Then it became a race to see who picked and cooked the first fully grown, ripened pumpkin. We all exchanged and shared and compared our vegetables. In various stages and means, our children weeded and planted beside me and loved to pick and eat fresh beans and carrots from their own little garden patches.

The Aboriginal families were like us in that they were creatures of habit, except that some of their habits were as totally foreign to us as ours were to them. My nursing standards and expectations fell on deaf ears. They resisted change because they had recognised no need for it.

When sickness struck, I was expected to 'make 'em better'. They seldom contemplated the cause of the illness. Until they sought change my efforts would be largely futile. There was no hostility between the two cultures; some things were just not negotiable. The Aborigines had great faith in cough medicine and rubbing medicine, or liniment, and used them as cures for all ills.

I implemented our own trachoma programme and organised vaccinations and treatment for head lice. As our general station conveniences were expanded, I was thankful for septic toilets, running water, a second refrigerator and even a 32-volt mix master. However, I repeatedly discovered evidence that the ablution blocks were being ignored. It was not just that old habits died hard; they seemed impossible to break.

'Where's your new hot water jug?' I asked Sheila when I discovered the electric cord on her kitchen bench.

'Might be in new fridge, keep 'em cool.'

I opened the door of the recent addition to their kitchen. The only thing inside the fridge was the electric jug of cold water.

Janey, whose fear of the debil debils never changed, had returned from Halls Creek with tiny twin daughters. On the day that I found her smaller bundle sucking tiredly on a propped baby bottle blocked with tea leaves, I almost despaired. The young inexperienced mother was exhausted and indifferent. I tried every tactic to help Janey and her babies. In time Janey welcomed and depended upon my help with her growing daughters. This regular involvement and friendship added to my distress when, during the following walkabout holiday, one of the twins drowned in a swollen creek crossing near town.

One day, John returned earlier than expected from the stockyards, and as his footsteps approached, I sensed a change in their rhythm. As I walked quickly down the hall, I saw a pale face bloodied from scalp to chin. He sat quietly as I carefully unwrapped the crude but effective bandage, a strip of his shirt, positioned like a pirate's eye patch. I washed away the hardened dark red crusts to expose an ugly gouge through his left eyebrow. It ended just short of his eye.

'Bloody humbug! I finished the draft even though blurry spots kept appearing. Something told me that this headache wasn't going to go away.'

When I had completed the seventh suture, he continued: 'Cheeky bugger too. I told him to wake up and watch the gate and next thing, as I turned away, he king hit me with a stone.'

The stockman responsible was of similar stature to me and obviously the angle of impact had worsened the injury. Refusing to rest, John departed. I knew the fresh white bandage wouldn't stay that colour for long.

Back at the yard, the stockmen awaited the wrath of the Boss. They were ready to 'pull out' if he went crook. John had a deadline to meet with the delivery of cattle and he could not do it on his own. They completed the work and the unspoken understanding between them all was that tomorrow was another day.

Indeed, relations soon returned to normal, but another shock was in store for John. When Jim Tough arrived to erect a windmill, completely undeterred by his fractured leg in plaster, I was horrified. However, my concerns were dismissed by the experts. The only discomfort our groomsman had ever admitted was wearing a black tie at our wedding. A week later, John and little Patrick delivered fresh meat and vegetables to our contractor friend, who, from the narrow wooden platform forty feet above the ground, was grappling with the enormous sails of the windmill. As John warily but confidently completed his climb, he glanced down with unspeakable horror into the face of his three-year-old son a few steps beneath him. Without hesitation, John spoke in a normal tone, telling Patrick he had forgotten something and they would have to go down again. Back on the ground, one little boy honoured his responsibility to look after the motor car while Daddy climbed back up to give his groomsman a hand.

Our every movement by road continued to be via Inverway. Our one attempt to transport rather than walk cattle met with disaster on the steep ascent of the jump up. One trailer jackknifed, spilling cattle everywhere and almost killing John in the process. We desperately needed our own direct access to the main road. However, government policy dictated that there was one only access road provided for each pastoral lease. Riveren was still an out station of Inverway and therefore ineligible for official assistance and services. If we wanted our own access road we would have to grade it ourselves.

From his intimate knowledge and practical understanding of the land, John mapped and marked the new and all important road that crossed rivers and creeks, red desert country and black soil plains. Flying our recently purchased Cessna 182, his bird's-eye view confirmed the suitability of the chosen route. Once again the grader was borrowed from Inverway. John climbed aboard the open cabin, dropped the huge curved steel blade and began grading. Weeks later, when he eventually completed this mammoth undertaking, the new dimension in our lives caused enormous satisfaction. Riveren homestead was joined to the main road by a new road stretching forty-two kilometres. We erected a hand-painted sign post indicating our turn-off to the rest of the world. One of our blackfellas chuckled to John as he pointed towards me, 'You make 'em long way, eh! Too far Missus walk back to Mummy.'

When Aboriginal couples had a disagreement, the woman often walked out. She went bush or back to her extended family. Dreamer thought John might have planned our road taking into account that factor.

The semi-retired carpenter who drove up to our gate explained that he was travelling through our region, looking for limited work before final retirement. Our homestead was bursting at the beams and an extension had been discussed often. It was really a matter of when, and deciding upon the most economical and reliable means of building. The carpenter's arrival and availability brought hopes and dreams to a head. Plans were drawn and materials ordered. John flew the carpenter to Springvale Station where a mining company was conducting a closing down auction. They decided to purchase a large building, suitable for dismantling and re-erection at Riveren as our men's quarters.

Six weeks later the carpenter returned with his wife from Melbourne and commenced the foundations of the men's quarters to be followed by a new wing on our homestead. The caravan of this homely couple offered another world to little Marie, who loved to dress up, put on 'lik-stip' and, carrying her handbag, wander across to the caravan beside the shed for afternoon tea. One middle-aged city woman entertained one little bush girl, both chatting incessantly and gaining great pleasure from their time together. It seemed almost a pity to separate Marie from her new friend so that she could start school, though of course we had all been looking forward to this momentous day.

The Katherine School of the Air was initially a branch of the South Australian Correspondence School based in North Adelaide. From there correspondence sets were sent to pupils and returned for correction. This South Australian system was the first correspondence school in Australia to operate independently of the Royal Flying Doctor Service or any other network. Its motto 'Knowledge Is Power' was embraced by those it serviced, including schools of the air, radio schools, overseas missions, lighthouses and hospitals. Marie's enrolment coincided with the year of enormous change when correspondence sets for all primary grades in the Top End were issued and corrected in Katherine.

'How do you know? You're not a teacher,' commented my little one.

I patiently explained all over again that in fact I was the teacher because we lived a long, long way from town and town schools. We were all going to learn in our home school room together. The trial governess had proven disastrous and subsequently it became my intention and unequivocal commitment to make the vital primary education years work effectively for us. John pledged his support.

We were fortunate to have a special area where we all contributed to the creation of a school room. There was adequate space to display the children's paintings and charts. After bedtime stories each night, I conscientiously planned our school programme for the following morning. As we still worked on Western time, it was 6.30 am when Marie nervously sat beside the school radio for the first lesson of the day. In vain she pressed her microphone button to answer her teacher. No-one could hear her. Radio reception remained erratic and it was many weeks before radio contact with the pre-school teacher from Katherine School of the Air was established.

Every morning we heard the same greeting.

'VL5 SK, this is Katherine School of the Air calling all pre-schoolers. Who is on air this morning? Can anyone hear me? Over.'

'Yes Miss Wynne, I'm here. Marie Underwood's here. Good morning, over,' called Marie.

'Good morning Marie and welcome to School of the Air. How are you today, over.'

We were ecstatic. Voice contact had been made and our journey begun. A background of bursts of static and roaring sounds on high frequency radio throughout the telegram sessions had helped prepare our children for the same type of noisy interference on the school radio. Marie was one of eight pre-school children on air and yet she could only hear the voices of two other pupils.

This on-air lesson lasted for half an hour for each class every day. The remainder of the school day revolved around my delivery of the correspondence lessons. It became immediately obvious that the success of our school room was in the hands of those who occupied it.

There were no blackboards or bubblers. There was one teacher—
Mum—for all lessons. There were no school uniforms or school bags.
There were tables and chairs and lots of imagination and motivation. We
were now part of a classroom four times the size of the United Kingdom.
It was the biggest classroom in the world, and beyond our Riveren school
room we had the biggest playground in the world too.

Patrick and Michael played with pegs and blocks, pencils and crayons.
Little fingers strengthened as they squeezed playdough and fashioned
shapes they called cows and horses. They scribbled and drew; they learned
nursery rhymes and songs and they learned the phonetic alphabet too. It
was an essential component of communicating by radio for young and
old. Likewise they became familiar with phonics and flash cards.

After breakfast every morning, faces and hands were washed, teeth
cleaned and hair brushed before school. On the day that I suggested
marching into school, they queried, 'What's marching, Mum?'

We formed a line and I demonstrated marking time before we briskly
marched through the breezeway to the sleep-out verandah with the school
room at the far end.

All parents have the privilege and responsibility of nurturing, moulding
and guiding their offspring. My responsibilities were overwhelming. As
parents in isolation, John and I were the major source of information and
influence for these hungry, impressionable minds. When things went
wrong at school, I had to prise little fingers from around my neck and
disregard the children's pleas: 'I love you Mummy. Can I go outside to
help Daddy now?'

Ever aware of my dual role, I would reply gently but firmly, 'I'm not
Mum. I'm your teacher and you know that you can't leave until you have
done it properly.'

The mother–teacher conflict was inevitable. However, it simply had to
be worked through. There was never less love and laughter, but to be
effective we had to observe boundaries.

Though we tried to keep school confined to weekdays, we never had a
'day off' specifically for relaxation. Living on a cattle station meant that
every day involved productive work which could sometimes incorporate
an element of leisure and pleasure if so planned. To check the paddock
fence at Pelican Hole afforded us a picnic lunch by the river bordered by

stunning serrated cliff faces. John performed the age-old ritual of cooking on a shovel, much to the delight of our children. Just as he had wooed me, he educated them.

Outside activities revolving around cattle production progressed relentlessly. Inside, at school, we commenced each morning with a prayer, followed by the identification of the day and date. School, station and personal diaries were meticulously kept.

The building projects were almost complete. We were assessing the value of our new wing when we heard the carpenter's vehicle drive in. He and his wife had just returned from their weekly recreational fishing excursion to one of our many beautiful waterholes. Five minutes later a panic-stricken voice called from our back door, 'Can you come quickly please? My wife is not well.'

Even though I was beside her within minutes, there was nothing I could do. Despite all my resuscitation attempts, I could not revive her. She had breathed her final breath. Signs and symptoms indicated that this kind, considerably overweight woman had suffered a massive heart attack. It was so difficult to tell the totally distraught husband that his wife had passed away. He had left her conscious, complaining of severe chest pain.

His anguish was understandable. To offer condolences seemed almost a mockery. I sought permission to attend to his wife and was thankful for my nursing training when I finally wrapped her in a white sheet. As John and I withdrew, I prayed for them both and their family. Beyond his present torture, only time could assist healing. Throughout the night he grieved beside his loved one. The dim yellow glow from the depth of the caravan reached up feebly to the myriad of blazing stars overhead.

It was evident next morning that directions had to be given and decisions made. John suggested the man in mourning take his dog for a walk. With the assistance of the only employee present on the station, John lifted the deceased woman onto a wooden door. Archie Sturt had lost the sight of one eye as a youngster and at that instant he closed both and lost all desire to lift one end as instructed. He shakily mumbled about the debil debils and disappeared. Acutely aware of our predicament, John by means unknown secured Archie's return to ensure the transfer of the body from caravan to cold room.

Every morning Everett, the radio base director, pre-empted the first telegram session with vivid descriptions of the weather in Wyndham. He then routinely called for urgent traffic before announcing the stations for which traffic or telegrams were on hand.

'Sierra Uniform Mike, Sierra Uniform Mike,' John called repeatedly, as static once again drowned out his voice. Persistence paid off and Everett at last acknowledged our presence. However, when John requested an undertaker and a coffin, Everett's change of tone dictated his disapproval.

'Very poor taste John, very poor taste indeed on April Fool's Day. Now is there anyone with a genuine emergency?'

Our frustration intensified as John called back to persist and elaborate. At length he convinced the base director that a death had occurred and certain procedures needed to be expedited.

The charter plane delivered a ruddy-faced, flabby-bellied person who gave loquacity a whole new meaning. He said he was the local undertaker. Having rolled a smoke, he recounted the latest jokes, with rumbles of laughter pre-empting the punchlines. His rowdy and untimely insensitivity was ignored. However, upon opening the cold room door, we were horrified to discover that the fresh killer had dripped a pattern of red right across the makeshift shroud. 'No worries, she'll be right!' the undertaker announced as he proceeded to organise the body into a plastic zip-up bag.

Fortunately, Liz Noonan's sister, Frankie, was visiting and she distracted our children from events beyond the gate. The carpenter and I remained behind while John drove the pilot, undertaker and the deceased woman to the aerodrome. To add to his dreadful burden, the carpenter's dog had disappeared during the night. Yet it seemed that pain on pain could inflict no deeper hurt and misery. The man stood beside me in silence dressed in his grey striped lounge suit and dark felt hat.

It seemed a long time later that I watched with disbelief our plane rise and slowly gain altitude as it headed north. Had John gone mad, I wondered. The plan had been for me to wait until the twin engine charter plane carrying the body lifted off, then to drive the carpenter over to the aerodrome. He expressly declined to fly with his deceased wife and so

John would fly him to Wyndham in our plane. This wasn't a good time to get it wrong John, I thought. Eventually our vehicle returned, driven by the pilot almost incoherent with distress. With the body and the undertaker strategically positioned on board, he commenced taxiing for take-off only to drive his left propeller into one of the marker drums. With great difficulty, John and the undertaker had transferred and manoeuvred the inflexible, bulky zip-up bag into our small plane as the departure for town could not be delayed.

That night the carpenter in his caravan refused food and company and the pilot, fearful of losing his job, retired early. I read to my little ones and kissed them good night.

Late the following afternoon an engineer arrived with a replacement propeller for the damaged aircraft. Later still the carpenter was flown into Wyndham to be confronted by processes and procedures that accompany unexpected death.

Marie missed her chatty, thoughtful friend. Three months later the carpenter returned to complete the final stages of our homestead extension; however, not surprisingly, he became so immersed in painful memories that he reluctantly admitted defeat. Subsequently his carpenter son, wife and baby travelled to Riveren to finally finish the job unwittingly abandoned due to tragedy.

The highlight of our family gathering at Riveren was the marriage of my sister Libby to Sandy. Mum and Dad helped convert the school room into a chapel. Prior to the arrival of Father Willis we decorated every space with abundant bush flowers. The radiant bride walked through the chairs to the altar table accompanied by my cassette recording of Shirley Bassey singing 'Ave Maria'. At the wedding supper, recorded ballads from Slim Dusty and Trini Lopez and live from Father Willis ensured night long celebrations. Our children had never seen a bride and now had another game for dress ups under the rainwater tank stand.

It was Libby who had asked if Gwen, an elderly city dweller seeking twelve months of alternate lifestyle, could visit Riveren. The right kind of spare hands were always helpful, so we agreed on a trial period. While pegging out the washing on the morning of Gwen's arrival, I suddenly spied a huge king brown snake writhing and wriggling on the lawn. Dropping the basket I grabbed the little boys, screaming to Gwen to lead Marie inside instantly. As she opened her mouth to speak, I shouted, 'Now! Right now! Don't talk, move!'

Fortunately the gun was in the broom cupboard. Even as I proceeded to pump bullets into the snake, Gwen's spluttering continued. I ignored Gwen until I was certain that the snake had sufficient lead in it not to threaten us. When finally I gave the all clear, a timid Gwen quietly told me that John had killed the snake earlier beside the shed. He had brought it across for her to photograph. Of course snakes writhe long after death, but depending on who related the story the winner was hero or heroine. Marie's allegiance was absolute. 'Clever Mummy killed the snake,' she told her brothers, dolls and pets.

Gwen really wanted to ride a horse. In order to placate her and negate our somewhat shaky beginning, I urged John to comply with her request. Having witnessed many accidents and suffered his own, John always worried about women around horses, even experienced women. Somewhat reluctantly, he led Beau, the quietest horse on Riveren, into the garden area. Beau, every child's first ride, was as gentle as a lamb. Gwen handed me her camera before she moved towards John who was going to help her into the saddle. At the very instant that her leg was raised and she was halfway across Beau's back, he pigrooted, tossing Gwen high into the air. I felt ill. Gwen's long grey hair tumbled free from her hair net and she was all arms and legs. John moved quickly to break her fall, breaking his watch in the process. Afterwards he muttered, 'Any more bright ideas?'

A badly shaken and deeply bruised lady decided it was time to return south. I could imagine her dining out on a whole new version of *Annie Get Your Gun.*

It was an eternally long night as the haemorrhaging commenced well before midnight. A new coldness enveloped me. I was afraid. I was afraid for my little ones. I thought that if I closed my eyes and slept, I wouldn't wake up. As he held me, John whispered, 'You'll be all right, because we love you and need you.'

With Mum and Dad still resident after Libby's wedding and able to care for our little ones, John flew me at first light to Kununurra for the earliest possible treatment. The doctor on duty admitted limited experience with miscarriages and thought observation appropriate while he awaited inspiration. I felt quite desperate. Eventually a Perth specialist holidaying in town was located and within an hour I was transfused and transferred to theatre. Were bush women ever going to be less vulnerable? As an inevitable sense of sadness and loss overwhelmed me, I wondered how on earth my predecessors had coped.

As John's birthday was around Melbourne Cup time, it became an excuse for a party. The main road grader drivers, Merv and Gill, arrived early, or sparrow fart as they called it. Vet David flew in, followed by stock inspector Gavin and girlfriend Cookie by road. Our neighbours were mustering and unable to join us. We ran sweeps at smoko time. The above-ground pool installed specifically to teach our children to swim became the party venue. In tepid water waist high for John and chest high for me, we listened transfixed and noisily rode the winner home in the main event. Later still we enjoyed cold beer and corned beef curry. After dark the calico sheet rigged on the clothes line became our movie screen.

It was usually a John Wayne western or a James Bond thriller passed on from Inverway. They ordered films from Darwin on a monthly basis. There was much anticipation and preparation for 'picture night'. The blackfellas, young and old, streamed through the showers in preparation for this special event. There had never been a movie shown to less than total attendance. During the bitterly cold winter nights, forty-four gallon drums containing blazing fires magnetised movie buffs like day-old chicks to a battery.

Station entertainment was both basic and satisfying. There was not much choice and subsequently no great expectations. Television, telephones and regular radio coverage beyond short wave and Radio Australia were beyond contemplation. Only the self-sufficient thrived. The very nature of the bush dictated the survivors. The culture and the challenges drafted the people who drank the water (which according to Outback folklore would ensure your return) and wore the dust beneath their fingernails. A diversity of folk embraced the Outback for a variety of reasons, which were not always immediately obvious. Some were plain anti-social creatures who embraced solitary living with great relish. They were referred to as 'adders' as in death adders. Others were on the run from life itself, while others genuinely sought new rural experiences. Then there were the helpless alcoholics. One stockman was brought to me for evacuation following a bullet piercing the fleshy part of his hand beneath his thumb. Much later I discovered that the wound was self-inflicted as 'his hide was cracking properly'.

For every inveterate roughened, toughened, die-hard stockman, there surfaced a gullible one. At Catfish Waterhole, John attended the Wave Hill muster and caught up with Sabu Sing and Lynny Hayes, the stockmen from Wave Hill Station. Apparently their latest recruit, a Pommy jackeroo, had requested urgent access to pharmaceutical goods.

'You've got to be joking, mate! There's no chemist around here for hundreds of miles.'

They extracted sufficient information to diagnose his problem. The first aid kit was inadequate. Until penicillin could be organised, their advice for dealing with the unpleasant aftermath of his illicit romance was simple. They told him about the foolproof bush cure for burning and swelling. All he had to do was soak his old fella in cooled corned beef water at first light and again at last light. Between five or ten minutes at a time, they said. They even organised it with the stockcamp cook. He thankfully followed their advice. Just beyond the flickering camp fire he faithfully squatted, a lone silhouette with concertinaed jeans around his ankles. Just how and when he discovered that he 'was being had' was only known to those who could take all they gave.

Each day seemed busier than its predecessor. As the mighty furnace that illuminated and warmed the world burst over the horizon yet again, this imprint of the Author of the Universe was recognised with great joy. There were no real distractions or interruptions to this family below. There were no insurmountable challenges. We would survive the ongoing meat crisis just as we had survived droughts. Family love, enthusiasm and energy intermingled and united. Our hopes were high for our future.

CHAPTER 11

TO RIVEREN AND THE NORTHERN TERRITORY!

....

Uncluttered horizons, purity of air, spaciousness and solitude all finely tune the senses. I heard the faint whop-whopping well before the speck in the sky became visible. As the helicopter touched down at the house grid, the pilot alighted. Beneath spinning silver blades he crouched and ran towards us. Waving a creased map in front of me, he shouted, 'Excuse me ma'am; mind telling me where this here place is? It ain't on my map anywhere.'

I explained that we were working towards being placed on all maps as soon as possible. For much of the world we still did not exist. When I pinpointed our exact location on his map, the American was greatly relieved.

'So I'm not off course or lost after all. Much obliged ma'am.'

We watched in wonder as the first helicopter to land at Riveren accelerated, rose and swooped forward and upwards. Finally, seeming no bigger than a dragonfly, it disappeared from sight. Then it was back to school.

Completed work was sent into the class teacher for correction. Our fortnightly mail from Riveren via Inverway to Katherine and back took at least one month. To ensure minimal impact on my pupils, I corrected the work at the completion of each daily school programme. The town teacher wrote comments around scratch and smell stickers on various pages. Although rather sickly sweet, the raspberry, cherry and banana odours proved great incentives. For additional encouragement, I implemented a gold star system. On the last day of each month, the children counted their stars and a small prize was awarded to the winner. Whenever possible, John would attend the ceremony to applaud his children, whose competitive natures ensured they were all regular winners.

Despite the static and the often ineffectual communication system, I persevered with the on-air component of our school programme. This radio contact was a luxury, not to be depended upon but invaluable when I needed to establish the performance level of other children. It was an all important yardstick. Overall, our links with Katherine School of the Air were of enormous consequence to the children too. Marie, Patrick and Michael were gradually exposed to other voices and in later years, face to face contact became possible at the occasional school functions we were able to attend.

My first trip to Katherine in nine years was to establish school contact. Eventually we changed to central time and became more orientated to the east, or rather to the Northern Territory. There was still limited wireless reception, no television and only tentative talk of a telephone one day. We were totally consumed by our own world, largely uninformed about day-to-day world events, and of the Northern Territory we heard even less.

We still did not travel to any town very often. John was more mobile than I as he continued to build yards and fences. He would travel alone to follow our cattle from hoof to hook at the meatworks, or to attend a bull sale or industry meeting. A full school programme and non-stop activities around our homestead complex, still in its infancy, provided my ongoing challenges. Interestingly, those women who travelled to town in between the annual race meetings were regarded as unsettled and unlikely long-term residents of this last frontier. I had long since surrendered any dependence on town and the community services with which I had grown up. In fact I had tried so hard to conform that town held little if any appeal.

It was the arrival of cattle buyers one day that alerted me to our children's fear of strangers. With a six year old hiding under the bed, a five year old clinging to my skirt and the four year old screaming for the security of Mummy's arms, it was difficult to produce lunch for an additional five people at short notice. For the sake of the children, I inwardly resolved to socialise more frequently if any such opportunity arose. However our geographic location and lifestyle ensured that social interaction remained largely between family members.

There seemed to be no room for new players on the chess board where the pawns continued to be moved by the same people. In a multi-generation, multi-location family business, decisions had to be made for the overall convenience and suitability of all. Stores, supplies and wages were still controlled and dispensed from Inverway. Cattle sales occurred in the Dry Season only. The resulting limited seasonal income placed restrictions on the cake that would be shared by the established property, Inverway, always in need of maintenance and upgrading, and our virgin block, poised at the beginnings of expansion. Although the situation was recognised, our frustrations increased as did the need to control our own finances and make our own decisions. The adage 'the man who made time made plenty of it' was wearing thin.

Our identity crisis deepened. Our home was still referred to as 'that place at the other end of Inverway'. Similarly, I was still referred to as 'John Underwood's wife'.

Announcements were constantly issued from Inverway regarding positioning of people in the plane, vehicle or truck. At times I felt like property. It was as though I was a heifer in the paddock to be mustered, drafted and relocated as deemed appropriate. If it was difficult for John, it was more than difficult for me. Pressure continued to mount. My safety valve proved faulty on an occasion when I felt not just outnumbered, but completely cornered and utterly defeated. John had often concluded his courtship letters by writing: 'Well, I'm not here.' They were my parting words as I bundled the children into the already dusty vehicle and departed with a roar in a cloud of dust. Too quickly I drove into the darkness of the night that swallowed the station wagon as it consumed my thoughts. Where to go? What to do?

Reason and the needle on the petrol gauge penetrated my broodings and I slowed, stopped and eventually turned the vehicle around. Acutely disappointed that John had not followed, I drove carefully and thoughtfully along the homeward stretch. As the bend in the road exposed the homestead area in the distance, every light globe burned to guide us back. Beneath the magnificent Southern Cross the early morning wail of a distant curlew accompanied the groan of the last gate. Our reunion and reconciliation were inevitable. To yield was to gain humility and strength. Love and understanding assisted in my acceptance of what must be. A tiny stitch in the tapestry of life regained its tension and balance.

There was never anywhere to duck or weave or hide in the Outback. There were no distractions from reality. Why had I considered even momentarily that I could resolve problems on the run? If I was to complete my life race fairly and squarely, endurance and tenacity were vital.

To face up was to survive. When John broke in young horses, he taught them just that. To watch a frightened, shaking colt respond to his touch was a real treat. John coaxed and reassured as he worked the youngster through the preparatory stages of education. He talked as he stroked. He urged rather than demanded the horse to 'face up'. 'What's the matter now? Come on, look at me, look at me,' he would murmur.

There could be no denial of the almost indefinable element of coping in the bush that demanded each individual to face up too.

Horses were an important part of life on Riveren despite the increasing mechanisation of station activities. We all followed with great interest the arrival and growth of new foals. Was this long-legged beauty destined for the race track or the stockcamp? With thoroughbred and quarterhorse stallions and a good line of mares, our horse population swelled. Apart from meeting our own requirements, we sold broken and unbroken horses to regular purchasers.

At the beginning of the stock season, each ringer would be given horses to look after and work. This included shoeing, riding, and after the mustering removing the shoes before 'bushing' the horse back into the paddock for a well earned break. Most people learnt to shoe a horse the hard way. Few horses would stand on three legs submissively in order to let the horseman nail in a shoe. Often the more edgy the horse, the more shouting and cursing there would be. I treated many injured hands jabbed or pierced by horseshoe nails. Infection was always a concern and one of the prerequisites for working at Riveren was tetanus immunisation. It was a joy to watch a good farrier and this was one of John's many skills. However, standing bent over a horse's uplifted leg for hours on end did not help his already fragile back.

'Steady on old man. Don't be silly now. Pull up, whoa.' He talked reassuringly all the while to the owner of the hoof in hand.

To increase their feelings of ownership and responsibility, John always asked the stockmen to name their own horses. With our stallions called Ginger and Ned Kelly, there were some predictable names like Trigger, Blaze and Biscuit. John had two freshly broken colts, Ice Cream and Lollypop. One of the stockmen, Frankie, could not get his tongue around the name of the latter and called him Lollycock. There was Nurse, Creamy, Hector, Drybone, Beef Bucket, Cloud and Motor Bike.

Frankie, whose surname was McHale, always looked as if he had been in a good paddock. He enjoyed working and losing weight, but told me often he'd never catch up with his brother Henry who was half his size. Frankie's blue eyes were unusual and he proudly told us that he might have a little bit of Irish blood way back somewhere.

Horses' names were one thing, bloodlines another. Years ago when Pat brought Laura Doll into the country, she was in foal to King's Realm, an early son of the legendary Star Kingdom. At the time there was much discussion and debate about the foal. Would it be accepted as district bred? That first foal, Kingdom Come, was by now a champion racehorse. Having won his Maiden by ten lengths, he went on to win over thirty races including every district bred cup in the country. Kingdom Come won numerous Halls Creek and Negri Cups and even ran third in the Wyndham Cup, which was an open event. The day that fourteen-year-old Kingdom Come won the Negri Cup carrying thirteen stone was a day for the history books.

When naming thoroughbreds, consideration was again given to the names of the sire and dam. In keeping with our designated prefix 'River', we named River Slick, by Nunsoquick out of River Nurse. Our mare River Irish produced River Patrick and River Colleen by our stallion Son of

Showdown. With district-bred racing dominating local race meetings, the home breeding programme continued to be an integral component of station life. Racehorses had to be not only officially identified, but named as well. The paper work was endless. This so called sport of kings was also a labour of love and dedication in our situation.

Having sat on horseback with their father from nappy days, Marie, Patrick and Michael loved their ponies. John was not an obsessive horseman, unlike some who had their children riding more or less from birth. However, he taught them basic riding skills and horsemanship. At fifteen hands Beau was not a small horse, but despite his unfortunate rejection of Gwen, his nature was ideal for a child's first mount. Our children learned enough from him to graduate to real ponies. Lynny Hayes presented us with Denim, a small grey gelding who would take each child through many gymkhanas. The little grey stallion, Boxing Gloves, was equally undersized when standing beside the stockcamp horses. However, no stretch of the imagination was necessary to work out why he was so named.

My city riding experiences were not transferred to Riveren where years of pregnancy and motherhood proved a practical deterrent. However, I discovered that with both feet on the ground, I had limitless opportunities to appreciate and enjoy our magnificent horses.

Jack Dalzell, the cattle buyer from the Wyndham meatworks, advised his expected arrival time. In preparation for a rare overnight guest, I cooked my special chocolate pudding. The following morning a telegram advised his unavoidable delay for twenty-four hours. This was extended three times and so it was many chocolate puddings later that we finally heard the sound of an approaching plane. In the yards John continued to draft the mob and I asked Patrick to collect our visitor. As the apparently driverless vehicle continued towards him, Jack savagely shook his head in disbelief. Always an observer of eight hours from bottle to throttle, Jack discounted alcohol-related hallucinations. As the vehicle came to a halt, he noticed the tip of a hat level with the tip of the steering wheel. For one so young and small, Patrick drove with unerring accuracy.

Jack's sense of humour was as unique as his continually amended estimated time of arrival at Riveren. Our visitor told John that if he'd married me to shorten the breed, by the look of the chauffeur son things were on track. He inspected our cattle and with the 'guesstimate' of weights, the price was negotiated. It was agreed that Jack would order the roadtrains to transport our cattle to the Wyndham meatworks.

Noel Buntine himself arrived on the gigantic trucks that bore his name. He wanted to check out not just our new access road, but the new station belonging to Big John. They were mates from way back and were also bonded by their individual commitment to the beef industry as well as the racing industry. Their passion was racing; they bred them and they backed them. They planned and dreamed and in doing so spent time and money to support the culture of the North as well as to fuel their obsessions.

That night over dinner John recounted how not long after they had taken over Inverway from the Leahy brothers, his old man had a mob of bullocks on the road for Wyndham. Three weeks down the stock route with just one week until delivery, word was received that the meatworks had closed down for the season with no beg pardon. The cattle had to be walked home again. It was in the early 1960s that Noel Buntine had seen the need for trucks to take over from the drover in Outback Australia. He started carting cattle to Wyndham despite the attitude of the meatworks' manager of some thirty years who threw up his hands in complete horror. Any change, let alone dramatic change, was just too difficult for him to comprehend.

Perhaps it is in retrospect that the real impact of change is recognised. We were in the midst of enormous change and side by side with those who wrought it. For Noel to make road transport of cattle work proved his ultimate challenge. He told us he had started with one truck and a single-deck trailer. This great innovator had redesigned trucks and crates to meet the challenges of the outback roads. He had pressured politicians at all levels to build better roads. Noel influenced body and crate builders to design and build gear that would make loading and unloading easier on the cattle.

John continued the story of progress, highlighting the phenomenal impact made by roadtrains. Various diseases had threatened the cattle industry over the years. Pleuro-pneumonia in particular had ravaged large numbers of cattle held in close proximity for weeks on end during the long droving trips. Quick and secure transportation of cattle by roadtrain helped prevent the spread and ultimately eliminated that dreaded disease. At the same time the incidence of redwater or tick fever, a constant threat for drovers, was dramatically reduced. As beef roads were gradually developed, cattle were transported more efficiently and better links were forged between cattle stations and markets.

The eradication of other potentially distastrous cattle diseases was proving similarly controversial due to the attitude of a stubborn minority of station owners. At Riveren, we were amongst the first to adopt the Brucellosis and Tuberculosis Eradication Campaign and subsequently veterinarian David Bradley became a regular visitor. Known as the 'Flying Vet' he serviced outlying properties over enormous distances. When the mustered cattle were yarded, David, assisted by a government stock inspector, would inject tuberculin into the caudal fold beneath the tail of each beast. Seventy-two hours later, he returned to feel the injection sites of the same mob of cattle to check for reactions. A reactor beast was destroyed for autopsy purposes. The completion of this compulsory complex programme would dominate our cattle management for many years. The end result would be a better managed, disease-free national herd.

The following morning we loaded our cattle onto the roadtrains straight after breakfast. Noel departed the way he arrived and John left to fly the bores. He had airstrips beside each watering point enabling him to land to assess or fix any problem on the spot. As Mother's Day cards were being glued together with extraordinary and equal amounts of flour and water and love, we heard him fly overhead. A bore run in the plane took hours, whereas by road it could take days. Minutes later I heard the untimely arrival of the stockcamp vehicle and hurried to the gate to investigate.

Both stockmen were agitated as they pointed towards a bulky swag in the back. They explained Ralph had taken a bad fall from his horse and had been knocked out 'properly'. He was deeply unconscious having sustained serious head injuries. The Aborigines found illness and injury distressing and out of sight was out of mind in most cases. Nervously, they helped unwrap Ralph and we moved him onto the verandah. They told of his horse clipping a beast, falling, then rolling on top of him. The signs and symptoms indicated a fractured skull and until the medical plane arrived, I recorded frequent observations. In the following days we learned that this fine young man had indeed sustained a fractured skull. Tragically, in months ahead, we learned that his recovery was limited and necessitated permanent nursing home care.

The threat of accidents and injury was ever present. John was working in the shed, making a 'small adjustment' with a twelve pound sledgehammer when a minuscule metal chip ricocheted and penetrated his calf muscle. By the time he had walked one hundred metres from the shed to me, his lower leg had swollen to double its size.

'Don't worry about a medical call. I'm not going to humbug around. Pack me a toothbrush and I'll fly myself in straightaway.'

Aware of the futility of arguing, I complied. His leg looked dreadful and I felt strongly that he deserved a pilot. However, I could not disagree about the time factor, for a medical evacuation always added three or four hours to treatment.

Tony Noonan reassured John that with the assistance of a local anaesthetic he should have the foreign body removed in no time. On the radio medical session the following morning, Tony advised me that the procedure had proven a little tricky, John was resting comfortably and should be able to fly himself home within the next few days.

Upon his return, John's well-bandaged leg did little to disguise his limp. Tony's excavation had proved to be extremely complicated. Upon entry the chip had moved at a right angle into the muscle before becoming deeply embedded. There was belated consideration of a general anaesthetic as extensive probing failed to locate the elusive prey. The perseverance of the doctor and the stoicism of the patient at length paid off.

'You don't believe in travelling lightly, do you?' John groaned as he carried our luggage to the door. I reminded him that one suitcase was entirely filled with school work. Ahead were at least five weeks in Sydney revolving around the imminent birth of another baby. Naturally I was prepared for correspondence lessons to continue if my rather bold alternative plan did not eventuate. We were still loading our plane when to our amazement Ratsy arrived at our aerodrome, puffing and panting, but determined to see us off if she could not come too. At Inverway John had lost his dog Copper when he walked into a moving propeller. Ratsy was hunted home. Her refusal to leave resulted in John directing her onto the back of the vehicle. She was not only still there on our take-off, but apparently still there on John's return the following day.

There were limited landmarks across the Tanami Desert and the flight to Alice Springs took almost four hours. Marie, Patrick and Michael were very excited at the prospect of flying in a colossal jet.

'It's really, really big,' they observed as the inevitable comparison was made with our Cessna 182. They kissed John goodbye. As I clung to their father, no-one could have wished more than I that John was coming too.

The three bush children were completely overawed by the movement of traffic and people. The sights and sounds of a vibrant city were arresting to us all. Everything and everyone seemed entangled. Wherever we looked our senses were assaulted. Even my routine visit to Dr Bob McInerney proved slightly overwhelming to my little ones.

It was no surprise to alight from the lift on the eighth floor of the Macquarie Street consulting rooms and find the end of the queue before me. Dr McInerney remained immensely popular. When the inner door finally opened to admit the Underwoods, Dr Bob appeared before us flourishing a rather terrifying, genuine Samurai sword.

'Well little people, have you been good for your mother?'

He was delighted to meet the three he had delivered. I was relieved to receive a good report and to commence the countdown until 'B' day.

As I entered the side gate of my old Pymble convent school, I could visualise the crates of white bottles as though it was yesterday. The lacy trees were ineffective in keeping the crates cool. Playlunch was the time for the compulsory consumption of bottled milk. Pretending to drink became an art until Sister looked elsewhere, allowing the lumpy liquid to be passed on.

With some trepidation I approached the entrance door. My appointment with the new Mother Superior was to inquire if three highly spirited bush children could be absorbed into appropriate classrooms for one month. The rattle of beads and swish of long black habits had previously forewarned of the approach of my teachers. Although I was aware of the dramatic changes adopted by the Church, I was nevertheless unprepared for the woman who suddenly materialised. Rather than the traditional greeting: 'Good morning and God bless you,' she heartily shook my hand and said, 'Hello Terry and welcome.' Her humaneness leapt out at me, demystifying the nunnery. I recalled the day that my school friend Maureen whispered that she had seen one of the nuns coming out of the toilet block. I frowned my lack of understanding, so she expanded: 'Can you believe it? They go too!'

Sister Anne, a youthful principal, was dressed simply and sensibly. There was no doubting her energy. I was gladdened by her understanding and insisted on giving her a candid background of my three children, who had not only never seen a school or classroom, but had rarely experienced life beyond Riveren.

'Don't worry, they'll be all right,' she stated. 'There is only one proviso. In the morning when you deliver your children, you should leave immediately.'

'Thank you very much, Sister,' I agreed.

The pact was in place. However, her reassurance did nothing to alleviate the knot in my stomach. I hoped they would cope. They had not asked to be born in the bush. I owed them so much.

I hastened back to attempt to describe the adventures ahead. It was a waste of time for they were preoccupied with each new experience as it unfolded. Having discovered the postman, Patrick waited with infinite patience for the wonderful man who blew his whistle as he handed him the letters. Michael noisily drove his new bright yellow grader dangerously close to Gran Gran's garden border, while Marie supervised her brothers and with tireless enthusiasm helped her Nanna with the housework.

Chattering children swarmed across the crowded playground. Some negotiated the monkey bars with dangling legs, others stared at the children not in uniform, while the queue for the bubbler lengthened. Mine knew the score. The time had come to say goodbye. As I quickly kissed each of them the reactions were immediate. Big tears silently streamed down Marie's cheeks. Patrick bellowed and twisted like a cleanskin bull in a yard for the first time and in desperation he bit and kicked the strong adult who guided him, despite his struggles, into the classroom. My departing vision of little Michael was his puzzled expression as he jumped up and down in his brand new riding boots and clung to the arm of another nun. It was a long day for us all.

At three o'clock that afternoon Sister Anne's approach was overtaken by three pairs of legs that raced toward me. They held me tightly. I was quietly informed that apart from one son chucking a wobbly, they had reacted more or less as expected.

'Tomorrow will be easier, Terry, particularly if the little fellow has less noisy footwear.'

❖   ❖   ❖

Rebecca's welcome was like no other. Soon after her arrival, three youngsters each wearing riding boots clattered through the hospital corridors searching for their new baby sister. They loved her with uncontained joy. So did I. We five visited the school at Pymble once more to express our heartfelt gratitude for absorbing bush children into their life so tolerantly and generously. My tiny bundle was nursed and admired by every nun in the convent and all the classmates of Marie, Patrick and Michael.

On our return flight to Alice Springs, the captain moved through the cabin as he conversed with various passengers. We occupied the entire back row and at length he pulled up beside us. With a warm smile, he marvelled at my family and our destination. Observing my hands and arms filled to capacity, he voiced his admiration.

'They can't possibly all be yours.'

'Four under seven,' I nodded with enormous pride.

'What a lusty lad your husband must be,' he chuckled.

When I explained that John was flying from Riveren to Alice to meet us, he asked the call sign of our aircraft. From the sophisticated cockpit, he established radio contact with John and reported that his family were on board and in great shape.

Inside the terminal, my great big John held with wonder and tenderness his new baby daughter. A voice from behind laughingly commented, 'I was right, all right. He is a real son of Australia. Take care all.' The affable captain winked as he and his crew passed by.

It was so good to be home. Baby Rebecca was beautiful. Her gurgles of happiness and contentment were encouraged by Marie, who automatically assumed the role of number two mother. Patrick and Michael melted into gentleness and never tired of hugging and helping their little sister. She was never spoiled simply because there can never be too much love.

The spare cot was firmly ensconced in the school room and somehow I juggled breastfeeding, books and bouncinettes. Despite the time pressures, short cuts were never a consideration. I expanded lessons and developed concepts. We faithfully carried out experiments, recorded tracks in the mud, played in sand pits, made playdough, painted, sketched, glued, researched and entered every competition.

During each of the three terms, we received a patrol visit from our school. As we were one of their most remote families, ours was always by air. The visiting teacher, usually the class teacher of one of our children, would learn much during the day in our school room and the overnight stay in our home. It was an opportunity to assess the children, the stability of the school programme and any additional factors relevant to school. The proximity of the kitchen to a school room would be important to teachers who conducted cooking lessons. Other families conducted school in caravans or separate buildings. For me, now firmly established as wife, mother, teacher, nurse, cook, book keeper, cattlewoman, gardener and counsellor, our school room within the home was a blessing and a necessity.

Meanwhile, John had not only mastered aerial mustering, but, like increasing numbers of people in our region, acknowledged it as an essential component of effective, clean musters. Piker bullocks and mickey bulls, the rogue cattle that hid in the scrub year in year out, were located by this aerial cowboy. They could now be flushed out and yarded. An outside speaker on the plane's wheel strut allowed John to sound a blaring siren or give instructions from the cockpit to his men on horseback.

'Over there you dopey bugger!' he chastised the ringer who appeared to have fallen asleep on his horse. The aircraft wheel almost dislodged the hat of the now wide awake fellow. Sam Long, our head stockman and an accomplished horseman, galloped past in a flash. In partnership with a horse that knew its job, he knocked off balance the breakaway mickey with a mind of its own. All in one movement he jumped off and with his bull strap tied its hind legs together. With the horn saw from his saddle pouch he dehorned the beast and then with his ever-sharp pocket knife castrated it.

John continued to muster both Inverway and Riveren. I constantly worried about the strain imposed by this intensive exhausting flying, apart from his ongoing workload of improving Riveren. I detested the sight of the swooping and looping, the diving and rapid escalation of the small aircraft as it criss-crossed the skyline like an inebriated eagle. The change in engine sounds I monitored too as he flew up and around in pursuit of each beast. It was exacting and highly skilled flying and when coupled with experienced cattle knowledge produced top results. Never doubting his performance, I still worried about all things mechanical. The safety margin associated with low-level flying was also of major concern to me.

At Victoria River Downs a large helicopter and fixed wing fleet, Helimuster, was established by John Weymouth. In conjunction with the Brucellosis and Tuberculosis Eradication Programme, pastoralists were utilising this costly but efficient method of mustering. Over large tracts of land, up to three helicopters were sometimes hired to muster widely scattered cattle in a different type of country.

In the meantime our first bullock paddock was being fenced, and we prepared a submission for Riveren to be acknowledged as an independent lease, separate to Inverway, for consideration by the Department of Lands.

Our submission was caught in the usual bureaucratic jungle. Proof of the viability of Riveren was sought. There were inspectors, reports, applications and explanations. At length John accompanied his parents to town and at long last the anticipated outcome was realised. Riveren was to be a separate pastoral lease. Our brand JUT was struck. It was not symbolic for John Underwood and Terry, as I had presumed. The T was a Territory requirement for registered brands!

The relief was overpowering. The first leaf in our cheque book was in payment for Riveren. From here on it was our challenge and our future.

On the Esplanade in Darwin the Northern Territory flag, incorporating the three official Territory colours—black, white and ochre—and the official Territory floral emblem—Sturt's desert rose—was flown for the first time at the ceremony marking self-government. It was acknowledged with a 19-gun salute from HMAS *Derwent*.

It was 1 July 1978. At home we celebrated Independence Day for the Riveren Underwoods and all Territorians. With profound love, optimism and commitment we raised our glasses and toasted our future: 'Here's to Riveren and the Northern Territory.'

The middle of nowhere was at last becoming somewhere.

CHAPTER 12

TRYING
TO BE BRAVE

....

In a time when roadtrains had already replaced drovers, other remarkable changes were threatening to sweep the country. Conservative, hard-working, cautious people instinctively resisted. Pathways of familiarity had always been embraced even by independent and resourceful individuals. Yet the keepers of the land could not hold still the wheels. They were turning.

The fading of the Negri Races into history, with the sale of Vestey's western properties, symbolised the end of an era. They were my first true bush race meetings and although they were a Vestey affair, other stations were invited to attend and compete. At the last meeting we realised that there could never be a substitute for the station camps, the creaking wooden dance floor and the mateship enjoyed at the Negri racecourse and surrounds in the back of beyond.

The English brothers, Sir Edmund and Lord Vestey, commenced their investments early this century. Their original intention was to breed and fatten cattle for slaughter in a Darwin abattoir to be built by them in return for the Australian government building a railway from Darwin to Alice Springs. Both elements of the agreement were ultimately unsuccessful.

However, like the famous Durack pioneering family who survived mammoth cattle-droving treks into the unknown interior and settled the North, Vesteys played a significant role in the development of this country. Few know that the first live export ship to Asia left our shores as far back as 1884. Vesteys had shipped over fifty thousand head of cattle to Manila before the trade was banned in 1930. Who could have dreamt that this market would prove to be our future security, in fact our salvation? When domestic markets were subdued, the live shipping market remained buoyant. Even now, our neighbours and companions on the Flying Doctor radio network were predominantly Vestey employees, as well as Quiltys and Underwoods.

Previously the Negri races had been relocated from the Negri River, after which they were named, to the Linnacre River, another tributary of the Ord in Western Australia. By my time, they were firmly entrenched on Nicholson Station at a bore site six miles west of the station complex. So important was this annual event that in 1952 when severe drought had resulted in race cancellation, the Inverway manager, Bill Hamill and his wife, had subsequently hosted a sports meeting to fill the unwelcome gap in the lives of the station people. Apparently they came in droves and Ces Watts, nicknamed 'Fearless', was amongst the winning riders. The bullock ride was replaced with buckjumping donkeys and from all reports those wild sulky creatures, spurred on by lively cattle dogs and cheering spectators, were pretty much unrideable and highly entertaining.

Fearless was one of John's many friends whom I still had not met. He was just another voice on the radio. It was on a return flight from Wyndham that I had become nervous about our altitude. Flying in our light aircraft was a convenience rather than a thrill. The children often became airsick as we bounced through tropical skies. When John darted or dived to check a mob of cattle, the best-settled stomachs were put to the test. The problem this time was that we were too high! Upon take-off, we had climbed above the puffy cloud base and the surreal flight started to change with the instant build up of cumulonimbus. All around us mountainous clouds escalated with the speed of Jack's beanstalk. Gaps in the cloud cover below were closing rapidly and we seemed to be in danger of becoming ensnared within a woolly white world in which monumental storms were brewing. Where was the ground? When John, to my great relief, eventually nosed downwards through a splinter opening, we were confronted by a blackish purple sheet of rain that completely curtained the horizon. Savage lightning taunted us. We turned back to town.

On our cloudless flight home the following morning, I was startled to see a larger plane fly right past us. Over the radio, the pilot called John. 'Pull your wheels up, Underwood, and you'll go faster!'

It was Fearless himself! Ces Watts was the pastoral inspector for Vesteys and flew a twin engine with a retractable undercarriage. It was an extraordinary encounter in the vast northern skies.

On the Vestey properties surrounding Riveren, small communities of people lived and worked. There were specific people for specific jobs. The bore mechanic and boundary rider were of necessity happy with their own company. There was a resident book keeper, a store keeper, a camp cook and a station cook and, depending on the size of the place, one or more domestic staff. A governess was usually employed if a school warranting a full-time teacher did not exist. Similarly, a nursing sister was engaged at places like Wave Hill, where four stockcamps were needed to muster the largest of the Vestey properties.

It was all in great contrast to our privately owned operation where the two of us covered all aspects of station management. John was stockman, bore mechanic, vehicle mechanic, fencer, pilot, yard builder, horse breaker, butcher and much more. I was continually learning new skills and felt by now that I was earning my keep. More than comfortable with our intimate family existence, I cherished our unity and lifestyle. I embraced solitude and did not envy those who formed part of a larger team.

We were both well used to new challenges. With a new infant, my school programme and other station commitments, it was much easier for me to meet my challenges by staying home. I had no desire to join the families heading for the Timber Creek Races. It was there that John issued a challenge of a different kind.

'I know that's a ring-in! You won't get away with it! I'm not the only one who recognises your horse from the first race.'

If anyone knew horses, John did. However, on this particular occasion, this particular horse owner would not heed John's advice. His muttered response through clenched teeth and look of thunder might have deterred some. Not John.

As the horse in question was already being saddled up, John's next remark was even more pointed. Like a torpedo from a cannon, the short, thick-set owner of the ineligible horse hurtled across the saddling enclosure and lunged at John who stood on the other side of the fence. His brute strength created by anger and charged by indignation caused John's shoulder to dislocate. John's natural defence was to follow his arm over the fence. As he hit the ground in agony, he grabbed his dislocated arm.

In my absence, John's mother came at a gallop, wielding her sun umbrella and shouting, 'Get away! You great big bully! Just look what you have done to my boy.'

Hot on her heels was Reg, forever ready to defend his brother or act as backstop in a fight. John received the necessary assistance just as the starting stalls sprang open. As generally happens, the horses belonging to both protagonists were unplaced.

My days were never more frantic. Being voluntarily tied to our school routine, I used any spare time to catch up elsewhere. After dinner I mopped floors, and at midnight wrote letters while the biscuits cooked. I was well on the way to becoming a true bush woman who could take her place amongst all those women I had met at our engagement party at Halls Creek. Not infrequently I missed opportunities to drive around to witness the wonder of new foals and calves, or to monitor new improvements. It was both demanding and satisyfing to live and work together day in and day out. However John felt it was time we shared a family outing.

It had been disappointing to miss the wedding of John's long-time mate Ken Warriner to Sally, the eye-catching Halls Creek rodeo queen. John was determined to prove to me that for once our lives did not revolve exclusively around work and annual race meetings.

Still nursing his tender shoulder, he contacted Tony Clark who had been transferred from Wave Hill. The outing was organised. It would brush away any cobwebs, John said, and be comfortably undertaken with minimum disruption to school and my daily routine. Tony and Sue were delighted that we were flying across to their new home at Nutwood Downs for an overnight get-together.

As usual, our departure was later than anticipated, but eventually we were airborne. Unfortunately, the appropriate map for the area had been left on the table where John had studied it before filling out his flight plan. It wasn't a problem, he reassured me. He knew the heading from Birrimba Station over which we were presently flying. Within half an hour we were surrounded by smoke rising above bushfires burning out of control on a wide front. John noted the disused airstrip at Daly Waters as we continued east, hoping that our destination would soon materialise despite the smoke screen. I started to envisage all kinds of things, the best option being a night in the scrub. At least baby Rebecca had foolproof nourishment. Apart from the standard emergency rations, we had a carton of beer and a container of Anzac biscuits. Outside was becoming horribly murky. Blackened tree after blackened tree stabbed the smouldering desolate landscape. It was both uncanny and unsettling.

'We're going back,' John stated.

What a relief! I couldn't wait to leave the smoke-shrouded sky. He had judged it to perfection and we landed safely on the deserted strip at Daly Waters just before last light. I was contemplating the best way to arrange everyone for the night when a man suddenly appeared from inside the dilapidated hangar not used since the war. He introduced himself as the caretaker and offered to drive us to the nearby roadhouse. As he disappeared towards his utility, I groaned, 'I didn't bring my wallet.'

John was furious. How could I leave home without money? I hotly retaliated that he'd left home without the wretched map and we argued long and hard with the relief of being on terra firma. Upon our arrival at the roadhouse, we pulled up right beside grinning stock inspectors Bluey Lunn and John Kieran. They offered money, friendship, icecream for the kids and whatever else we wanted. Next morning we flew 'IFR' (in this case, I Follow Roads), to Nutwood Downs where wonderful hospitality and friendship were concertinaed into a brief visit.

We seemed constantly to be confronted by occasions when one was put on notice and it was a case of sink or swim. We all knew from first-hand experience that God helps those who help themselves. There were times, though, that I desperately wished for professional advice and assistance.

One such occurrence was my increasing concern that Michael seldom spoke. He made sounds rather than specific words. Despite John's reassurance that he too had not said anything of significance until he was four, my alarm increased. According to John, his first words were: 'I think it's going to rain today.' This was confirmed by Peg, his mother.

When Michael started pre-school, the on-air teachers had trouble interpreting his messages. Their routine responses such as, 'Oh, that's interesting,' covered most news items; however, I could not sense any real progress. Oral activities were of paramount importance and his participation was as imperative as that of his siblings. Particularly when John was home and able to participate, we acted out plays and poems. Our puppet shows were constructed as though for Albert Hall. We converted two beds into the ground floor of a large department store and worked out bargaining, money and change. Although we comprehended what Michael meant, I worried about other people understanding him. Marie and Patrick alternately teased and spoke for him. Most of all I worried for Michael, and determined to seek help for him at the first opportunity.

A mother knows her child like no other and the mother–child bond is like no other. As mother and teacher, I had to acquire yet control an analytical attitude and furthermore balance the need to reinforce, persevere with and consolidate skills. I knew each child's strengths and weaknesses and was in the best position to anticipate and solve problems. When Marie persisted in spelling 'wish' as 'whish', I would find myself at smoko saying, 'Sit up darling, watch your cup and spell wish.'

My even-keeled husband, when present, would interject, 'Come on, this is meal time. Family time.'

However, on any six hour drive to town, we would squeeze in a tables quiz and revision exercises in between the usual games of I Spy.

We were by no means foolproof. When pressure in the school room became almost unbearable, we would break to sing or play charades. One particularly explosive, long hot afternoon we defused the tension with an impromptu performance of the hokey pokey. We were all loudly and happily putting 'backsides in and backsides out' when out of the corner of my eye, I noticed a huge king brown lying inert in the corner. I signalled to the children to climb onto the table while I went for the gun.

They quickly obeyed. However, as silence reigned, the snake uncannily slithered away like greased lightning. Several days later the reptile returned to witness our Health Hustle, a physical exercise routine to music. This time it was despatched to heaven, much to everyone's relief. Was it coincidence or musical appreciation? We wondered because we had learnt at school that although they have no external ears, snakes are sensitive to vibration.

Another trying morning when concentration spans seemed to be in shreds, when tricks were executed repeatedly, when I'd had minimum sleep and I was expecting a tribe for dinner, I lost control and started shouting. With little effect I shouted, despite my ever-increasing volume and frustration. From the yard John registered the situation. Within minutes heavy footsteps ploughed through the house and my consciousness and a concerned voice demanded, 'What's going on here?'

The big-brimmed stock hat herded the breakaway mob and they were told by their Dad to give Mum a fair go. He stayed half an hour. They read about Digger, recited poems and related to a new person in the school room. They expressed their apology by almost sitting on top of me.

At other times, John would visit us at school intermittently. He played the school inspector. He praised and balanced. He helped me enormously to remember that it is all a matter of perspective: 'To a worm, digging in the hard ground is more relaxing than going fishing.'

Our school routine was demanding, flexible and rewarding. Each child kept a word book into which he or she copied favourite descriptive words and phrases. We all had insatiable appetites for reading. Amongst my many expectations were adjectives preceding nouns and sentences never ending with prepositions. Though my motherly duties including reading to the children at bedtime, on one particular night I was especially weary and, hoping for a quick session, I selected a book that was not anyone's favourite. My inimitable Patrick asked: 'What did you bring the book I didn't want to be read to out of up for?'

I always gave points for imagination and having a go at teacher Mum.

Marie's fixation with her one spelling problem did not prevent her winning the Northern Territory poetry competition held in conjunction with the International Year of the Child.

ME

This is the year and I am the child
Blue-eyed, blond, meek and mild;
My home is filled with laughter and love,
Although we all work without a shove.
Cattle are mustered, ponies are ridden,
Our school room is hectic and some things are forbidden.
Sunrises, sunsets, green grass and pets,
Are all enjoyed in between correspondence sets.
Oh children everywhere all over the world,
I whish you happiness as flags are unfurled.
It's good to be a young girl in 1979,
I whish you the joy and peace that are mine.

The letter of congratulations informing Marie of her win also invited her to personally accept her prize at a special awards ceremony in Darwin. The letter arrived a fortnight after the event.

It was quite a shock to learn that whooping cough had claimed victims sporadically across the region. All required immunisations were religiously given at Riveren by either a visiting health sister or myself, so we felt quite secure as our shots were up to date. However, the mutation of the causative organism makes it impossible to completely contain this dreadful childhood illness and the Aboriginal infant mortality rate was of great concern.

Unfortunately, our four little ones contracted whooping cough in order of age and one at a time. There was little sleep for months as the night time whoops always culminated with vomiting and sheet changes, often numerous times a night. School continued and became a mini hospital in the process. Baby Rebecca was the last to display the symptoms. She was so frightened and helpless when the dreadful climax followed the uncontrollable coughing.

It seemed no time had passed before Michael was ill again. He was pale and listless. For a little fellow who was eternally happy, his quietness was of great concern. At school he lay on the bed next to his sister's cot, either listening to our activities or sleeping. He tolerated fluids better than food. I prayed that he would soon be well; John suggested antibiotics. I watched and waited.

Ten days dragged by before tell-tale signs pinpointed the problem. In the sense that a life threatening condition was no longer a possibility, it was a relief to know that Michael had hepatitis. Once he stabilised, we drove the six hundred kilometres to town to visit the doctor and establish the state of play for other family members and the Riveren workforce. It was amazing that upon our return, the Aborigines had somehow got wind of the fact that I had a 'big needle' for each one of them. They were terrified of injections and all my powers of persuasion and explanation came to the fore as the queue trickled tentatively towards my medical table and chair.

The ordinary days afterwards when everyone was well again were appreciated as never before.

In Katherine, the annual supervisors' conference for teacher–parents was held in conjunction with the school camp. We decided to attend for the first time, though we arrived late and would depart early due to home demands. Camping for two nights with other correspondence pupils at Tindal, the skeletal remnants of the RAAF base, was a great adventure for our children. During the day, they visited the fire station, the library and the spectacular Katherine Gorge.

We parents and supervisors attended lectures and discussions led by teachers and experts on every conceivable topic. Panels were formed and ideas and methods exchanged to make life in the home classroom effective and harmonious. The problems that were aired so honestly were common to all. Distractions and discipline topped the list.

There were some mothers who sensed failure in their inability to teach their own children. A few simply did not have the necessary education standards. Usually the children who refused to co-operate for family responded to the efforts of an outsider. However, not everyone could afford a governess or accommodate one either. A young enthusiastic governess often proved an asset, becoming friend to Mum and children. However, there were others who were determined to scoop the pool and catastrophically marriages disintegrated as the governess ultimately replaced the wife. On other properties the children were also the stockcamp and work force. In that situation lessons had low priority when thirsty cattle had to be relocated. For us all it was difficult.

Remoteness affected schooling in many ways. A trip to town would encroach on school time because with one day in and one day out for travelling, it was never less than three days away. Subsequently, weekends would become school days. The continuing and increasing complaint over the years was that there was too little free time at home. We always seemed to be making up school time.

Listening to others, I appreciated our situation all over again. Our children were wonderfully energetic and my pupils remained extraordinarily co-operative. Motivation seemed almost congenital in our family. We did not drift. We planned and played. We learned and grew together. The children trusted me implicitly. Several mothers mentioned enviously: 'You are so lucky that your children are such good pupils.'

My reply was instant: 'I certainly am.'

I grasped the opportunity to seek advice for Michael. The principal, Mike Forster, was immediately helpful. He organised an experienced, highly qualified speech specialist to spend a weekend at Riveren. The children had no reason to associate this lady with school, nor was there the slightest indication of a hidden agenda. We explained that she was a friend who loved to visit families and children in the Outback.

As Rosemary shared our usual daily activities, she assessed Michael's problem and devised games to help overcome it. Co-ordination activities were implemented for all the children. Specific sounds were targeted and limericks and rhymes written to highlight them. What appeared to be great fun had a serious agenda. These were her skills.

How fortunate we were to have her professional advice. When things went wrong in the bush, help was a long way away. Young children with a physical impairment or learning disability created enormous pressures on bush families. Talented and gifted children were not catered for either. Distance and limited resources highjacked every agenda. We knew of broken families as a result, or alternately a family in need of full-time guidance exchanging station life for a town existence. The father, a stockman through and through, would then struggle to find other work. It was not uncommon to find such a man behind the wheel of a roadtrain, at least affording him a continuing role in the cattle team.

With John in Alice Springs for the routine hundred hourly service of our aircraft and the stockmen out on a fence line, the children and I had enjoyed being on our own for a week. However, we did look forward to John's homecoming as it was never quite the same without him.

In view of his expected return I drove the children to the airstrip to meet him. Marie discovered a beautiful dried bush pumpkin vine, the boys intently watched ants in cavernous ant beds, and little Rebecca happily wriggled her bare toes in the warm red dirt. When last light faded, I gave the boarding call for home. To my dismay the vehicle battery was completely dead. I jiggled and fiddled as I had seen it done before. I lifted the bonnet, and in the poor light, I peered and poked. Nothing happened. The vehicle was going nowhere. It was a long walk home in the darkness unaided by a new moon. For three long kilometres, I coaxed and carried, encouraging and urging forward tired little legs. Finally the distant house lights beckoned us onwards.

Next morning as the plane buzzed overhead, I announced to the children that we were not going to admit defeat, but would display some of the good old bush initiative always applauded by their father. They clambered upwards to board the roomy cabin of the gigantic bore truck which resembled a drilling rig. With continued encouragement from five enthusiastic voices, it sluggishly surged into life with black smoke billowing in all directions.

'Hooray Mum!' the children cheered. Very slowly and deliberately we rumbled towards the airstrip. It was like manoeuvring a skyscraper, as overhead massive steel ladders and poles stood upright and unyielding.

Neither driver expected the other vehicle and at the bend we almost collided. John was behind the wheel of the vehicle I had abandoned as broken down the previous night. His look of total astonishment was shared by three passengers. I was having trouble pulling up and as there was nowhere to turn I continued to the airstrip where I eventually executed an about turn. John had pulled up trying to guess the name of the game I was playing. Minutes later I idled beside the mirthful men.

'Flash car your wife drives,' a stranger laughed.

I desperately wanted to know how he had fixed the utility, and didn't have to wait long.

'Remember those things called battery terminals, Terry? When they are loose, they have to be secured.'

I groaned as I proceeded homewards in the dust of the all-male vehicle.

We had prepared for this Riveren Christmas with a great sense of pride. Our newly completed wing afforded adequate sleeping for a crowd. We were also anxious to share extensive improvements beyond our homestead gate. These feelings were matched by the growing anticipation and impatience of the children as they waited for Santa.

Early scuds or small floating storms announced Christmas Eve, and that evening John's family arrived with mud rather than dust on their vehicle. Patrick's and Michael's noses left definite smudges on the homestead windows as they gazed into the increasing darkness for the first glimpse of reindeer.

After a couple of rums, Grandad Pat told the children, 'Old Santa might not make it here tonight. I saw him up at Laura Bore, bogged to the eyeballs. Too many presents on board! Loaned him my shovel and he reckoned he'd be right. Better cross your fingers, kids.'

The expletives that routinely floated through the air when things went wrong could never have fallen on deaf ears all those formative years.

'Shit!' shouted the little boys in unison.

I appeared from the laundry with a packet of washing powder, just as a reminder. Whenever the children's vocabulary became too colourful, the thought of soap in mouth was usually an effective dampener.

The tree was decorated and the cake and carrots positioned for Santa and his reindeer. Adult snoring and muffled whispers penetrated the stillness. It was almost morning before all four children had slipped from their watch to the land of dreams, and so Christmas slips were finally filled with Santa's goodies.

Our numbers increased dramatically with the arrival of two neighbouring families. After hot turkey with all the trimmings the men had a siesta, while the women enjoyed the antics of the youngsters sharing armfuls of new toys. As the blistering heat became less acute, we prepared for our river expedition. With the vehicles loaded, a head count revealed that the one and only jackeroo was missing. The obvious places were double checked. He was repeatedly called by a chorus of impatient anglers. When John found the cold room door unlatched, he discovered more than the cold water containers. Fred was sitting in the centre all on his Pat Malone, playing his guitar and singing 'Pub With No Beer'. He was equally surprised to see John.

'I couldn't find anyone, but I found this cool dark place instead,' he grinned.

It was law for all cold rooms to have an internal door catch so that one could never be trapped inside. But what if one wasn't even aware of one's location? John quickly organised Fred into a vehicle and we set off for Mucca Waterhole.

With the ghostly river gums in sight, John called a halt at some scattered wooden posts. Pointing to the remains of a yard built by the Farquharson, brothers, John told us why this place was called Mucca. It was their uncle, Nat Buchanan, the legendary Boss Drover, who formed Wave Hill in 1883. Before the three brothers, Archie, Harry and Hughie Farquharson, took up Inverway in 1894, it was crown land. Once they established their base at Moonlight Hole, the droving brothers led a party south to bring back another large mob of cattle to stock the new station. Nat Buchanan had blazed trails across the continent taking cattle into the harsh inland. His nephews, nicknamed Sweaty, Skinny and Squeakie, also underwent epic journeys in the years when the real opening up and stocking of the North commenced and stock routes were formed.

'Anyway, on this particular trip the returning drovers with the mob of cattle intact were unable to relocate the crude homestead at Moonlight Hole from which they had departed the year before. They ended up erecting a temporary base right here. It was a complete muck-up, all right. Hence the name "Mucca" was given to this waterhole.'

With a sense of reverence I closed my eyes, trying to imagine the fortitude and perserverance of those pioneers whose courage had made possible our presence. They had opened up this hostile country in the face of every known adversary. Three generations of Underwoods and their visitors moved on to the waterhole where fishing and swimming were the order of our ongoing Christmas celebrations.

Another mustering season was under way after generous rains and promised record brandings. The stockmen were drafting their horses when a hullabaloo at the door interrupted school. A breathless Sam Long shouted, 'Come quick! Hurry now. John's on ground in round yard. Moaning, everything. Hurt properly.'

I ran. John's shoulder had dislocated yet again. With my foot in his affected armpit, I somehow mustered the strength to pull on his arm, allowing the weakened joint to slip back into its socket. In the ensuing months, coughing or sneezing caused instant and increasingly painful dislocation.

It was back to St Vincent's and Dr Roarty for a shoulder repair operation. Sister Bernice, the mother superior during my training and now in charge of the new St Vincent's Private Hospital, welcomed us with open arms. She was thrilled to meet the offspring of her graduate nurse and patient from Ward 3 and often dropped into John's room for a chat with the children. My brother Johnny had specialised in Anaesthetics and was working at St Vincent's, so at the completion of his theatre list each day he also called in. As always it was wonderful to catch up with family and friends.

Before leaving Sydney, we attended the necessary interviews at Marie's future school, Kincoppal Rose Bay, Convent of the Sacred Heart. Though the school and staff were known to be excellent, we were not looking forward to the beginning of the much talked about boarding school years.

Once home, John continued to muster at Inverway. He was there the day that a fierce electrical storm brewed. Great claps of thunder growled menacingly as blinding lightning zigzagged across the darkening sky. I knew that electrical storms were renowned for starting fires, particularly early in the Wet Season. I was now seeing it for myself and watched the greedy tongues of fire with horror.

The westerly wind was fanning the fire towards the aerodrome. Concerned about the car parked at the hangar and the drums of aviation fuel, I started in that direction. I felt secure in the knowledge that from the air John would have seen the now towering cloud of smoke and be homeward bound. The fire intensified and I turned back. I could see the terror on the faces of my four little ones. Marie nursed Rebecca. Patrick held Ratsy and Michael clutched Cuddles, our new blue heeler cross puppy.

Without warning the wind changed. It accelerated as it swung east, whipping the flames into a frenzy. A gigantic fire front roared towards the homestead. Outside the humpies I screamed to the Aboriginal women and kids to get in the car quickly. One started to wander back inside. Dear God, I thought, as I raced after her.

After the monthly wages were distributed in cash, there was always a big card game. Some blackfellas seemed never to lose, others lost their entire wages in a single night. Sometimes having run out of money they bet their possessions. As Nora reached out for her new wireless acquired at last night's game, I pulled her towards the car. 'Hurry up,' I shouted. We could feel the intense heat and the thick smoke was blinding and choking. The other four women and three frightened children had already followed their five dogs aboard. I slammed the door and instantly accelerated. From a hilltop beyond immediate danger we watched. The dog fight might have been predictable as snarls and fleas were exchanged. Not so was the death of the fire at the road beside the homestead complex. It was unbelievable and quite miraculous that the force of the wind had not caused the fire to jump the road, in which case everything could well have been totally devoured.

Upon his return much later John informed me that there is only one weapon with which to fight a fire and that is fire itself. Had I not thought to light up from the road edge and burn back to the fire front? I hoped that the advice received would never have to be used.

To keep our children beside us would be the essence of selfishness. With the broadening of their horizons they might return home by choice, not because it was all they knew. Although the necessity for secondary boarding school had been part of living in isolation and always discussed openly and positively, none of us could ever have been ready for the separation. All too soon it was time. Leaving Sydney without Marie was leaving part of me behind. I cried inside all the way home.

We rearranged the desks to cover her gap; however, Marie's presence was constantly missed by us all. After milking the goats at first light, she had exercised racehorses before school. No-one's indispensable, John always maintained. I maintained that it was as though I had lost my right arm. In my letters I assured Marie that her love and laughter filled our home and hearts even in her absence.

The installation of the long-awaited radio telephone fortunately just preceded the boarding school wrench. There were about twenty stations on one channel and only one could use the system at a time. It was a High Frequency system, which meant that in addition to the queue for telephone use we remained at the mercy of the elements with static and interference. There was also a time limit of twelve minutes on all calls.

'Hello 1 3 4 5, I have a reverse charge call for you from Sydney. We have a backlog of traffic today, so please restrict your call to nine minutes. Go ahead, over.'

Marie had had to wait for a long time before the call was available at our end. The public phone for the year seven boarders was right outside the office of the boarder mistress. Due to the static and squelch, Marie had to shout at the top of her voice and repeat everything several times for me to understand anything she said.

She sounded so far away. Her forlorn little voice quivered as she repeated, 'Hello, Mum. Can you hear me? Can you hear me, Mum? How's everything at home? I miss you all, over.'

'Hello Marie, it's so good to hear your voice. Everyone is well and busy. Tell me about school, over.'

When the operator intervened to insist on goodbyes, I concluded, 'Remember we must all be brave darling; goodbye Marie; over and out.'

At least we could talk to each other. Although we exchanged letters written weekly, to be able to speak to each other was vitally important. Both forms of communication were not just comforting, they were essential.

As the eldest and the first to make this journey, Marie's hill really was mountainous.

CHAPTER 13

THE BULL

....

'Good morning all grade four children. This is Mr Nepia calling. Today I want you to tell me about your favourite pet. What is its name and what is its favourite trick? Firstly, we'll go out west, almost as far as the West Australian border, to Riveren and to Michael Underwood. Go ahead Michael.'

'Good morning Mr Nepia. We have lots of pets but our blue heeler Cuddles is the cleverest because she can ride a horse by herself, over.'

'Well, there is no doubt about the Underwoods. Next they'll be telling us that Cuddles runs the stockcamp.'

In the entire litany of climbing cats, talking birds, burping poddies and limping lizards, Cuddles was unsurpassed as the most unusually talented pet.

A somewhat sceptical teacher was dumbfounded when he subsequently received a photograph of Cuddles riding Son of Showdown. With reins around her neck she was as balanced as her mount was unconcerned. As the stallion thirstily drank chlorinated water from the swimming pool, Cuddles watched the circling crows caw in disbelief at the strange sight below.

It was a special skill to retain the attention of unseen children on air and some class teachers readily excelled at this challenge. However, it was important for new teachers to gain information and preferably early exposure to the nature of this land and its people. There was nothing more crushing for a child who ecstatically reported overdue rain than this response from an ignorant teacher, 'Oh dear, I hope it fines up for you soon.'

Not only did our workforce embrace an infrastructure and discipline, so did our family and personal lives. Regardless of circumstances, everyone everywhere washed faces and hands and combed hair before eating. Water was water whether it be from creek or trough or hand basin. At night the evening meal was religiously preceded by a shower and change of clothing. Our remoteness would never be the cause of any drop in standards; however, it did gradually increase our awareness of the need to be actively involved in education, industry and community events. For me the school radio provided the perfect medium enabling contribution from home.

I became an inaugural member of the world's first Penguins of the Air Club. In 1937, during the Depression, the club's founder showed great vision when she realised that if women were ever to reach their full potential, they must be trained to be confident, concise, convincing speakers, competent in chairmanship and meeting procedure. As Eleanor Roosevelt said, 'Nobody can make you feel inferior without your consent.' While town Penguins dressed for their dinner meetings, I was one of many isolated women who applied lipstick and perfume before taking up my microphone to speak either on the topic of the day, to pass a motion, amend a motion, or to give an impromptu talk. The associated research and social interaction Outback style were stimulating and loads of fun.

With great enthusiasm, I embraced my new role as president of the Katherine School of the Air associates. There was no school council and so the functions of the associates extended beyond fund raising to include decision making relevant to many aspects of distance education.

There were long days when after our school programme was completed, I would chair an on-air meeting. Whenever static drowned out a voice, the message might have to be relayed several times by those who could hear for those who could not. These inevitable delays extended meeting time considerably. On occasions such as these, it could be 6 pm before I crossed the threshold of my school room to swing a mop before preparing dinner. Late at night patches were applied to jeans, school lessons prepared, the diary entry recorded and letters written.

Despite the fact that there was never a spare moment day in and day out, I continued to embrace new challenges. As fund raising was not just tedious but a real struggle in our situation, I decided upon a substantial and unprecedented means of boosting the coffers as well as involving our extended community. Having thoroughly enjoyed the hilarious wedding satire *Dimboola* on our last visit to Sydney, I decided to bring the production to the Northern Territory. It would be a far cry from my Cinderella performances in our Albury garage; however, I thought it was the kind of play that would suit our ever adaptable, dedicated inhabitants of the inland.

Playwright Jack Hibberd was fascinated to learn that his most successful play was to be produced, directed and rehearsed by parents and teachers from the Katherine School of the Air over the radio network that delivered lessons to the isolated pupils. For months I deliberated, plotted and planned.

With an extraordinary amount of contemplation, the characters were cast. Given the near impossibility of the undertaking, I selected those who were not just fun-loving and bold, but reliable and trusting. It was also important to take occupations and location into account.

With the script and cast list before me, I booked eighteen calls through the astonished radio-telephone operator. In mimicry of the change-room supervisor in the clothing section of a large city store, this lady imposed a restriction on the number of calls I might make. Consumer convenience had little to do with regulation. I explained that in a sense each call was interconnected, each would be less than three minutes and that I would be more than grateful for her assistance. Somewhat begrudgingly, she relented.

When Jim Cobb, proprietor of Dunmarra Roadhouse, agreed to play the role of Horrie he had no possible conception of the demands which lay ahead. Jim resembled a youthful, slightly overweight Omar Sharif. His twinkling brown eyes, bristly moustache and ready laugh made him the perfect candidate for the rather unreliable Master of Ceremonies. Horrie detoured to the pub on his way to the church and as a result made a cheerfully noisy late entrance at the wedding reception. Jim's wife Lorraine, a young looking mere slip of a girl, asked who rang.

'Oh, that was Terry wanting me to attend some school meeting in town at show time. It's something to do with fund raising.'

There remained seventeen affirmatives to extract.

That meeting in town was in fact our introduction to the play and for some people to each other. I had divided the script into four parts, with a proposed timetable for rehearsals on air and deadlines for memorising lines. We had six months in which to conquer the script and prepare for our stage debut. There were no cultural phobias attached to this rendition of a kind of wedding reception that rang bells with most people honest enough to admit it. The deputy principal Mahlon Nepia, the same Mr Nepia who was still coming to terms with horseriding dogs, was to play bridegroom Morrie. With perfect inflection and a poker face, he practised his one line from the play: 'No worries. No worries. No worries at all.'

To substantiate my commitment and belief in the outcome, I took on the role of Shirl the Girl the Bridesmaid, as well as the duties of director and producer. John's involvement was vital and I invited him to be understudy for all nine male roles with the proviso that 'no' would not be an acceptable answer.

'You're crazy,' he said. 'You can't ask this much of anyone, let alone your husband and friends.'

'Trust me. I'll prove to you that we can do it,' I replied with unfailing conviction. Two of the cast of twenty took fright and were immediately replaced. For the newly formed group of thespians, the sails were hoisted for the voyage of a lifetime.

To helicopters, cattle yards, school rooms and roadhouse we returned with our scripts. Lines were recited and repeated as windmills were climbed, cattle mustered, customers served, school lessons delivered and sleep attempted. Our first on-air rehearsal at seven o'clock one evening highlighted the surging roar of night noises, hopelessly drowning all voices after my initial rollcall. The need for daytime rehearsals was obvious. Less obvious was how the actors would manage to attend. My cast included men and women from diverse backgrounds, all of whom had enormous responsibilities and commitments.

At last, our first daytime on-air rehearsal was under way. John was taking the roles of three absentees when he glanced by chance out of the school room window to witness stockmen in the distance taking the mob of cattle back to the wrong paddock. He thundered outdoors to rectify the situation. I lowered my voice several octaves and played four roles. Schoolteacher Leonie Rosevear played the piano. Wendy Edison, who played Astrid the flower girl, tap danced and sang 'Rubber Duckie', despite the fact that she could not hear the accompaniment. As director I could see neither of them. In fact, none of us could see each other and, as events unfolded, it became increasingly difficult to hear each other as well. Despite the fact that many people expressed frustration that they were talking to themselves, words and music, singing and dancing were somehow co-ordinated.

John Armstrong, better known as Captain Armstrong, was chief pilot and operations manager of Helimuster, based at Victoria River Downs. He co-ordinated all the fixed wing and helicopter movements in the region as well as personally mustering long hours away from home base. He was rarely able to attend our rehearsals. When attendances repeatedly became impossibilities, I reminded my actors that this was less about torture and more about love and a cause. Despite all odds, it was going to be a never to be forgotten production that would raise much-needed funds for the education of our isolated children.

All forces were marshalled for the first 'in the flesh' rehearsal in town. Family and food were loaded aboard the various vehicles and from north, south, east and west we headed for Katherine. It was an occasion to ascertain entrances, exits, interaction and outfits. Our twelve hundred kilometre round trip was eclipsed by Ros Lavercombe, who played Mavis, mother of flower girl Astrid and brow-beating wife of harassable Horrie. From Nathan River in the Gulf of Carpentaria, Ros drove an incredible eighteen hundred kilometre round trip. Five flat tyres did not deter this amazing woman intent on not letting down her fellow thespians. With the assistance of her young son, she patched and repaired and valiantly drove onwards. At Dunmarra they collected Jim (Horrie) and immediately adopted their Dimboola personas. Many kilometres further north an unusual apparition materialised from within the shimmering haze. Roadside stood a gaily dressed woman, complete with a large lime green hat bearing a single rose stem and swathed in matching tulle. Her script rested upon her upturned swag. Sharon Sutton, who played Florence, mother of the groom, climbed aboard.

Across the other side of the Territory at Victoria River Downs, Carol Armstrong carefully loaded her original bridal gown into the family car. She was Dimboola's bride, Reen. She and her real-life husband, John, joined the convoy of vehicles further down the track. John Armstrong and his mate Gerald Dayes were to act the roles of drunk and wit, or wit and drunk, or drunken wits. They insisted that it was six of one and half a dozen of the other. Only their lines were different. During our rehearsal the cold amber liquid lubricated parched vocal cords. At intermission, we all enjoyed a lively evening meal. Throughout the six hours of togetherness, numerous children absorbed rare companionship. They thrived on this feast of friendship.

To effectively imprint new identities, I suggested the cast assume stage names as they learned their lines in the undertaking of normal daily activities. The community at large was caught up in the Dimboola preparations too. Gerald, the manager of Camfield Station, one of the largest properties in the Northern Territory, was startled to be flagged down and greeted by a main roads grader driver, 'Gooday Bayonet! How're you going?'

Our Patrick, who had an almost photographic memory, could recite the entire play. He sometimes called me Shirl with a great deal of affection and, I suspected, a touch of admiration. There were gales of laughter from children whose parents seriously performed outrageous roles.

As the weeks turned into months, I wrote regular letters and made numerous phone calls of encouragement to all eighteen players. They rehearsed and recited pages of the script as they went about the business of their daily lives. With the passage of time and the dedicated repetition of words, sentences and paragraphs, they assumed their roles with increasing ease. Mike Forster, our conscientious school principal, portrayed the sloshed Irish Catholic marriage celebrant as convincingly as if he'd been born in a Dublin pub and absconded from a seminary days before ordination.

However, the days of *Dimboola* did not dent our school programme. That would remain my major priority for eighteen years.

Barking dogs and a cloud of dust announced the approaching vehicle and yet another interruption.

'It might be those Baptist people coming for lunch again,' suggested Michael as he peered through the window. I thought most people realised by now that at Riveren school stopped for no-one. I instructed Patrick to continue his project on *We of the Never Never* and Michael to finish his maths. Rebecca remained totally absorbed in a multi-media painting of her pony, Mini.

'I won't be long,' I remarked as I hurriedly left the school room. From experience I knew that my sons, nineteen months apart in age, needed little temptation to bicker or to tussle on the floor like grizzly bear cubs. Returning sometimes to broken rulers, giggles or sobs, it would take three times the length of absence from school to restore calm and a working environment. They knew that whoever was about to invade would be offered a cup of tea and placed on hold until our official school break for smoko.

Two familiar gentlemen alighted from their vehicle. Bob Cruise and Peter Hoare from Elders greeted me with beaming smiles and the predictable inquiry.

'How're you going? John home?'

'Unfortunately he's out for the day. They're doing a destock and with a yard full of scrub cattle I don't expect anyone back until dark.'

Even as I spoke I heard another faraway sound. I thought out loud, continuing, 'That's strange. Here's the old Toyota returning now. I hope there's nothing wrong.'

With increasing alarm, I watched the vehicle approach at snail's pace, cross the grid and veer towards us. Three heads turned as did the vehicle. The driver was not John and I knew indeed that something was very wrong.

It seemed to take forever to focus on the reality of what was before me and yet I had still seen nothing. Whether in slow motion or a sprint, I reached the passenger side of the cabin and put my hand through the window to touch him. Like a spectre he seemed to be elsewhere. John was bloodied and grey. He was in deep shock. As I opened the door I spoke.

'What happened?'

His disembodied voice answered.

'A bull.'

Bob and Peter were beside me and with stockman Eric carefully stood John up. He sagged. Gently but deliberately they directed him towards the house. One leg after the other, in automation he walked. Although he was upright, they were doing the walking for him. He was levered up the steps and lowered onto the lounge. I wondered how I could have managed without the extra help. Bob was as strong as an ox and although Peter and Eric were visibly distressed, they were capable offsiders.

His saturated clothing was ripped haphazardly. I cut it away with scissors. He lay very still. As I washed away the top layers of blood and dirt to assess the injuries, John said very quietly, 'I'm all right. There's no serious damage to my vital organs or I wouldn't still be talking.'

His logic and control sliced through my mental turmoil. As two sons and Rebecca clung to his off side, he slowly turned to them and smiled. 'Humbug properly, aren't I kids?'

Peter assumed the role of teacher while Bob hovered around John. Having discovered four horrific points of entry by the horns of the maddened beast, I established immediate radio contact with the Flying Doctor base. The chest injury was of urgent concern as flying in an unpressurised aircraft at an unsuitable altitude could cause further serious damage. During our lengthy consultation, I gave my assessment of John's injuries and requested that he be delivered directly into the care of experienced surgeon Tony Noonan, who was now working in Darwin. The medical plane at Halls Creek was to be diverted to Inverway as our airstrip was deemed inadequate in length for its landing. Fortunately John's brother Reg, who now piloted his own plane, had overheard my medical call and was able to provide the connecting link from Riveren to Inverway.

Unbelievably, there was another knock at the door. Loaded with newly purchased Brahman heifers from Queensland, a roadtrain had failed to negotiate the steep silty bank in our river crossing and had jackknifed into the river. The driver had walked ten kilometres to request assistance. Peter Flanagan, friend and stock inspector, arrived next to organise the destock operation in the yards. The Elders gentlemen offered to hold the fort; however, John was absolutely insistent that I remain at home to solve the problems and run the station in his absence. All the while we discussed the situation, I cleansed deep, punctured holes that were choked with shale, dirt and gravel.

Reg's plane flew overhead. Since baby days our children had never seen their father skip a beat. They wanted him repaired and returned as soon as possible. As they kissed him goodbye their love and concern were visible. I would return from Inverway within the hour. From the front seat beside Reg, I kept watch on John lying across the back seats as we maintained a low altitude to Inverway.

The medical plane awaited him. He was helped aboard. The doors were slammed, engines started and within minutes he was airborne. We followed. As John headed north-west to Wyndham, not Darwin, we flew east. Having returned me to Riveren, Reg took off again for his new home, Bunda Station, at the western end of Inverway. His recent marriage to childhood sweetheart, Janelle, had added a second city-born Catholic daughter-in-law to the Underwood family.

Once home, I contacted Tony Noonan to seek his intervention in having the Wyndham bound flight diverted to Darwin. Thank God for the radio telephone. The politics of the medical system paid little consideration to the nature of injuries and treatment required. Tony promised to do his best and he knew the system inside out. In the meantime there were a multitude of problems for me to address. Outside, we turned our attention to the roadtrain.

After dark I met the stockcamp vehicle and the blackfellas told me the story of John's near demise. It was one of the final chapters in the disease eradication programme to clean up feral cattle from areas adjacent to Riveren. They were mustered and trapped into the portable yards specifically erected to contain the mob of wild scrub cattle that had never seen man or captivity. Horns and heaving hides crashed and thrashed against the yard panels. They bellowed and pawed the earth, challenging and charging whenever room was adequate. John commenced drafting. Though the men were ever aware of danger, this mob represented double danger and everyone developed eyes in the backs of their heads.

One particularly agitated bull had John in line and charged. With instant reflexes, John leapt high onto the portable panel. Not to be denied or defeated, the crazed beast, snorting loudly, thrust his head between the rails and with malevolent force and locked horns not only lifted the panel but shook it as well. Losing his balance, John toppled to the ground and the bull had him.

In the corner John grappled with the bull's horns as he yelled at the monstrous charging beast. The cruel horns thrust forward repeatedly, penetrating chest, arm, groin and shoulder as though John was a papier-mâché figure. Seconds passed as the ringers, paralysed with fear and horror, witnessed the murderous attack on their helpless Boss. Something triggered action just as John's time was running out. Petrified though they were, they swarmed forwards. With no regard for their own safety, some waved hats and sticks, shouting and distracting the angry animal, while others dragged John away from danger. The lump in my throat was like a rock. How could I ever thank them adequately, I wondered. Their respect and affection for John governed their act of heroism and this would never be underestimated or forgotten.

Destined for the meatworks, the bull in question was branded many times. Thus he was distinguishable from his travelling companions. Jack Dalzell, a renowned listener to the Bush Telegraph, organised the salvation of the horns and their subsequent mounting. The weapons of destruction would be presented to us at a time in the future when physical and emotional scars were less painful.

John was transported from Wyndham airport to the hospital, where admission papers were organised while he was assessed as having sustained injuries too serious for treatment there. He was then moved back to the same aircraft and eventually Darwin bound, where Tony Noonan and his theatre team were on standby. Tony's telephone call advising me that John was on his way at long last was the only lightening of my burden.

'He should be on the operating table by 6 pm,' Tony advised. 'I'll contact you as soon as we are out of theatre. Try not to worry too much.'

John was moved into the ambulance at Darwin airport just as another remote area evacuation flight landed. Within minutes an Aboriginal woman was positioned on the bunk beside him. Feeling drained, John rested quietly with eyes closed. The wailing siren did not obliterate the woman's increasing moans. With flashing lights the ambulance announced to motorists and pedestrians alike that it was indeed on an important mission. Inside and invisible to the world, the woman struggled and heaved as John lay inert. She grabbed John's hand, her fingernails biting into his leathery skin as she groaned and panted. With involuntary relief, her final all powerful push released her baby into the world minutes before the ambulance pulled up outside casualty. It was quite an arrival.

Sleep had claimed them all and I sat alone beside the telephone. I had read the same page three times without any idea of the contents. It was now the second time that I had contacted the operator to see if there was a call for me. It was not only customary, but obligatory, for the lines to be kept open for a limited time on the hour to enable emergency calls to be taken. For the remainder of the time when calls were in progress, there was no mechanism to break into the system. It was often unsatisfactory, but it was as always a matter of working within our limitations. Annie was sympathetic and offered to ring the hospital.

'Are you still there, 1 3 4 5? I have been advised that Dr Noonan is still in theatre. They will ring as soon as any information is available, over.'

A new date on the calendar was notched before the long-awaited din of the deafening radio-telephone siren blasted through the stillness. I removed the handpiece before it reached the crescendo pitch that would waken our world.

Never one to beat about the bush, Tony stated, 'You don't know how lucky you are to still have your husband. The horn that penetrated between his ribs went within a centimetre of John's heart. Wound debris was shocking, however I'm hopeful that infection will be avoided with my treatment in theatre and massive doses of antibiotics. John is resting comfortably, Terry. I suggest you do likewise and I'll call you tomorrow for an updated report, over.'

I thanked him from the bottom of my heart. Upstairs and inside, I looked down at three young foreheads sprinkled with sun kisses and covered with blond tousled hair. As I gently kissed each one, I whispered, 'Your Dad has made it.' As always I was drawn outside and with arms and eyes raised upwards, I communicated with my Creator.

Two days later, I desperately needed to speak with John regarding cattle movements. I telephoned the hospital. There were no telephones for patients in any of the wards. However, the sister in charge kindly organised transportation of John's bed complete with intravenous stand and drainage bottle apparatus to the nursing administration desk and telephone. We talked briefly. My dilemma was instantly resolved. Not so his.

It was essential that deep puncture wounds heal progressively and thoroughly from the inside to the skin surface. Tony telephoned me regularly to discuss John's progress. Until now no mention had been made of John's precarious groin injury and its possible implications.

'Your man has extraordinary recuperative powers, Terry. In fact I have never met anyone quite like him. I'm constantly amazed at his resilience. However, there is one area that is definitely your domain. As soon as he is discharged I'm sure that you will take him for a test drive. Cheers for now. Over and out.'

Concerned about his damaged chest muscles, the physiotherapist urged John to stay. John was determined that his second week in hospital would be his last.

'I feel all right, really. I have to get back to the station. Besides which I'm married to a nurse. Ask Dr Noonan,' John reiterated as he packed his bag to head down the track with stock inspector and mate, Peter Flanagan, who happened to be Riveren bound.

Although John was uncomplaining and undeterred, the extent of his injuries had taken a toll. In the following weeks healing progressed slowly, thwarting his return to normal activities. For John these included the most demanding tasks, demonstrating his very real enjoyment of hard physical labour.

Water bags had been complemented by esky containers and at our *Dimboola* rehearsals all of them were filled to capacity. Beer cans poking through rapidly melting ice were consumed with equal rapidity. They seemed part of each part, the culture of the story and the setting of the scene. A little alcohol between lines accelerated the authenticity of each role and each rehearsal resembled an increasingly unruly wedding reception. When gatecrasher Mutton stated that he was as parched as a parrot, spinster aunt Aggie retorted that he certainly squawked like one. Arriving late on his bicycle, Horrie wobbled unstably through the scattering guests, intent on pursuing lubrication for his voice. As the antics and drinks flowed, John faithfully recited his required lines. Only I detected his air of detachment, bordering on a deep sense of weariness.

The Australian Broadcasting Corporation television network contacted me to ascertain the width and depth of the story about which they had heard whispers. Producer Janet Bell instantly sensed a winner and our combined total support was pledged to accommodate their filming of this unique production. Our victory over isolation coupled with the generosity of the participants left the film crew staggering in disbelief. Had we each pooled the cost of fuel, accommodation and time away from home over six months, total monies would have been five times in excess of those raised by our live performance for three consecutive nights in Katherine. However, there was more to this than dollars and cents.

Apart from the socialising aspects there were other direct benefits to the children. The annual school Christmas party was naturally held on air. However, this year many families involved with *Dimboola*, either as performers or 'wedding guests', were in town for the on-air break up concert and party. Children from all over the top half of the Northern Territory gathered excitedly for Santa's arrival by helicopter. They trailed behind the profusely perspiring figure as he shouted, 'Ho ho ho', and despatched lolly bags in all directions. Inside the school studio Santa spoke on radio to those other children still at their isolated locations, patiently holding their microphones in anticipation, and in turn performing a Christmas song, poem or short story. Within the studio there was a great hush and crush. For so many it was their first sighting of the jolly fat man in the red suit and white beard.

All too quickly it was 7.30 and the church bells were pealing to announce the *Dimboola* nuptials. Like veteran celebrities, we in the official bridal party performed for the wedding guests at Kirby's restaurant. It was transformed into the Opera House of the Northern Territory as laughter and disbelief intermingled and the hysterical lines of the play unfolded. On cue, the celebrant priest made a pass at Aggie before passing out, the Catholic and Protestant elements came to blows and the bridegroom collided head first into the tiered cream wedding cake. It was all so convincing and genuine. Wedding gifts for Morrie and Reen included a ridiculously fluffy, multicoloured feather duster. Congratulatory telegrams from guests attending that night's performance were contrived with unabated imagination and humour.

Part of the television production was the inclusion of the home school room at Riveren. Producer Janet, who hailed from 'Playschool', had a wonderful affinity with children as did her crew of three. During their four days at Riveren, adults, children and animals all became good friends. It was a fond farewell to the team from 'A Big Country' as they returned to Sydney to edit their seemingly endless footage.

Many of us involved in *Dimboola* were also members of the Isolated Children's and Parents' Association, which is primarily a lobby group targeting government for equal educational access and opportunities for isolated pupils. Rather than raise separate funds for this association (as well as for our School of the Air), we established a joint fundraising mechanism to avoid duplication. It was always the same people working for the benefit of the same children. *Dimboola* was the biggest single fundraising operation we had undertaken and the money collected was used in part to purchase a new printing press for our School of the Air.

The widespread and ongoing benefits did not bear a price tag. At the party signalling the end of our theatrical season, everyone agreed whole-heartedly, 'No worries! No regrets!' Goodwill and togetherness were as unlimited as the distances that separated us.

CHAPTER 14

GOING FOR
A FLY

....

Patrick was learning how to put on a school tie for the first time. He was enrolled at St Joseph's College, the leading rugby school in Sydney, but had never played football. Our children in fact were not familiar with throwing or catching a ball, lining up for the starter's gun or losing, let alone winning. My concern at our lack of sporting experience intensified. With a rising sense of urgency I lobbied the Katherine School of the Air for a sports day. This was at length reluctantly agreed to and only on the condition that it was organised and co-ordinated by parents, due to the teachers' workload. My desk was cleared and other matters placed on hold. It was now or never. More than one hundred children traversed hundreds of kilometres to compete at the Katherine Oval for the very first time.

According to their ages, they lined up for sprints, long jumps and high jumps and accuracy throws. There were relay races, tunnel ball and other team events and last of all a running race for the parents and teachers. The true value of that function, given the isolation of School of the Air families, was beyond doubt and sports days subsequently became an integral part of the school year.

Twelve months after we left Marie in Sydney, eleven-year-old Patrick stood at the impressive main doors of St Joseph's College, Hunters Hill, trying to control his trembling lip. Gruffly John cautioned, 'Hurry up and say goodbye, Terry, or you'll be here all bloody night.'

Although Patrick and I knew what he meant, it did not help very much. Nothing did. His road would be strewn with boulders too.

Patrick's acceptance into the largest boarding school in the southern hemisphere had been a miracle in its own right. Although we acknowledged the Creator and His kingdom in every aspect of our daily lives, the numerous Catholic practices inherent to urban children did not exist at Riveren. We were not exposed to Sunday Mass, hymns and many traditional prayers. Moreover we had been forewarned by friends that John being a non-Catholic might go against us in the final analysis. On the day that we were ushered into the presence of the headmaster for the all important family interview which would ultimately decide the future of one Underwood son, we were all slightly nervous.

A powerful presence, Brother stood tall as he smiled his welcome. Dark brown eyes explored each of us as he firmly shook hands and registered individual names. What if we fail, I thought. That was too terrible to contemplate. Our boys desperately needed dedicated educators and professional moulding during their critical years of adolescence. Sitting awkwardly on the edge of the comfortable lounge, John tried to appear relaxed. I succeeded in not speaking for Patrick as he answered the question as to why he wanted to come to this college.

'Because Mum and Dad want me to.' Then to my enormous relief he added, 'Also, because everyone reckons it's the best.'

Patrick's eyes lit up when asked about home. Instantly a myriad of splendid images and orchestral sounds of the bush burst into the room of beautiful paintings and relics and renowned violin concerto recordings. One passionate cattle boy launched into animated descriptions of protective cows with newborn calves, bellowing bulls, galloping horses, huge sand goannas preying on baby birds, shaggy paw lizards waving to no-one in particular and wild dingoes howling at daybreak. The headmaster was absolutely fascinated. So far so good I thought when unexpectedly he turned to us.

'Have you heard about the Pope?'

As it was a fortnight since the assassination attempt on the pontiff,

John automatically assumed that another attempt had been mounted and responded swiftly.

'No.'

Watching Brother scribble in his book something to the effect of 'no knowledge of Pope', I realised in horror the misunderstanding. Within minutes we were showered with beautiful books with titles like *Life of the Peoples' Pope*. Despite making some disappointing first impressions, thankfully we were accepted into the college family.

In the busy corridors, classrooms and playing fields of this college called Joey's, Patrick was one of nine hundred and twenty boarders who, of necessity, quickly adopted the rules of survival. For him, like Marie, the adjustments were monumental. He learned to substitute cement and buildings for bull dust and space, big mobs of people for big mobs of cattle. Firm guiding hands helped newcomers, though the rub of other people's characters meant it was not all beer and skittles. Patrick determined to keep up with the best of them.

Back in the school room we commenced our afternoon activities. Although we desperately missed Marie and Patrick, their absence resulted in interesting changes. Michael, at ten now taller than his older brother, became protector of his five-year-old little sister who was increasingly called Becky. Most noticeably, school pressures had diminished with the halving of pupils. The morning had commenced with an address from guest speaker, Mother Teresa from Calcutta, who spoke from the Katherine studio and happily answered questions from her widespread listening audience. Maths and reading followed and then a film strip and accompanying cassette provided much enjoyed audio-visual stimulation. Becky, having finished her impressively realistic painting of a bushfire, cleaned her brushes and started her recorder practice. Michael's bird project was progressing beautifully and his identification of over forty bird species at Riveren alone was astonishing. Michael sorted through his collection of feathers and John's voice overtook Becky's quavering notes as he called, 'I'm going for a fly. Won't be long.' His words of farewell were as predictable as my response, 'Be careful.'

An hour later, we concluded our productive day by singing 'Brumby Jack' to the accompaniment of home-made musical instruments. Bean pods from the rain tree rattled, rice in the milk tin shook and two wooden

sticks were tapped rhythmically. Brother and sister then worked through
their late afternoon jobs of watering and weeding their individual vegetable
gardens, and the homestead gardens, feeding poddy calves, chooks, the
cat and both dogs. Childhood for them was an apprenticeship where
natural pleasures were in another sense responsibilities. Our children
possessed wisdom and skills well beyond their years.

As usual I rushed from laundry to cold room, from cupboard to stove,
from shed to humpy and increasingly from clock face to empty sky. My
uneasiness grew with the lengthening shadows of the setting sun.

The final rays from the fire ball seemed to ignite the camp fires. The
orange and pink flames licking the twigs turned to bright red as the wood
was devoured. Grey twirling smoke merged with the increasing darkness.
White teeth flashed against favourite fresh rib bones as town plans were
made. It was race time again. The droning and intonations of the
corroboree had hardly begun when I interrupted.

'Hey, you fellas. Did anyone see that plane? John is not back.'

Only the crackling fire broke the awful silence. Then Eric, our head
stockman, spoke.

'Nothing Missus.'

Henry, however, stood up and pointed due east.

'I saw Boss fly that way, might be.'

'Straight line?' I queried.

'Ui,' he replied.

With thumping heart I returned home to explain to Michael and Becky
that we were going to look for Dad.

'He has probably landed at one of the bores and run out of daylight,'
I commented, with more assurance than I felt.

The governing factor in his absence was that tomorrow was our
scheduled departure day for the races, and only an unexpected and
monumental crisis would jeopardise that. The troops and horses were
rearing to go. I too was organised for the imminent departure. Where
was the Boss? Where was my man?

As I gathered blankets, torches, a thermos of coffee and extra water,
the children ate their dinner. They curled up in a swag in the back of the
station wagon and were dozing when I stopped by the far humpy, which
belonged to Eric and Alison.

'Better come with me please, Eric,' I said quietly.

'Ui,' he nodded gravely.

It was a crystal clear night and as we made our way towards the brumby shooters' camp site, I silently reasoned and wrangled with the possibilities. John had accumulated more than five thousand flying hours over many years in diverse weather conditions. Furthermore he knew this country intimately. However, he had booked the plane in for a hundred hourly service ahead of time as there was a leaking fuel cell in one wing. My scales would not balance and my pendulum was swinging wildly.

I recalled the time he had departed from Inverway late one evening. Although the savage storm was in his line of flight, he judged it to be east of us and the aerodrome. It was fast moving and directly over the homestead upon his attempted approach. With insufficient daylight to return to Inverway, John nevertheless turned around and flew west again with the aerial onslaught gathering momentum as it gave pursuit. He landed at the closest small airstrip beside a bore. Minutes later the rain squalls tugged menacingly at the wing tips and blotted out the darkness. He felt certain that I, hearing the plane on the edge of the storm, would be concerned for his safety. Furthermore, understanding my deep-seated fear of small aircraft accidents, he left the shelter of the cockpit and trudged twenty kilometres through blinding downpours and squelching mud in the wet, wild night to reassure me that all was well. It had taken me several seconds to comprehend the apparition; the muddy, dripping figure leaning over me. With his wonderful bear hug, he embraced me, whispering, 'I'm OK; don't worry.'

Needless to say, I had not heard the plane.

'I reckon he might be walking home right now, Eric.'

With a huge smile and visible relief, Eric agreed.

At Mucca Waterhole I heard the freezer motor from the pet meat operators' camp site. Tonight there was no card game, only blackness to greet me. The first fellow I awoke shrugged and yawned loudly. It was the fourth person who pointed east to indicate the direction of the low-flying plane he had sighted mid-afternoon. We headed for Neave Bore.

The road seemed even rougher at night. The two in the back, well used to bouncing around, slept on. I prayed. I prayed as I had never prayed before.

An hour or so later I drove up and down the airstrip at Neave. I pulled up. Eric and I left the Toyota and walked around, shining torches that pathetically strained into the blackness. I drove around and around, up and down the strip, positioning the headlights to thrust through the darkness. The chilly August wind had risen. It was cold. I was cold. I was fearful.

On our return home I was desperately hopeful to the point of being almost convinced that John would be waiting for us. Every light that I had left burning remained so. Only the throbbing of the generator broke the stillness. There was nothing else.

I told Eric that I would see him at daylight. When Michael and Becky were bedded down, the trembling began. Outside I paced and prayed, searching for smoke or any signal of life or movement. Away from the shelter of the building, I stood beneath the millions of blinking, twinkling diamonds repeating their nightly performance, shimmering and dazzling in their purity and infinity. They were John's canopy too. The silence of the night screamed at me.

I felt certain now that he had crashed. I thought he had a fifty per cent chance of survival. He was somewhere out there in the wilderness. I wanted desperately to find John. I tried to explain to God that I needed my man more than He.

I remembered writing to John after our engagement:

Five minutes without you is as though five years, five years with you would be as though five minutes.

To contemplate life without the one who epitomised living was beyond comprehension. As the hour hand dragged itself around the clock face, the constellations offered no hint of morning.

The telephone lines were out of order. When I tapped on the caravan door at 3 am, builder Dave's initial sleepy response was total surprise. He didn't know that John was missing. However, quickly registering my concern, he fuelled his car as we talked. I asked him to by-pass Inverway on his way to Reg's home, Bunda, one hundred and fifty kilometres west. There was no point in distressing John's parents until we knew more.

'Just tell Reg I need him here at first light. Thanks.'

The night was eternally long. Had the sun slept in? The children hadn't and over Vegemite and toast accepted with trust that Dad would be back soon. Everything was happening so slowly. Where was Reg? If he did not hurry I would have to call the official search and rescue operation. They would be contacted anyway if we did not find John quickly. Just as we three whispered a little prayer the distant sound of a plane engine penetrated the stillness.

Reg landed on the road and taxied to the house grid where I awaited him. 'John's back, isn't he?' he called hopefully as he hurried towards me. Even as he spoke he knew from my demeanour that the builder's story was true. We had not laid eyes on John since two o'clock the previous afternoon.

The children stayed with the builder's wife, while we took off to initially retrace my search pattern. Two pairs of eyes were straining and searching for our Cessna. For a quarter of an hour there was nothing unexpected, no clue, no suggestion. My eyes ached as they bored into the landscape below. It was difficult to distinguish the widely strewn, tangled, metal wreckage from the beige and silvery grey grasses sprawling over reddish earth. By its unobtrusiveness it was grotesque. By its implication it was heart-breaking.

We circled sobbing. We circled again. Time stood still. Only the grasses danced and bowed before their master, the easterly wind.

'Go around again, Reg, I think I saw something move.'

Through the gaping cockpit doorway a leg moved backwards and forwards. Hope was reborn.

Landing on the strip that I had explored hours earlier, Reg unclasped his seat belt even before the propeller blades died, and sprinted across the uneven terrain to his big brother. I was not far behind.

Surrounded by destruction and devastation, John's survival was an absolute miracle. He was less recognisable than the crumpled plane with the smashed instrument panel. Everything everywhere was mangled, broken and bent. The brutal impact had overturned the aircraft and upside down the damage seemed even more bizarre. These things were slowly absorbed as I hugged John. He whispered that he thought he had lost an eye. His face was so cut and grossly swollen that I couldn't tell.

'What's an eye?' I said, as I tried to warm him and assess his injuries. He was battered, bruised, bleeding, but far from beaten. His inbuilt strength and control were blindingly apparent. Thus he had been for eighteen hours. John was in shock and Reg left at once to fly home, organise the medical evacuation and then return by road to collect us.

The wind rose as we sheltered inside the shattered plane. Indescribable relief flooded through me as did unadulterated horror when John quietly mentioned some details of his incredible experience. The first thing he remembered was regaining consciousness just after sunset to find himself hanging face down across the shoulder harness in a topsy-turvy plane. He released the seat belt that had saved his life and somehow crawled through the wreckage into the darkening night. The coldness accosted him and he pulled the seat cover free before repositioning himself beneath his sparse 'blanket' for the duration of the long wait.

When hours later my headlights teased, he called to me. Over and over again he called. The shallow beam of headlights and torch were useless and the sound of my engine left running obliterated any chance of contact that night. I could only imagine how he felt watching our departure. How could I not have sensed his closeness?

Michael returned with Reg and in the instant he saw his father, he assumed adulthood. John was uncomplaining throughout the upheaval of transportation over one of our roughest roads. Michael and I tried in vain to buffer the bumps as we sat beside him on the tray-back vehicle. Michael even let air out of the new tyres in an attempt to lessen the impact of constant jarring and jolting. At home a silent group awaited us. Becky scrambled up over the sideboards and started to cry when she saw the injured person who bore little resemblance to her Dad. Eric stood back respectfully, making no effort to stem the rivulet of tears that poured down his face. I heard him mutter with enormous relief, 'Poor old bugger, that John.'

As I packed, I talked to Eric about the programme for the following days and hastily organised food supplies for Alison. The blackfellas were to prove their initiative as never before. Already the medical plane was circling and half an hour later John and his three greatest fans were flying to Darwin Hospital. That the aero-medical sister on board was St Vincent's trained seemed not just appropriate but wonderfully endearing.

Even as we steadily climbed, the smoke signals were spiralling upwards too. Through every medium the word was passed around that John had 'gone in', his plane was a write off, but he had survived. I wanted John to continue south to Sydney, for these serious injuries were right on top of those inflicted by the bull just ten months earlier. He would not entertain the idea for a second as his proximity to home was of paramount importance.

Upon our arrival in Darwin, Tony Noonan, our Gibraltar and dear friend, awaited John. Awaiting me were numerous messages offering any and every assistance. They extended from managing Riveren to minding the children. Family and friends cried in unison: 'What can we do for you?' We were touched and surrounded by overwhelming support.

Two days later, the air safety investigator put John's memory to the test. His head injuries amongst all the others made concentration and the required attention to detail a difficult task. Tony advised us that hospitalisation would be long-term as John's foot reconstruction could not be attempted until the massive swelling subsided. Marie and Patrick had returned from Sydney on school holidays, which for the most part were spent in the corner of their father's hospital room.

I worried about John. I worried about home. Friends worried about us. *Dimboola*'s Horrie and his wife, Lorraine, travelled six hundred kilometres from their Dunmarra Roadhouse to Riveren. Lorraine, in their car, followed Jim as he drove my vehicle a further one thousand kilometres to Darwin in order that I might drive home to ensure that everyone and everything was all right. We were surrounded by priceless friendships.

The blackfellas never did make the races that year. With the ten hour drive home behind me, it was a relief to find the team had coped well. Their concern, loyalty and special brand of friendship were acknowledged and never forgotten. For four days I organised and supervised and covered tracks. Then word came through that John's foot would be operated on the following day and so I repacked school and family suitcases. By radio telephone I wished him good luck before he was wheeled into theatre and my wheels crossed the house grid to commence the return journey to Darwin. He had never needed me more.

The television set was heavy, however I staggered along, finally reaching John's room. From the shopping bags carried by the children, tempting aromas floated through the sterile, disinfectant-scented corridors. The aerial was adjusted to deliver a clear image. It was 7.57 pm and three minutes to the premiere of 'A Big Country', featuring our story. In Katherine the cast of *Dimboola* had gathered in their play costumes to view the programme. The ward door burst open to reveal a glowering Matron. In a glance she absorbed one patient almost invisible due to his children sitting all around him, mouth-watering fish and chips and cold beers, and a foreign intruder in the form of a hired television set entertaining this family. I took a deep breath. Had she been obstructive or officious I would probably have burst into tears.

'Have a good evening,' she ordered as the door clicked shut behind her.

As though it was yesterday, we relieved the *Dimboola* rehearsals, the victory over isolation and the final performances. The documentary, entitled 'Everyone's Invited', captured the true spirit of our families and also put Katherine School of the Air on the national stage. Perhaps the most precious line came from our youngest. To the question, 'Do you know what *Dimboola* is all about?' five-year-old Becky replied, 'Well, it's kind of when everyone plays up.'

John's injuries were multiple. The least problematical, his fractured arm, was the last to be diagnosed. It was discovered days after admission. Although his eye was intact, it was permanently damaged. His facial muscles and nerves were particularly slow to heal. However, after many weeks he was finally allowed home again. Somewhat to my relief his leg plaster and crutches inevitably slowed him down. I threatened to hobble him if need be; however, he was not about to resist the impositions of Mother Nature.

Not only had a precedent been set for fund raising, but the theatrical fever pitch had taken a firm and lasting grip on players and audience alike. In anticipation of their next roles, they balanced on the crest of a giant wave. *Macbeth* had been mentioned; however, we had experienced more than double toil and trouble and the mood seemed to dictate something less tragic. In the months prior to John's plane accident, I had explored every possible option for a sequel to *Dimboola*. I read numerous plays and even wrote my own. Finally, to balance and accommodate the needs of all concerned, I had decided on one mammoth night crammed with activities, themes and participants. I had drawn up a plan and the Territory Talent Quest was born. Auditions were called, sponsors for prizes were instantly responsive and generous, and a venue that could stage maximum action for maximum numbers was finally unearthed.

Living in geographic remoteness continued to transform simple things into complex issues. So many mole hills became mountains thanks to the effective fertiliser named isolation. Communication restrictions further impeded progress. However, well used to challenges I remained undaunted. So too was my wonderful back-up team.

The appropriate authorities yielded to my seemingly impossible request and the Katherine Sporting Complex, which had been closed for years, was reopened just for the occasion. 'Play School' personality and actor John Waters and his actor wife Sally Conabere were thrilled to accept my invitation to join us in Katherine to act as judges for the evening. Not only would they judge the best in the talent quest, their experienced antennae would identify the winners of the old timers as well as the rock and roll dance competitions. Finally, they would select the best dressed male and best dressed female.

When John Waters inquired about the theme, I replied simply, 'It is reverse.'

'Does that mean that everyone walks backwards, puts their clothes on back to front, or dresses as the opposite sex?' he puzzled.

Laughingly I informed him that the latter was correct.

Our year of disruption unwound all too quickly. John's positive attitude dominated his every movement and moment. On the day that we drove back to the crash site we realised all over again just how lucky he had been. Having spotted cattle on a turkey nest where they should not have been and an open gate that should have been closed, John had circled at low altitude trying to hunt the cattle out. He maintained that the ground had got in the way.

We traced the probable impact of the amputated wing and the engine lying alone that had crushed John's foot as it disengaged from the body of the plane. There was nothing to salvage except the St Christopher medal that I found in tall grass beyond the propeller. I clasped it thankfully and placed it in my pocket. It would stay with John always.

Back at the homestead, school lessons continued and the preparations for the end of year function intensified.

'I'll do it, but only because you insist,' groaned John. The role of Jeanette McDonald miming 'If I Loved You' and 'Wunderbah' held little appeal for the battle-scarred cattleman. Ros Andrews, a diminutive mother and home teacher from Newry Station, enthusiastically planned her Nelson Eddy supportive role. John's elaborate gown was designed and created by Carol, alias Reen the *Dimboola* bride, and suitable gauge fencing wire was attached to the inner petticoats and skirt to establish the generous hoop effect. Countless others prepared a variety of outfits with flair and imagination.

The musty, spacious skating rink with low ceilings was transformed into a glittering entertainment centre. Electricity was reconnected and lighting installed. Tables, chairs, stage, bar and music facilities were in place. The late licence for 4 am was approved, but even so time might be inadequate for four hundred and fifty people dressed in reverse to absorb twenty-one acts and participate in a night of unprecedented audacious entertainment.

With flowing locks and colourful frocks, the men of the North teetered on high heels. Captain Armstrong and his mate Gerald, alias Mutton and Bayonet, wearing frothy tutus, fish-net stockings and ballet slippers, ran the busiest bar in the country. Jim Cobb, alias Horrie, served the excited throng as cigarette and sweets girlie. This multi-talented man later changed into an XXOS tutu to perform as Dame Margot Fonteyn in *Sleeping Beauty*. When the forest prince dubiously lifted the bush mosquito netting draped around the stockcamp stretcher to awaken the deeply sleeping maiden, there was a roar of surprise as this prima ballerina arose and plonked unceremoniously onto the floor. Jim's third act, the unfit and very funny back-up to Janelle Underwood's exacting performance as Olivia Newton John in 'Physical', delighted young and old. Disbelief continued as a convincing magician attempted to saw a trusting lady in half. Despite a few technical hitches, the performances were superb. Two sisters performed a unique song and dance routine to the well-known oldie, 'Two Girls who Can't Say No'. A self-choreographed dancer stunned the already disbelieving audience. Each performer was a winner.

The interstate judges had an unenviable role. However, few were surprised when first prize was awarded to local station manager Ross Alison for his heartfelt rendition of Mary Durack's wonderfully moving poem 'The Lament for the Drowned Country'. Only his wife Anne and I knew that the old Aboriginal woman carrying her fishing stick and billy can onto the stage was Ross in disguise. It was all the more meaningful to me because twelve years earlier I had heard on the two-way radio the hasty departure call from the caretaker at Argyle Homestead. Early heavy rains had triggered premature flooding and the beginnings of Lake Argyle.

There was unanimous spine-tingling attention as Old Maggie Wallaby mourned that same country, her born country, that was drowned by the man-made formation of this lake.

You hear them kids over there laugh this old woman?
She mad, old Maggie. She sit there fishing all day—
talk to myself and when she got a catch she let him go.
We seen *her let 'em go.*
Mad Maggie! Mad Maggie! Poor old Jilligan Numbajina,
Mad Maggie. You look now—she let that fish go …

You go back up there, that old station—Argyle station—
(poor fella my old boss, my old missus. Nothing left that house,
where I sweep'm every day!) You look out that house, you look out
windmill, tank, garden, kitchen, saddle shed.
You look out that store, that camp down there along crossing.
You look out that horse paddock, yard, mustering camp everywhere,
plain country, ranges. You look out that limestone pocket
where I come from my mummy—that place where I lie along coolimon,
(Poor fella my old mummy, pass away long time ago.)
You tell him, my country—me, old Maggie, old Jilligan—
she can't forget 'im, my country, she all day heart-crying.
You tell him my country that secret. You tell him old Maggie,
old Numbajina *woman belong* Mirrawung—*she got that dream.*
You tell him hang on! *Old* Jilligan *see what going happen*
long time, might be close up, might be fifty t'ousand year,
I think them old spirit fellow gone fast asleep …

Old Maggie, old Jilligan, *she tell that fish:*
'*You bring this message my country, down there underneath.*
You tell him hold on! *Some day that dream coming true*
then he can stretch out and dry himself, my country.
He can breathe that air, he can open up him eye.
Bye'n'bye the grass come back again, tree, spinifex,
all them lizard and snake and wallaby, bandicoot, porcupine,
flying fox—all that good bush tucker—everysing come back.
And bird too—big mob brolga—dance lika that—
And Jabiroo, emu, cockatoo—poor fella—I watch'm
flyin' over , lookin' down—Carr! Carr! What all that water?
What happen this good country? (That born place, my country!)
Little fish, you tell him—me, old Maggie, old Jilligan,
heart crying my born country. I got him here—
inside my heart, can't lose'm. I got that dream,
that message. You talk my country: Hold on!
Some time, you gonna look out that sun again. You gonna
see all that moon and star. You gonna feel that warm wind blowing.
You gonna see that sky!'

During the long drive home, I reflected on John's remarkable survival and our life together at Riveren. I remembered writing to John that he had won my heart probably before either of us was aware of it. Somewhere along the way his country had won my heart too. Like Old Maggie Wallaby and Mary Durack, my spiritual attachment to this land was totally consuming. The power of love thrilled and filled every fibre of my being.

CHAPTER 15

LITTLE GIRL LOST

....

'Ready; set; go!'

From the finishing line freshly drawn in the red earth, dog owners called their pets towards them. Schoolteacher Miss Lawrence shrieked in dismay when a fully grown doberman careered into her hound in its pursuit of a disappearing flock of bush pigeon. Just south of Dunmarra Roadhouse at the Hayfield Station turn-off, several cars had halted for a final practice for the dog race to be held later that day. With Cuddles an equally inquisitive onlooker, we watched the impressive form of our competitors. This would be a hard race to finish, let alone win and there was no doubting the seriousness of the people leading their assorted dogs back to their vehicles. The annual Katherine School of the Air Gymkhana attracted families from everywhere as it was one of the highlights of the school year.

There were horse events, bike events, athletic events and novelty events. The race open to all breeds of canine always provided unlimited entertainment. We screeched encouragingly to our very fast, short-legged Cuddles who was pipped on the line by that long-legged doberman. Most other starters had abandoned the race by turning towards cheering family on the sidelines. In a setting of spinifex and ant beds we celebrated bush culture and reflected on the achievements and disappointments of 1983.

Though the gymkhana was enormous fun, I was pleased to return home safely the next day. I was also relieved that there was no necessity for travel for the remainder of the year as long distance driving bothered me. On the contrary, town was becoming increasingly attractive to our Aboriginal families. With the mustering in full swing, we continued to work long hard days. At the appropriate or inappropriate time, they headed into town for 'that little bit long holiday'. Not infrequently, alcohol flowed in saturation levels, absorbing hard-earned wages in a matter of hours as accumulated friends joined the return to town celebrations. Fights would follow and another gaol cell would be occupied. It saddened us to receive the pleas from town, 'Hey Boss. You come bail me out, eh?'

There was no bar at Riveren and sore heads cleared quickly. Once back into the familiar routine they enjoyed their work, although for increasingly short periods of time.

Peter and Poppy and family had been with us for many years. Their little daughters Irene and Magdalen played with Becky after school. Poppy's lovely face was one big beaming smile until someone produced a camera. Then she froze self-consciously. On the other hand, Peter was not shy. Periodically and passionately he declared his loyalty, 'By Chri, I bin love this place. I bin love you mob too, properly, alright.'

Nevertheless, Peter asked for time off to visit his sick uncle. He was reminded that his uncle had recently passed away. Peter then remembered that it was his father not his uncle who was sick, and apart from his illness this tribal elder wanted to see his son on urgent business.

'Him give me present,' Peter explained. Not always receptive to the various explanations, we nevertheless believed in fairness and as the requested journey was merely a stone's throw in our terms, Peter was loaned the stockcamp vehicle. John insisted that the Hooker Creek trip be executed in time for the planned muster the following morning.

I was awakened by shouting and screaming at the front gate. The luminous clock hands indicated that it was three hours past midnight.

'Missus! Missus!' pleaded Poppy. 'You tell 'em Peter me proper good wife. You tell 'em for me. Dat new one no good.'

In the background I made out the faint silhouette of a small, slender figure standing next to Peter. Poppy was larger than life at the best of times and that night she cancelled her sobs to assume a personage angry and mobile, intent on giving 'dat present what for'. Brandishing a nulla nulla, she took to the young girl. The darkness gobbled them up, although the sounds of fury from a love-spurned wife echoed long afterwards.

At daybreak Poppy entertained misgivings. The law of the land applied to us all. The unforgiving nature of the land also applied to us all. She was once again calling for help.

'Might be you lend 'em motor car one more time?' she begged. 'Dat girl not anywhere. We go look about.'

Peter and Poppy tracked the missing girl for two days. She eluded them, probably preferring her chances in the bush to Poppy's wrath. We advised the police at Hooker Creek of the missing person. Unease was widespread for an entire week until we received advice that Poppy's failed replacement had walked into the settlement, footsore, but otherwise in good shape.

One could never plan too far ahead, for the uncertainty of the season and the tyranny of distance assumed equal dictatorships. From the very beginning I was frustrated by the lack of ability to plan beyond the hour and the activity. Urban dwellers faithfully followed meticulous diary entries. To alter or defer appointments in the city created inconvenience and could lead to a reputation for unreliability. In the bush, a spill of cattle created havoc and called for a remuster, or an empty trough might end up requiring the bore to be pulled. Versatility and flexibility were vital components of bush people. It was hour by hour, day by day. I had found this extremely frustrating in my first months at Riveren, until I grew to understand that the very challenge of the lifestyle was its unpredictability.

To my routine question, 'What are you doing today?', the reply would be guarded.

'Well, if we get water at Soak Dam before lunch, we'll go around the fence and muster that paddock tomorrow. Otherwise . . .' and the options and alternatives would be outlined to the raw recruit from the city. Unlike me, our children had grown and developed with Riveren. Their contribution to station life guaranteed deep-rooted understanding. Both their inborn and acquired knowledge equipped them for adulthood in the land they knew and loved.

In the absence of Patrick and Marie, Michael and Becky assumed additional responsibilities. With his Huckleberry Finn demeanour, Michael appeared a small replica of John in every way. They were built the same, they thought the same, they talked the same and they had even walked the same way before John's accidents.

Like his father, Michael's smile dazzled the world. He would without hesitation give away his last toy or drop of water. He had inherited John's acceptance of all people, and all mankind were their friends. With hearts of gold, together or separately, they were nevertheless capable on occasion of 'burring up' at the drop of a hat. As John's already fragile back was subjected to increasing pressure with the gradual collapse of his reconstructed foot, Michael became his shadow, bodyguard and responsible offsider.

Becky too performed her tasks with a sense of thoroughness, and her deep love of animals was manifest in her every action. Her latest poddy calf was secretly smuggled before me with the eventual invitation, 'You can come out now, Mum. Surprise!' Knowing how I shared their love of calves, my joy was predictable.

'Oh golly, isn't he gorgeous,' I exclaimed, and so he was called Golly. Michael and Becky continued to grow together as each child displayed diverse skills with animals and the land. Like their parents, Michael and Becky were great mates.

In recent months John's work rate had scarcely abated. In his specially made boots, he strode tirelessly and without complaint across paddocks, fence lines and up windmills, or crawled beneath the chassis of cars, trucks and tractors. Without fear or hesitation he returned to the skies in our replacement Cessna 182 VH-EIA. Ironically, his battle-scarred body would be subjected to less stress with bore runs being conducted once again from on high. Suppressing memories of the horror of his air to ground impact, I had to concede that as long as we lived at Riveren, we really did need an aeroplane. The convenience and cost-effectiveness had always been recognised, and now the welfare of the man who was also the pilot was another consideration all over again.

The thought of turning forty bothered me momentarily. Then I decided to tackle it head on and, weather permitting, host a party at home.

The weather held until sundown by which time most guests had not only claimed a space, but changed into their outfits too. As the downpour commenced, a plane flew low across the homestead roof. Reg and Janelle only just made it to my F party. There were Footballers and Fantails, a Frogman and a Feathered Fiancée, Footrot Flats and Flirts, a Fighter and a French letter. The Fart sat beside the Full stop and the Physician and the Flowing French Flag served drinks. As always, the theme was whole-heartedly adopted and it was an energetic and hilarious celebration throughout which forty full size candles burned brightly.

We had barely recovered when it was time to pack bags for Sydney again—to both attend to John's collapsed foot and settle Michael into St Joseph's, where Patrick had performed impressively in all areas.

The headmaster welcomed us back calling each of us by name.

'So Michael, you have come to us to learn the many things taught at this college. The boys here are good boys because those who disobey the rules do not deserve to remain. Now Michael, tell me who is the one about whom the boys learn most?'

Without hesitation, Michael blurted, 'The Pope!' Silence reigned. Should I prompt? John frowned. The children were puzzled. At length Brother smiled.

'God is the most important person and there is so much to learn about Him and even more that we, His creatures, can never understand. Welcome Michael. You will learn about many others including Blessed Mary and, of course, our infallible pontiff.'

Of course John had been booked into St Vincent's, and Sister Bernice's gentle smile filled the reception area as she moved forward to greet us. The years had not lessened her dedication or involvement and it was always heart-warming to be welcomed by our dear friend, unchanging and serene. My brother Johnny, one of my very best friends, was also on hand and called in at least once a day to say hello.

Dr Roarty seemed unsurprised by the complete collapse of John's foot and this reconstruction involved fusion. Like back, like ankle, he declared. However, this orthopaedic specialist, who had looked after John since his single days in Ward 3, was extremely concerned about John's future. Tony Noonan had christened John 'the Professional Survivor'. Our charming Sydney doctor gently admonished, 'Terry, you will have to transform him into a verandah manager. Does John really believe he is invincible?'

Everyone knew that to prolong the departure was to prolong the heartache. However, with John back on crutches, we were rather handicapped for a hasty retreat. It was important not to cry. Once I started crying I could not stop. For one who was supposed to lead by example in the bravery stakes, I was still learning to allow only inward tears to flow. As I held her closely for the last time for three months, Marie's tears fell uncontrollably. At Hunters Hill, our two young sons stood side by side, desperately trying to appear brave as goodbye time confronted them too. I thought I would choke emotionally. The boys watched their parents and little sister drive through the magnificent college gates to commence the long journey home without them. These were the penalties for the freedom and independence of living in one of the most remote and beautiful parts of our vast continent.

Back at home Becky's school routine and the accompanying discipline absorbed some of my emptiness. Now that Becky did not have Michael as constant companion, Golly became her shadow. When Becky fed the chooks Golly followed faithfully. As she collected the warm eggs, he stood amongst the white-feathered hens and ate huge helpings of laying pellets. This large honey-coloured calf trailed her to the stables to share chaff and hay with the racehorses. At the cold room entrance, Golly towered over two dogs as he gobbled his piece of meat. He assumed various identities as he received the love and attention of the little girl who'd saved and reared him. He won all our hearts.

Cyclone Sandy had been affecting our weather for several days. The ceiling was very low as pregnant grey clouds blanketed the sky. Normally fluffy and unthreatening, today they looked clotted and angry. Intermittent showers and whistling winds had dissuaded Cuddles and Bett, our new blue heeler, from any activity other than sleeping in a cosy corner. Becky's poddy calves were fed and played follow the leader to the stables where they would enjoy shelter for another night. Michael was missed every single second. It certainly did not get any easier when the next one left for boarding school.

Our last outdoor job was to feed the chooks. Becky collected twenty-two eggs and checked the newly born, fluffy ducklings. Two mother ducks fussed as they gathered their babies for bed beside their warm breasts and beneath their protective wings. I turned towards home and Becky, joined by the dogs, asked if she could quickly run down to the creek to collect some stones for her school project on collections.

'Please Mum, just a few more stones . . .'

'It's too late, Becky. Leave it until the morning.'

'Please please Mum. Look how much the dogs want to come.'

'Don't be long,' I insisted to the backs of one blonde head and two sets of pricked ears.

No sooner had I returned to my kitchen than I felt distinctly uneasy. From his lounge chair where he dutifully had his leg elevated as he read, John asked me to turn on the lights.

'It will be dark early tonight,' he commented. 'Most unusual to have this weather disturbance so far inland. Now that it's here, it might as well rain properly instead of all this piss and wind. Send it down, George!'

I wasn't really listening. An ominous feeling completely invaded me. I ran outside. There was no sign of Becky anywhere.

I turned to the One Uncle Tom invoked as Hughie and John called George, 'Please God, help me find my little girl.'

As though waiting for a signal, the wind intensified as I raced down to the creek, screaming: 'Becky! Becky! Becky!' Screeching winds mocked as they chopped the words off at my lips. With about five minutes of bleak light remaining, I had to decide which way to run. Left or right? I pounded along the creek bed, calling and straining through the increasing darkness and the penetrating cold raindrops. There was no sign of movement, no sound, no little girl, no dogs.

It was pitch black and raining heavily when I burst inside and announced to John that Becky had not returned from the creek.

'Settle down, we'll find her,' he calmly advised. As he rose and balanced on his crutches, I bounded ahead to collect torches and blankets before bringing our brand new bright red station wagon to the door. As I assisted John into the passenger's seat I whispered, 'If only Michael had been with her.'

Peering into the wild weather that surrounded us, John shivered. 'This would not have happened had he been here,' he agreed.

Cautiously I drove into the creek as overhead branches and boughs tossed and collided with the fury of the turbulence. Our headlights played across water that looked like black ink spilled along the creek bed, a spillage that was slowly swelling with each plop of rain.

'Get out and see how deep that water is ahead,' John instructed. 'If it's too deep, we'll need to back up and drive along the bank.'

It was pointless to call her anymore for the sounds of the squalls were as deafening as the rain was blinding. I walked through the middle of the creek where the car would follow and as the chilly water claimed me, I stepped into an unknown hole, lost my footing and completely disappeared from sight. Realising the depth of this section, I frantically signalled to John as I stumbled towards him that this was indeed treacherous. My mind rioted against the possibility that such a hole had also claimed Becky.

Misinterpretation was almost inevitable under such weather conditions. John, thinking that my waving of warning was an indication to proceed, pulled himself behind the wheel and nudged the station wagon forwards into the water, intent only on finding his little girl.

When John realised the water was getting too deep, he tried to reverse. The engine sucked in water and refused to budge. The sole glimmer in the darkness came from the cabin light which illuminated a shaken driver with his plastered leg resting on the dashboard. The rising water level already lapped the gear stick. A cold hand clutched my heart. Where was Becky in this night of nightmares?

'You stay there,' I ordered. 'I'll go and get help. The ringers will have to carry you out. Whatever else happens, your plaster must not get wet.'

It was no ordinary plaster for Dr Roarty had shaped it around John's specific injury. As I grabbed the torch and turned towards home, a strange swooshing sound behind me announced that this man of mine had a mind of his own. Did he have to prove it tonight of all nights?

'I'm coming too. We have to find Becky. Her safety is more important than my bloody plaster,' he insisted as through the water he waded, plaster, crutches and all.

Over at the humpies, the blackfellas were instantly alert and very worried. 'Look out for dogs too,' I asked. Immediately, the women, unconcerned about the weather, disappeared into the night to set up watch from the wall of the dam, situated between the creek and the homestead. We all knew that if the dogs returned without Becky, we were in trouble. In my mind their absence secured her consciousness. However, if for whatever reason the dogs did return, it was vital that the direction from which they came be noted. The men followed me back to John and together they did a mud map of the search area to be immediately covered.

As I depressed the switch, lights from the recently constructed tennis court warmed from a soft glow to a harsh bright light that threatened to infiltrate the smothering darkness. They had acted as a safety beacon to an overdue helicopter on a previous occasion. It had been well after last light and anxiety rode high until the distinctive whopping sounds signalled the approach of the chopper, guided to safety by the brilliant blaze.

'Like your inland lighthouse,' laughed the greatly relieved pilot.

Hopefully, the same bright lights would guide Becky home. John was ashen as he spoke words that dashed my hopes.

'Get used to the idea that you cannot expect to see Becky until morning. There is no way she will move tonight. She'll just burrow in.'

We silently held each other, aware of our emotional fragility and the menace of the night. The unthinkable had happened. My teeth were chattering uncontrollably and John had a violent attack of the shivers. The radio-telephone operator had not cleared the channel on the hour. The red light indicated that the line was in use. We would have to wait another whole hour until eight o'clock to send word of our predicament to the outside world. I made a thermos of coffee for my radio operator with his saturated plaster, gave him dry clothes and blankets, and added another pair of warm socks, a jumper and a windcheater to my two layers of clothing.

Outside nothing had changed. I walked down to the women on watch and beyond them to where the distant torch and motor car lights drew lines of light up and down and down and up in the general direction of the creek. Fearful and frustrated I called Becky's name over and over again. Mother Nature wreaked her vengeance without apology and I wondered how Becky could escape pneumonia if she was lucky enough to escape the numerous other dangers lurking in the darkness.

It was nine o'clock before we gained access to the operator. Upon taking full details of the missing seven year old, the officer in charge at the Katherine police station despatched a policeman to drive five hundred kilometres to alert our local policeman at Wave Hill of our predicament. There was no other way of contacting him out of hours.

John manned the radio telephone as all other calls were cancelled and the lines retained for our exclusive use. He sought assistance from Inverway and Bunda. Search parties from both places arrived after midnight and once again steaming coffee mugs were grasped as grid lines were drawn on our map. Our five workers pointed to the area already searched. The five new arrivals split up and headed off in different directions. Hoping to find daughter reunited with parents, our sister-in-law Janelle had travelled down to share our relief. Instead, as a relatively new mother, she crumpled. Imagining that it was her daughter, her tears were unstoppable as she shared our heartache. Although immensely grateful for everyone's assistance, I could not talk to anyone, nor could I sit down. Back into the night I went to confront the thief that had abducted my little girl. I prayed to the Mother of God, because she had survived the most brutal and repeated tortures of maternal love. Once again my thoughts turned to the patron saint of travel and I reminded St Christopher of my past gratitude to him as I sent out yet another monumental plea for help. She was so young, so trusting, so defenceless.

At 3 am, fresh nourishment was served. Reg announced that it was now too boggy to drive vehicles and he was adamant that Becky was not in the designated paddock. Some talked, some dozed. Outside I paced and prayed, fearful that if I blinked an extra blink I might miss a sign or a signal. This was the very longest, coldest night of my life.

Reg offered to search in John's plane at first light, however it was too wet to drive to the airstrip. John Weymouth from Helimuster was in contact with the police and we were advised that a helicopter search and rescue team would be with us as soon as daylight permitted. It was an insidious transition from night to morning as the dark, leaking clouds appeared low enough to touch. From the dam wall to the phone room to the creek and back again I ploughed with my boots collecting and depositing huge clods of brown, sticky mud.

The constant wailing of the telephone no longer registered as a deafening intrusion. Rather it signalled another offer of assistance or message of hope and support.

Marie, who usually rang from school every Sunday, called to say hello. It was a Friday morning and to this day she doesn't know what prompted her to telephone home. When she asked how everything was going, her father told her that her little sister had not been seen since the previous evening, but that we hoped to locate her very soon. Someone found Marie sobbing by the school phone and soon after the entire school congregated in the chapel to pray for little Becky Underwood.

The three helicopters circled in formation before landing close by to discharge the two policemen. The officer in charge's children attended Katherine School of the Air and he proved to be a great balance of efficiency and understanding. Once again people pored over maps as the official search was to commence from the creek bed with each helicopter working in ever increasing circles. John, Reg and brother-in-law Johnny from Inverway, each holding blankets, prepared to board. As I opened my mouth to protest, John said, 'No way! You are better here on standby.'

Those who had endured the sleepless night of searching sat on the rain-soaked ground in silence, watching the choppers take off and like droning giant bees commence their stirring of the sky. They remained in sight as they circled and searched, methodically and deliberately. As they progressed further west, we estimated their location by sound. I could see only two, then one, then none. Faces were upturned as were my thoughts and prayers. The minutes ticked by.

Suddenly one helicopter tipped the horizon and flew directly towards me. I could not see clearly through the perspex bubble and until the chopper landed was unsure of the head count. Matted blonde hair and wide blue eyes peered over John's huge arms. Like a joey in a pouch Becky nestled against her Dad. He passed her to me. We were all crying with disbelief, relief and joy.

The message was relayed instantly and even as we moved towards the homestead, Cuddles and Bett arrived by individual helicopters. They weren't enjoying their rides and quickly ran beneath the house to avoid the unusual activity that surrounded them.

The warm bath soothed Becky and she was nearly asleep before I had gently cleansed her multiple cuts and scratches. Her clothing too gave evidence of the fright of the night. After a glass of warm Milo and a bite of sandwich, she snuggled into bed while I brushed her hair. She was in remarkable shape given her ordeal and just when I thought details would be best left until after she had slept, the policeman in charge called me outside. He needed information for his report and asked me to question my daughter at once.

Energetically the dogs had romped and sniffed, chasing lizards and birds as Becky stooped to select some unusual stones. All of a sudden they were chasing shadows. It grew dark and cold as the rain fell.

'Come home naughty Cuddles, come on Bett,' begged the little girl as the dogs raced away in the opposite direction. Fearful of losing contact with them, she hastily followed. Through prickle bushes and spinifex and tussocks of grasses they tore. As the cold wet blackness enveloped her, she stumbled and stopped, not knowing where she was or what to do. As she crawled under the closest leafy shrub, the panting blue heelers returned, jumping over her and leaping all around her as though to say, 'Come on, we've waited all day for this adventure. None of those other boring people come out at night.'

Her sobs sobered them. Cuddles licked her streaky cheeks and Bett, who was just a pup, nestled beside Becky and, resting her head on one bleeding knee, drifted into a sound sleep. To close out the world, Becky drew her knees to her chin, then by pulling open the neck of her T-shirt, she popped her head inside the opening like a turtle withdrawing into its shell. Positioned on either side of her, the loyal, loving dogs kept her warm and safe. Throughout the eternally long night she thought she imagined distant moving lights. The only sound with meaning was the soft snoring of the dogs. Beyond her makeshift nest, cyclonic conditions and steady rain continued to deluge the earth without apology or consideration.

Thinking the helicopter had not seen her, she stopped running to frantically wave overhead. It was merely circling to pinpoint her location to the other pilots before landing to collect her. With her two companions, Becky was five kilometres from home. Since first light they had kept moving in the hope of finding us soon.

The report was written. The weary group enjoyed a well-deserved barbecue prepared by Janelle, then the helicopters and officials departed to pursue their normal daily affairs. Having quickly and emotionally thanked them all, I returned to Becky's bedroom where her guardian angel, assisted by dolls and teddies amongst numerous photos of calves, kept watch.

Patrick and Michael were completely incredulous. How on earth could anyone get lost at home? The Bush Telegraph, having relayed our loss, just as faithfully relayed the recovery and joyful celebrations. One of the most experienced stockmen in the country stated that similar weather conditions had proven disastrous on other occasions. In the grip of Cyclone Sandy's influence, Riveren was like a small plane trapped in thick cloud. Orientation and direction were elusive, and danger stalked anyone who left their familiar dung hill.

Who could guess what images taunted and haunted Becky? Her nightmares continued for weeks. For hours I sat at her bedside as she whimpered and wandered in her land of dreams.

CHAPTER 16

A NEW SUIT

....

Feebly the newborn calf regained its standing position. Swaying on wonky legs, it wobbled unsteadily. With her nose between its back legs, the cow nudged her baby towards her engorged milk bag, where all four teats were bulging. Desperately thirsty, the little one butted in the hope of releasing the milk. Desperately sore, the cow propped the calf against her udder, urging it to suck.

From nearby bushes, two lean dingoes emerged. Slowly and deliberately they moved towards the cow and calf. The mother sensed their presence before she sighted them. With lowered head and bellowing protests, she charged the wild dogs. Their cunning combined with hunger anchored them and they darted and dodged the lowered head and sharp horns of the mother protecting her baby. She knew they represented death and they knew that the calf lying in her shadow was theirs for the taking once she eventually left to walk to the closest watering point.

As witness to the law of the jungle yet again, I felt frustration at the horrible unfairness that one must be sacrificed to feed the other. I was in the only station vehicle that didn't carry a rifle so I drove home quickly to secure one, hoping that I would not be too late.

In bygone years, ringers young and old had collected dingo scalps and extra pocket money. Today there was no longer a bounty on dingo scalps, nor was any financial incentive necessary to reduce dingo numbers. It was heartbreaking to find a defenceless calf ripped, torn and clawed until pitiful moos were silenced as the last drop of life blood stained the already red earth.

At all times safety measures associated with firearms were observed by us all. During my initiation period at our bough shed camp site, John had taught me to shoot as surely as I had learned to sharpen butcher knives. With rifle and bullets, I returned immediately. Four dingoes rapidly withdrew from the dead calf as I drove up. The outwitted cow watched from a distance. Feeling angry and despondent, I returned home to bottle feed the new poddy calves and mow the lawns.

Though the laws of nature never changed, man-made changes and improvements continued gradually and deliberately at Riveren. John Tilley, the founder of the Northern Territory airline, Tillair, offered to include us on his mail service delivery from Katherine. The realisation that we could count on our own mail bag and mail delivery and our own postal address after all these years was almost unbelievable. As our calico windsock was already in place, it was just a matter of completing the necessary paperwork that would initiate the revolutionary change in having mail delivered to Riveren. Three kilometres instead of seventy; weekly instead of whenever! This was unprecedented progress and from such dizzying heights I felt intoxicated with excitement.

Katherine was our centre not only for mail distribution and school affairs, but for obtaining foodstuffs and spare parts. As John loaded the empty aviation drums and gas cylinders onto the Hino truck, he tucked my extensive shopping list inside his notebook and farewelled us all. The road to town was unsealed for the first one hundred and fifty kilometres, and from there it was single lane bitumen. He hoped to return in three or four days from this business trip.

My days seemed short-sheeted. The stockmen drafted and branded the yarded cattle. School lessons continued inside and outside the classroom. Our measurement and mathematics skills were in constant practice, either through cooking recipes or refuelling vehicles. Since Alison's illness I had been cooking for the stockcamp too. Her pleurisy left her frightened and exhausted. Every few hours I went across to the humpy to give her chest percussion, encourage fluid intake and generally monitor her progress.

John's return was eagerly awaited by us all. When the well-stacked truck stopped at the shed, the Aborigines eagerly clustered around to collect their special town orders of hair dye, lollies and high-heeled riding boots, unavailable from our station store. As it was dark the unloading would wait until morning. Over dinner a tired husband announced the unexpected passing of one of the Territory's unique characters. John had arrived at Top Springs Roadhouse, halfway between Riveren and Katherine, just after the policeman who was summoned to certify her death.

John knew something was wrong the moment he laid eyes on a very sombre Norm, offsider for Mrs Hawks since time eternal. The man behind the counter was visibly distressed as he confided that his employer and friend had passed away that very morning. Norm's shock was understandable as Mrs Hawks, or Ma Hawks as she was affectionately known, had always appeared indestructible. As they drank to her memory, Norm and John agreed that the roadhouse would never be the same again.

How vividly I recalled first meeting Mrs Hawks on my journey to Inverway in the red Bedford truck containing our six tea-chests of wedding presents. Heavy rain was falling as we pulled up beside the petrol bowser. Inside the sanctuary of the roadhouse, John proudly introduced his new wife. The stony silence matched Mrs Hawks' look and somehow her nickname Leather Tits seemed appropriate at the time. There was no doubt that we stood before the law maker of Top Springs and God help the law breaker.

The sequel to this story occurred seven months later. Senior Constable Bob Bruce was in his Wave Hill police station at 6 am as usual, when tracker Roy Yunga tapped loudly on the window, gesticulating wildly and demanding attention. Bob pointed to his watch to let his reliable offsider know that it was too early for work; however, the tracker became increasingly agitated. When Bob opened the door, Yunga, talking excitedly, led him to the nearby residence of the junior policeman. Before them lay an extraordinary spectacle.

The lawn that had been treated with top soil days earlier was being dug up by the constable's dog and in every direction dollar notes were flying through the air. They rose like droplets of water in a highly pressurised fountain. Before a brisk breeze they floated across the yard, through trees, down to the horse yard and on to the river. Grabbing garbage bags, the two men went after the money. They 'emu bobbed' the entire area before returning to where the puffing dog had finally captured his prey, a small green frog. It had been unearthed from a shallow hole, which also contained a torn plastic bag filled with wads of old notes.

The junior constable looked positively ill when he arrived on duty to confront his boss sitting behind a desk piled high with money. His greeting sealed his fate.

'I hope you don't think it's mine.'

The Senior Constable replied, 'You always were a lazy so and so. Our jurisdiction is an area of seventy four thousand square kilometres and you buried your loot in two inches of sand at your back door. You deserve to be caught!'

When the head of the Criminal Investigation Branch in Darwin arrived to question the constable, the latter again spoke first.

'I'm sorry I took it.'

The amount recovered was $28 450. He was duly sentenced.

Was it dog's justice they later wondered? The dishonest policeman had backed the police van over his dog, which somehow not only survived its injuries, but on the very next day uncovered the money his owner had literally planted.

The constable had been called to Top Springs upon the death of Mrs Hawks and had been unable to believe his eyes—and unable to resist the temptation. He thought no-one would ever know about the new money if he handed in the old. The authorities were staggered to receive approximately thirty thousand pounds in old currency. Mine Host at Top Springs had trusted no-one, least of all the banks.

Following my *Dimboola* production, I was encouraged to apply for a position on the inaugural Northern Territory Women's Advisory Council. Previously, my involvement in community affairs had largely taken place from home, via the school radio. To take on the obligation to regularly attend six meetings a year at various Territory centres would place enormous pressure on not just our cattle activities and workforce, but my school room in particular, though certainly it was a little easier having just Becky as a pupil. However, I recognised my responsibility to represent the viewpoint of the remote Territory woman—and family. The longer I lived in the middle of nowhere, the more I realised how little understanding existed about us beyond our front gate. If I did not make the effort to go out there and beat the drum, who would? After prolonged deliberation, I applied for the position and was selected along with fourteen other Territorians.

Our charter was to act as a vital vehicle of two-way communication between Territory women and the Northern Territory government. One of the highlights during my two year term was the End of Decade Celebration Luncheon I organised in Katherine. Seven guest speakers from diverse backgrounds spoke to a capacity-filled restaurant on the theme: 'End or Beginning—What of the Future?' I felt strongly that the ripples in the pond would be far-reaching.

The greatest eye-opener for me during my time on the council would prove to be my limited tolerance as I listened to debates and discussions sometimes immersed in emotion to the point of drowning. As our deliberations would ultimately influence government policies, my involvement was charged with responsibility. My honesty was never in doubt and I was never backward in coming forward. Furthermore, years of living in isolation had highlighted my listening and speaking skills, so that I heard what others said, and tried to think before I spoke. At Riveren we never chatted simply to hear our own voices.

I continued to serve as vice president of the Katherine branch of the Isolated Children's and Parents' Association, which worked constantly in its lobbying of governments for equal educational opportunities for families living in geographic isolation. Although our meetings were conducted on air, there were annual conferences at state and federal levels to organise and attend and I remained actively involved in the ongoing necessary business of fund raising.

However, above all else I longed to be involved in the lives of my three elder children, so far away in Sydney. Not only did I physically ache for them, I also no longer had access to their learning and study progress. After years of intimate involvement there was suddenly nothing except their school reports. It was inevitably frustrating not to be able to attend in person any of the southern boarding school activities.

To our great delight, the Marist brothers at Joey's realised that the sporting, cultural and fundraising functions that were a way of life for urban families would always be beyond our reach. They decided to bring the college to us. As these wonderful men became regular visitors, their time at Riveren proved a dramatic eye-opener. The boys from the bush who initially struggled to secure a school tie could fix a bore, change a tyre, drive a truck and castrate a male calf not only with the dash of speed demanded by their father, but with a standard of excellence.

One special Joey's visitor was eighty-one year old Father Jordan, retired college chaplain and long-term resident at St Joseph's College, who was driving at leisure around Australia. In Kununurra he decided to rest and recharge his batteries and was delighted to accept an invitation from Father Paul, the current parish priest, to accompany him to one of his most distant outlying stations for a First Communion celebration.

In the meantime, the matron of St Joseph's College, Joan Lloyd, and her four sons were visiting Riveren during school holidays. With Patrick's class mate 'Ringer' visiting as well, our verandah uncannily resembled a Joey's dormitory. Marie and her school friend Sandra were happily surrounded by young men and Riveren was bursting with youthful exuberance.

Joan had helped prepare an elaborate supper and everyone had been forewarned that bogey time or showers should be early for Becky's big event. Above the rowdy sounds of the teenagers' music, the barking dogs announced the arrival of strangers and we quickly rinsed cake crumbs from fingers before rushing out to greet Father Paul. He introduced his snowy-haired companion who slowly alighted from the car, and as I turned to introduce Joan and the line of Joe boys the air was filled with shrieks of disbelief and joy. Father Jordan was astonished to travel a long way from anywhere to find almost an entire Joey's football team to greet him.

Beautiful Becky, dressed in white, was supported by an impressive congregation as Mass began. Halfway through, so did the giggles. Eleven youngsters were hopelessly out of control. The more I frowned, the louder the muffled struggles. With mouths pressed to clasped fists they dared

not look at each other. The two priests intoned the age-old prayers and
Joan and I faithfully gave the required responses, while intermittent
outbursts of spluttering and choked giggles continued. When Becky, as
honest as her father and the day they were born, received her First
Communion she said plaintively, 'Mum, I can't swallow the bread.'

The giggling started all over again. Looking across at John for moral
support, I suspected a smile played on the face that was lowered on his
gnarled, grease-stained hands. They were the hands of a working man
and I shivered with delight as I remembered my first visit to Inverway,
when he had led me protectively through the night to the fallen log beside
the stockyards, where the symphony of brilliant stars overhead was ours
for the counting. We had shared undreamed-of tears and laughter since
then.

Everyone ate breakfast with voracious appetites. The excitement of the
muster was unmistakable. Outside the morning star appeared luminous
as it twinkled and sparkled in its attempts to entice mankind from inside.
Nobody else spoke while John pointed to the map and outlined the plan
for the day. Captain John Armstrong had done this muster before and so
had Andy. They knew that Mucca was always a particularly demanding
muster, and although the workforce on the ground had dramatically
increased in numbers, the task of putting together two thousand head,
taking them around the end of the permanent waterhole and into the
Mucca yards was unchanged. The objective was to get every beast in the
yard.

There was a patient queue of visitors for a ride in the helicopters and
later they all compared the exhilaration of the muster, impossible to
describe unless personally experienced. After a delicious lunch of sizzling
rib bones cooked over the stockcamp fire, I returned home to water the
garden, feed the poddy calves and prepare dinner. I'd only just commenced
my afternoon chores when the unmistakable sound of the chopper alarmed
me. The musterers were not expected back until last light and I hoped
that no-one had been hurt.

Landing at the house grid, Captain Armstrong waited until Father

Jordan was clear of the blades before rapidly accelerating and lifting off to return to the stockyards. I hurried to meet the old man who walked uncertainly and appeared ruddy-faced, flustered and overheated. We slowly returned to the homestead where he thirstily drank a cup of sweet black tea. When he advised me to keep a closer eye on John, my heart lurched as I wondered whether yet another mishap had occurred.

'My goodness he gets upset, he does. Shouts and roars like a lion. Has a colourful turn of phrase too. Can't do his blood pressure any good, that's for sure. Watch him, pet. Settle him down.'

Thanking Father for his concern, I left him to enjoy a quick siesta before sundown, the return of the teams and the evening meal.

There can be no greater luxury than water when you are so dirty even your teeth are coated with dust and grime. Food and drink take on a new allure after a yardful of cattle has been drafted and branded and calves mothered up. For the teenagers from the city their excitement reached fever pitch as they recounted the near spills and thrills of the day.

Long after the last light was extinguished, John quietly railed about the danger and humbug of ignorant visitors. Poor old Father Jordan in his long-sleeved white shirt had stood in the centre of the yard gateway. He was well positioned to capture on camera the endless corridor of bellowing boisterous cattle that surged towards him. He was also well positioned to cause a bloody big spill of cattle and to get trampled in the process. They would inevitably baulk when they saw him and the cattle that had taken two helicopter pilots six hours of intensive flying to bring together would scatter and spill every which way. John's voice was stretched to the limit as he yelled and signalled to the man about to unknowingly create havoc, and a disastrous domino effect on the moment, the day and the week. Thankfully Father was removed in time and flown home to me. It was on another occasion that the near calamity was explained to the gentle old man. Deep sleep claimed us and without resistance we slipped into the unfathomable land of slumber and renewal.

With the departure of Marie, Patrick, Michael and the visitors, an emptiness descended on us. There was never time to dwell on the negatives as the routine and the discipline marched us through our programme, both predictable and unpredictable. However, I always felt incomplete until we were a family again.

Every week I wrote separate letters to Marie, Patrick and Michael. Each week we received equally detailed accounts of boarding school life in the big city. While none of them compared letters, their first pages were incredibly similar as question after question filled line after line.

How's everything at home?

How is Golly?

Is Golly still jealous?

Has there been any rain yet?

How many calves did you brand from Rudi's?

How did Burtawater muster go?

Is Fault next?

Do you still call our racehorses 'chase horses', Dad?

Is the country still holding on?

How do the bullocks look?

Did you get all the bores pumping again?

How is school, Becky?

What set are you up to, Becky?

They all wrote to Becky too, and she wrote back. Our school system involved a lot of writing. When some correspondence children struggled, their parent or supervisor substituted cassette tapes for other work in order to minimise the pen and paper output of their pupils. On the contrary, I applauded this writing practice which kept us in good stead throughout the eternally long months of separation. For us all, letter writing was not only effortless but rewarding. It was as automatic as washing before meals and as important as breathing.

Golly viewed Becky's newest poddy calf called Chocolate with a degree of suspicion. He was a rich brown colour and beautiful. The strong little calf emptied his bottle noisily and then watched wistfully through the fence as big Golly sucked vigorously from the teat projecting from his flour drum of Denkavite. His tail swished from side to side like a giant windscreen wiper. His grass-tainted burps mingled with great sighs of contentment as though someone was squeezing a large set of bellows. Beneath a shady tree in the vicinity of the school room they collapsed side by side, awaiting the next break when their little mother and best friend would return. Golly's mistrust and deep hurt were short-lived, for the dreaded day of branding had been and gone. Tears from Becky and roars of protest from Golly had filled the air as the new brand for all poddy calves 'PUT' had made its imprint on his nearside rump. He had always known to whom he belonged. In the order of officialdom, the world now knew that he belonged to the Riveren Juniors' herd. The eventual sale proceeds were earmarked for the bottomless pit labelled education fees.

Our other pets were not happy. Poor little Bett had eaten a bellyful of ratsack and her death was dreadful. Sorrowfully, we buried her beside Ratsy and Kyber. Cuddles was only distracted from the grave site when a savage early storm laid puddles everywhere. She pounced on tadpoles and water bugs with boundless energy and would stay by the freshly created water until it dried up. Evaporation was usually rapid; however, the Wet Season represented paradise to this funny little dog whose loyalty to each of us, and since their long night together to Becky in particular, was unquestionable.

Some months later we named our new puppy Precious, much to the consternation of the boys.

'How do you think a bloke feels telling his mates that our dogs are called Cuddles and Precious?' groaned Patrick. 'Why didn't you call her Spot or Patch or something normal?'

Halley's Comet was a once in a lifetime experience for most people. Naturally Riveren would be the perfect viewing point. The Noonans packed their high-powered telescopic equipment and tennis rackets and headed down the track. Our court was already a great success. In conjunction with a previous New Year's Eve party, we had created a tennis tournament and engraved a trophy with the words 'Riveren Cup'. Tony Noonan had been the reigning champion for two consecutive years and

Celebrating in December 1982 the on-air performance of Jack Hibberd's hilarious satire *Dimboola*, which was rehearsed over the radio network that delivered lessons to the isolated pupils and was performed by parents and teachers from the Katherine School of the Air. From left to right: Flower girl, Astrid (played by Wendy Edison); Dimboola's bride, Reen (Carol Armstrong, in her original wedding gown); and bridesmaid, Shirl the Girl (Terry Underwood, producer and director).

Tony Noonan, our dear friend, competent surgeon and compassionate doctor, dressed appropriately as a flying doctor, at Terry's fortieth birthday party where forty full-sized candles burned brightly throughout the energetic and fun-filled celebrations.

Left: Cuddles, the horse-riding dog and 'cleverest pet on School of the Air', mounted for another day in the saddle. Later, Cuddles would shine as a little girl's bodyguard in a night of terror when Becky was lost overnight at Camel Creek.

Above right: Becky, in 1987, helping a slow learner to suck from a specially made 'calfeteria' that allows twelve or more poddy calves to drink simultaneously. As they suck vigorously, frothy milk bubbles appear around their mouths, and their tails swish backwards and forwards with contentment.

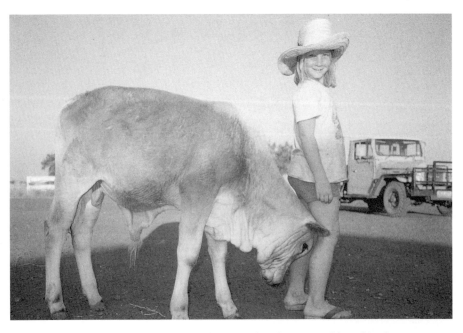

Becky's shadow, Golly, lovingly nudges his playmate and best friend.

Bush friends: Michael nursing Puss, surrounded by panting dogs Mandy (behind), Cuddles (left), and Precious the snake dog (right). Fleck, the poddy calf who loves potato chips, is sitting behind Cuddles; and just making the photo is poddy calf Orange, who sadly was later killed by dingoes.

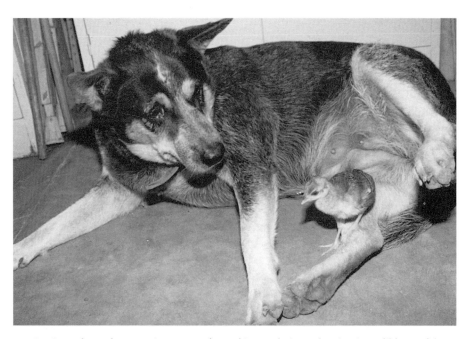

Precious, the snake executioner, transformed into a doting, adoptive, incredibly careful mother of an orphaned peacock chick.

Michael, John, Becky and Patrick having smoko – as always at Riveren it's a family affair, year in and year out.

'Hey Hey' guru and honorary Territorian Daryl Somers at Riveren with stockcamp cook, Chatterbox, who recognised with great excitement his favourite TV personality.

Following hours of aerial mustering by helicopters and stockmen on horseback, the Mucca yards are filled with cattle and dust. After the horses are washed down and the musterers have had a quick drink of billy tea, the drafting of the mob will begin.

Riveren stockmen on the top rail at the end of another long, hard but satisfying day: Snaps with his master Scott Munro, and Albert Murray, Lesley Chatandgi and Frankie McHale.

Cattleman John and our favourite Brahman bull, Jerome – two sires like two kings, side by side in silent communication and intangible understanding.

Father and daughters – John, Marie and Becky – at the historic Buchanan Yards, which were laboriously constructed by the Farquharson brothers and named after their legendary uncle, pioneer Boss Drover Nat Buchanan. The yards are now a heritage site.

The Riveren Underwoods today – Michael, Patrick, Marie, Becky, Terry and John – as a storm approaches and rain drops fall from a darkening sky with the promise of follow-up rain, the family is aglow with optimism and togetherness.

The Riveren homestead today is surrounded by well-grown trees, planted and watered by hand over many years, and a beyond that stretches forever. The Aussat satellite dish beams radio and television to this remote area and the telephone tower affords the luxury of a normal or real communication system.

Aerial photograph of Riveren Station after rain – stockyards, stables, shed, humpies, homestead, tennis court and cottage all nestled in close proximity. The tree line denotes Camel Creek, the site of our first bough shed camp and also where Becky was lost. As far as the eye can see, Riveren, the headwaters of the Victoria River country, unfolds.

he planned to have a hit and hold his title for the following year. It was no small victory as quite a few people played a mean game of tennis, none more so than John. Like everything else, we all took our tennis seriously. The ladies championship was up for grabs as were the junior sections.

The magic of Riveren always touched Tony deeply. Upon arrival, he visibly took a deep breath as though to permanently absorb every detail and moment of their stay. From the tennis court, he waved his racket in all directions at the neverending horizons as the translucent golden light bathed and enveloped us. All too soon it would be ambushed by twilight.

'Look Liz, look kids! Can you believe the backdrop of this tennis court?'

I shared his reverence for this mighty land.

As fortune or fate dictated, cloud cover restricted our vision of the celestial wonder. We managed to view craters on the new moon as small partings in the clouds appeared intermittently. The disappointment was borne with good grace as acceptance of inevitability was ingrained in both families.

Since the amalgamation of three cattle industry bodies in the Northern Territory, John had taken the position of the inaugural Chairman of the Katherine branch of the Northern Territory Cattlemen's Association. His grassroots experience, practical skills and vision were exemplary and he had now been selected as the Northern Territory representative on the national industry body, the Cattle Council of Australia. I was thrilled for John and our industry, for I knew that this man would bat with conviction for the minority at home against the big guns down south. My role as manager during his ongoing absences was of less immediate concern to me than the pressing problem of his wardrobe.

As John would be required to regularly travel interstate for the next three years, I casually mentioned that he would have to buy a new suit as soon as possible. John thought he could borrow one. However, there were other occasions looming in our lives for which he would need a suit, including Marie's vale and graduation. Just when the one in the wardrobe had been last worn we could not remember.

Out on the run, fence lines were pegged and paddocks extended. The specific requirements of the ongoing Brucellosis and Tuberculosis Eradication Campaign programme influenced these developments. Unmusterable cattle were shot. Efficiency was the name of the new game.

Inside, school days were pressure free as Becky was an intelligent and willing pupil. As the same number of hours were still committed to the school room despite the number of pupils, I was continuing to juggle balls in order to keep up. The more involved John and I became in our relevant organisations the more acutely aware we became of the lack of understanding of our lifestyle. Blindly and conveniently too many outsiders attributed the myth of an idyllic existence complemented by fat wallets to pastoral families. It remained staggering that there was so little understanding of our challenges and even less concern for our vulnerability. We knew and understood then and now that it will always be up to us to initiate communication and discussion to succeed in breaking down misconceptions.

CHAPTER 17

FRIENDS

....

Independence was vital for survival. Dependence on company or friends could prove a short cut to treacherous quicksands. Having left behind nursing mates and adjusted to extreme isolation accentuated by limited communications, I did not seek or expect friends. Family and animals proved ultimately satisfying and we were all contented with our lot. Because outside companionship was never a consideration, the formation of a friendship that blossomed and grew was a bonus. However, the expectation of sharing regular time with friends remained an absolute furphy. Nevertheless, friends trickled through our lives and were always more than welcome.

There was so much to share with them all and yet nothing actually changed because of the presence of visitors. Riveren was like a slow-moving train, upon which one boarded or disembarked according to the particular activity. There was always a queue for flights with John. The aerial perspective of the property never ceased to amaze everyone, even rural folk.

Our best man, David Sheil—son of that Northbridge couple who had so generously, though unwittingly, hosted John's party upon his discharge from Ward 3—came to visit with his family. The Sheil youngsters were intrigued by the disciplined routine that turned the wheels of Riveren. Patrick, home on holidays, confided with a mischievous smile, 'I tell you, it's a relief to get back to school after a holiday dominated by Mum gonging bells and Dad cracking whips.' Then catching my eye with a wink and a big grin, he added, 'Only joking, Mum!'

The killer was another top attraction for the Sheil kids and the two fathers competed to educate their audience as the hide was carefully removed and the various cuts of meat identified. With half a dozen willing offsiders, the beast was butchered in record time. Everyone helped load the utility, and once back at the butcher shop they hung the meat for several hours before eventually transferring it into the cold room. There was a correct way to hang each section and there were other cuts that were salted and soaked in the large deep tub of water for cooking as corned beef. Like everything on the station, nothing was accidental. There was a method to follow and a hygiene standard to comply with, John and David explained, as they expounded upon the attributes of quality meat. As colour and fat-covering relevant to the age and sex of the beast were deliberated, our children, who had heard it all before, feigned interest. Cuddles and Precious with drooling tongues also listened and watched as they wandered through the many legs hoping for a fallen scrap. Whenever John roared, 'Out of the way, you useless bloody mongrels,' they backed off marginally. They knew at the end of the day the great big Boss was a real softie.

Just for old times' sake, John decided to make a greenhide rope. As he salted the hide and wrapped it up for the night, he explained that in bygone days the hide fresh from the killer was treated in the same way. Next day it was stretched, often on a wagon wheel, for weeks on end. These treated hides were then stored, because rope and hobble making had been a Wet Season job. Next morning, John unrolled the hide and stretched it out with steel stakes. The circling crows instantly descended to help clean up any remnants of meat or fat. Eventually the hide would be soaked, then cut into strips. Individual strips would be twisted before being twined together and finally stretched to make the rope. Sadly, many such bush crafts were in danger of being lost as superior manufactured goods were readily available. John's father, Pat, was one of a minority who still had the time and skill to pursue this art. Pat Underwood made the best greenhide ropes in the country.

The Aborigines also had visitors. The brand new tractor and large trailer had negotiated the back road from Hooker Creek at a snail's pace to discharge the greatest number of visitors we had ever seen at any one time. At least a dozen adults and an even greater number of children gathered happily and explored inquisitively the place where Auntie Poppy and Uncle Peter lived. With her gummy grin, Alison arrived at the cold room carrying her beef bucket. Standing shyly behind her were several children, hoping to carry some extra rib bones back to the humpy kitchen. Their needs remained simple. Their ultimate joy was to sit together around the camp fire cooking fresh beef washed down with scalding billy tea that was so overloaded with sugar it was almost too thick to stir. The corroboree after the great occasion of a fresh killer always seemed to reach unheralded heights, as the unique rhythm of song and tapping sounds of the music sticks filled the air with the potent magic and mystique of the culture of these people.

Even though John was starkly aware that his back was fragile, he was forever subject to the unpredictabilities of the land, its products and the infrastructures installed with blood, sweat and tears. Furthermore there was never a time to hang up the branding iron or shut down the welder. Apart from ongoing repairs and maintenance, we were still developing further out. The arrival of the Thorncraft cattle crush for the homestead yards signalled progress and a more sophisticated level of management.

The various components of this crush, including a head bail, allowed cattle to be immobilised for the appropriate procedure—branding, dehorning, speying, artificial insemination—or to help a calf with feeding difficulties suck from its mother.

We regularly sold horses to neighbouring properties and on one occasion, a station manager arriving to inspect and select his horses was most concerned to find John bent over double. My man shrugged off any concern, saying that he had done his back in yet again and it would come good in a few days time.

Fury, scorn, anger and near despair were not just tactics. They were the emotions that flooded my heart, mind and soul when I witnessed my tireless man working in a hunched position. His tall broad frame seemed sometimes reduced to half its normal size. It was as though he needed placing beneath a giant ironing press to be straightened out. Furthermore, he who never complained increasingly mentioned the acute pain that crossed his buttocks and scissored down his legs. Something had to be done.

John was due home and my deliberations about the earliest and best method to have his back assessed were 'on the table' awaiting his response. As I crossed the lawn to move the sprinkler, I saw the most incredible sight. On the other side of the house fence a blue heeler grazed beside Chocolate and the new poddies, Fleck and Orange. In perfect unison with the herbivores, Precious with head down ate the grass too. When they moved forward marginally, so did she. The intimate sharing of their blissful existence had created an identity confusion. As I laughed out loud, Precious turned and raced towards me in the hope that it was walk or milk time. From beneath the laundry steps, Cuddles opened one eye and cast a look of reproach upon the delirious young delinquent.

With school holidays drawing to an end all too quickly, I mended and marked clothes. The behaviour pattern of Marie, Patrick and Michael changed noticeably during their last days at home. They fought their own private wars, with the difficulty of leaving home dominating every thought and word and action. I understood yet remained helpless as I witnessed the swings in mood and conversation. Home was not just their anchor, but a way of life which they cherished with real passion. I endeavoured to maintain the calm and the norm. While no-one suspected that I was being ripped apart as I prepared them for departure, there was no alternative other than to surrender to the unbearable ache of the looming separation.

My plan to remove John from home paddocks was unsuccessful. He could not accompany us to Darwin because the station workers were laying poly pipe and his presence was essential for positioning the troughs and connecting them to the storage tanks.

'Take it easy, won't you,' I farewelled him as three city boarders reluctantly said their goodbyes.

'Off you go, billy lids,' he smiled encouragingly. 'Be good at school and don't do anything that I wouldn't do.'

The Noonans, whom we had not seen for ages, had invited us for dinner and I intended to seek Tony's assistance in organising some resolution to John's back problems. As soon as we entered their front door I knew something was wrong. As Liz handed around drinks and we flopped into chairs and bean bags, Tony delivered his bombshell. Always one to call a spade a shovel, he quietly said, 'We've just found out that I've got cancer and six months is a generous estimate of my time left to be with the people I love.'

Silence broken only by weeping was short-lived as he outlined their plans to relocate immediately to Adelaide in order to buy a home and settle the little boys into school. I looked at Liz and then at the man who had carried us through every known and unknown heartache. He who had given his all and more was being called. I could not speak as I looked back at Liz and their two younger boys, Matthew and Josh. After dinner, goodbyes were difficult. On the footpath we stood and talked about irrelevant things until Tony opened the driver's door and all but pushed me in.

'You had better get going,' he said. 'It's late.'

A quick kiss to each of them from each of us and we were gone. I did not look back, but we all knew that we would never see Tony again.

At Darwin airport, we mingled with other parents farewelling their children, most of whom were red-eyed and visibly upset. How quickly tears dried after the kids fastened their seat belts, I never did find out. Mine continued all the way home. I was never ever 'all cried out'.

I had telephoned Sydney from town and John's back review with Dr Roarty was secured. Upon hearing of Tony's illness John too was devastated. What a waste, he kept saying, what a terrible waste. I prayed that Tony's suffering would be minimal and that Liz would find the courage to fight the fight they were predestined to lose. John's resolve that Riveren could not survive without him had reached a low point through this unhappy distraction. Grasping the moment I told him the date of his appointment and proceeded to book the flights.

If St Vincent's Private Hospital kept a visitors book, surely our surname would have appeared as one of the most frequent to occupy beds. Sister

Bernice showered her affection and support upon the bushies from afar. The stress of the plane accident was still taking its toll. Dr Roarty performed a decompression laminectomy and gave his patient the advice that John knew he could no longer water down, delay or ignore. He really had to look after himself.

One of the best things about living in the Outback was that one's neighbours were as refreshing and stimulating as the lifestyle itself. Distance and work commitments prevented regular contact; however, that mattered not. One of our neighbours was one such bush character. Frank Dalton was just an ordinary kind of bloke, who had arrived some years earlier, and yet we felt he had always been there and that we had known him forever.

Along the Buchanan Highway some four hundred kilometres south-west of Katherine an arresting sign greets travellers.

CAUTION. DROP BEARS. NEXT 15 KILOMETRES.

A privileged few apart from the stalwart locals know that not far away nestles the headquarters of the Wave Hill Drop Bears, the most remote cricket club in the world. Frank was founder and captain.

The club's rules are marginally different from traditional cricket in that each player on the fielding team must bowl an eight-ball over in turn. When all eleven players have bowled, they start again. An extra ball must be bowled for wides and no balls. Overs are unlimited and the innings is over when all the batsmen are out, with the last man batting on with a runner at the opposite end. Batsmen have to retire at the end of the over in which they reach a score of twenty-five. Unless he makes three ducks, the batsman can't get out without scoring.

Many a battle for the Ashes has been played in this remarkable setting, and the plastic seagulls placed strategically across the grounds have witnessed amazing scenes. With the calling of drinks after the falling of the first two wickets and every two thereafter, it can take days to finish a game. That matters not in the heart of Australia, where there remains a sense of timelessness.

Having left his home town of Melbourne to travel, Frank ended up at the Wave Hill settlement and it was there that he met his match. Lorraine Carter, the granddaughter of the Boss Drover, Matt Savage, stole Frank's heart. The local priest from Katherine married them minutes before the broadcast of the Melbourne grand final, giving the groom time to change into his going away outfit of black and white footy jersey, stubbies and footy socks. After Mass the following morning, Lorraine and Frank's son was baptised Robert James Dalton. The Drop Bears' members stand was subsequently named after this little fellow.

Naturally the bar area surrounded by extensive cricket memorabilia is called Frank's Bar and Grill. Apart from the odd game of cricket, tribute to two outstanding Territorians has been made there. The third presentation of 'A Territory Story' along the lines of 'This is Your Life' was in the pipeline. Our assistance was sought to entice one unsuspecting Noel Buntine, road train entrepreneur, to Riveren, and on his return to town a quick beer at Frank's would evolve into an unforgettable evening.

It was all that and more. Noel's entire extended family had been smuggled in. Every driver who had ever driven for Buntine was surely present and when asked to stand to identify themselves they did so with great pride and a glint in many an eye. The stories both unofficial and official continued as night turned into morning. The cricket match between the World Eleven and Buntine's Eleven commenced after a generous breakfast of rum and rib bones all round. Following the declaration by the Rest of the World at 0 for 200, Noel's Eleven were 9 for 45. It was then that Noel sent his 88-year-old mother in to bat. When Captain Jack Taylor couldn't coax any of his team to bowl to the old lady, the Rest of the World, gentlemen at heart, immediately conceded defeat.

Whenever in doubt about progeny, everyone referred to Becky. She had always displayed an extraordinary natural ability with livestock. Her memory seemed photographic. Marie, Patrick and Michael usually asked her to drive them around for an update on their first day home on holidays. From a very early age she knew which calf was by which bull and how many calves each particular cow had had. John sought her opinion when drafting stud cattle. They discussed temperament and conformation as cows were drafted off to go into another paddock with a different bull. As soon as she could write, Becky took over the record keeping of the stud paddocks.

After school, I followed Becky to the yard where the best looking young cattle were awaiting my inspection. Each beast was introduced by name backed up by parentage, weight and age. There was Tina and Spot, Sunny and Noddy, amongst others. The subjects under discussion tried to pretend they weren't really there, because in the beginning that would be their preference, had they a choice. Whereas dogs and horses lead instinctively, cattle do not. Winning their trust was part of the breaking-in process that required infinite patience and the investment of many hours over many weeks. Becky's skills were amazing. I watched as she tied each one to a rail using the special knot that prevented escape. The frightened calves tried various tactics to evoke sympathy and secure premature release. One threw itself head down and tail up with eyes firmly closed. Lying in this awkward position it appeared dead.

'Don't play possum with me, you rascal,' Becky cajoled confidently as she uprighted and reassembled her charges.

Using the special cattle stick as an extension of her arm, she gradually closed the gap between girl and beast, until her hand touched the hide and rubbed and stroked. She talked constantly to the calves as she worked, knowing that the underbelly and between the back legs were the areas to produce the best response. When the tail lifted involuntarily, the calf was responding.

A friend telephoned with the sad news. Tony had lost his battle with cancer on 1 November 1987. In the church calendar it was All Saints' Day. It was two months after Tony's last letter.

> *I doubt if I will have the energy to write again but know that you are all frequently in our thoughts and conversations. Some of the stories of our times together are reaching the status of bush yarns. Just the other night I had to recount in detail for the two little boys the story of John's air crash. Of course John is now taking on an*

aspect larger than life in their minds and I am afraid that they
worship you from afar.
   God bless you both and all the kids.
   Love
   Tony

We mourned Tony's death and sensed the enormous loss. He had touched us in so many ways—as a good friend, a competent, compassionate doctor and surgeon, a seeker of excellence, a family man with a great sense of humour and a man of deep faith. We were thankful for his legacy—the imprint Tony had made on our lives.

Henry the stockman's passing also followed a prolonged illness. Upon receiving the news, I located his brother, blue-eyed Frankie McHale, to tell him in the best way I could of his loss. His reaction was predictable. Sorrowful bellows and howls of grief echoed throughout the stillness for many hours. Having witnessed terrible injuries self-inflicted at the receipt of sorry news, I was aware that the Aboriginal people had their own way of coming to terms with personal grief.

Despite John's absence, the mustering was in full swing. When I checked the programme with head stockman Eric, he said they were a little short-handed. Apparently Frankie had not surfaced for days, so I knocked on his door. I called his name as I opened the door. Frankie lay face to the wall and ignored my presence.

'Frankie, are you all right?' Silence. 'Eric might need a hand.'

He sat up and turned to me.

'You don't know nothing. You don't know how I feel bout these things. I can't work when my brother bin die. You don't understand blackfella way, Terry.'

'Do you want to tell me, so I can know too?' I asked as I sat on the step. From his bedside Frankie glanced at me and at length said, 'Ui.'

His inside hurting spilled to the surface. He told me many things as I listened without interruption. When I departed to take my bread out of the oven, I noticed out of the corner of my eye Frankie pulling on his boots and looking towards the yards. He was back on deck at last.

Although we seldom saw them, Ken and Sally Warriner had become special friends to us. When Ken and his two partners sold Newcastle Waters to the Consolidated Pastoral Company, we followed with healthy envy the changes occurring under new ownership. It was around the time when Kerry Packer initiated World Series Cricket and the impressive new improvements such as stockyards and bores were named after cricketers. Newcastle Waters quickly became the jewel in the crown of the Packer pastoral empire. In their role as managers, the Warriners moved from the original station homestead into the newly completed Big House, above which towered the massive chimney bearing the station symbol brand of a wine glass.

Sally was very much outnumbered with the arrival of baby Sam. Surrounded by Ken and five sons, she showed no signs of supression. On the contrary, Sally continued to run the family and huge homestead in her powerful and flamboyant style. Our invitation to attend Sam's christening was accepted with delight, particularly as I was to be his godmother.

'I'm ensuring the spiritual and material well being of Sam are beyond dispute,' Sally confided. 'K. P. has agreed to be godfather and I'm always under the impression that you have a direct line to the Almighty. Lucky Sam.'

I laughed. 'There's a direct line for everyone, Sal; all you have to do is pick up the phone.'

The tin walls of the tiny church in the Newcastle Waters township were draped with masses of scented bush flowers and freshly gathered foliage. Family and godparents occupied the front hay bales. Kerry Packer nursed a wriggling Sam throughout the christening service performed by the Flying Padre, the Salvation Army minister from Darwin.

At the celebration barbecue afterwards, the interstate visitors mingled happily with those who worked the land. After the cake cutting, Kerry Packer spoke of the moving christening and his high regard for Ken and Sally. Having bathed and bedded down my new godson, I joined the stayers on the extensive lawn between the homestead and the near empty lake. There was talk of Dr Victor Chang's brilliant cardiac surgery and the marvellous story of his young patient Fiona Cootes, the recipient of a successful second heart transplant. I fully identified with Kerry's respect for Sister Bernice and St Vincent's Hospital. As discussions continued beneath the vision splendid that was for us a nightly extravaganza, someone sighed, 'If only we could roll up this brilliant Territory sky and transpose it to Sydney.'

We were barely home before it was time to leave again. It was difficult to grasp the reality that Marie's journey at the Rose Bay Convent was over, and yet we all recognised that the end signalled the beginning of the rest of her life. There were no spare seats in the beautiful chapel. As the procession of school leavers, each lovely face illuminated by a flickering candle, walked up the aisle, I felt completely overwhelmed. Our eldest had travelled this pilgrimage without our presence. On many an occasion my brother Johnny had provided stand-in parental support. It had never been possible for us to see her play sport, participate in a school recital or share her presentation of an assignment. And now it was too late. Some of the passing girls shared my inability to control the tears that trickled, despite very best intentions not to cry.

When one of Marie's best friends sang very poignantly 'Do You Know Where You're Going To?' there was not a dry eye in sight. However, Marie knew. During her boarding school years her closeness to home, if possible, had increased. Marie was returning to the Territory, to be close to her sun and dust, family and animals. The plan to move in a specific direction was in place, for her application to enrol in the hospitality course at the Beaufort Hotel in Darwin had been accepted.

The dinner afterwards was a moving reunion with families and friends seldom seen since our daughters commenced boarding school six years earlier. However, they had become part of our lives through this school connection. As always it was a matter of cramming in maximum time together, for all too quickly I would be exchanging stilettos for riding boots. Tearfully, I attempted to express our gratitude to all who had taken Marie into their homes and hearts over the years. Many promised to visit us one day. Realising that our location was still inaccessible to many, we urged them to come if and whenever possible.

As the crush of the cantankerous city became a memory, John casually asked me, 'Do you know how many people you have invited to Riveren in the last three days?'

The answer had to be in the hundreds.

The rips were freshly inflicted. Poor little Orange lay beside the grid, as though she knew we were due home. Becky was heartbroken as she placed the torn body across her lap. Gently she cradled the bleeding head, stroking and reassuring her little friend. It was too late. The devilish dingo had won another round.

CHAPTER 18

IF YOU ARE EVER PASSING BY

....

Everyone from Inverway travelled down to Riveren for Becky's birthday. It was a lovely party and one of the few occasions when we made time to congregate. I was pleased to welcome back Pat and Peg, the consummate grandparents who cherished every family gathering. As Cuddles and Precious lined up for cake, bellows of objection from the front gate announced Chocolate's indignation. Becky ran to her friend. He slurped her sticky fingers as she handed him some cake and, feeling slightly less miffed, joined the crowd on the lawn. Like Golly, he considered himself one of us. His growth rate was exceptional and he looked as good as any young steer in the paddock. That this impressive big calf with his deep red shiny coat would one day have to leave Riveren seemed unthinkable. However, Becky knew cattle were raised for a purpose and that one day she would have to farewell her friends.

❖   ❖   ❖

We approached with determination another year of consolidation. John's confidence with flying had never faltered and our Cessna remained a reliable beast of burden. Sound, functional improvements supported an ever increasing herd. Our commitment to upgrading this herd was ongoing and as finances permitted we purchased new bulls. The continued infusion of Brahman blood lines over Shorthorn was exciting to plan, implement and monitor.

The Brahman breed originated in the United States in the early 1900s and developed from the amalgamation of four Indian (Bos Indicus) cattle breeds with some infusion of British-bred cattle (Bos Taurus). Hindu priests used the term 'Brahma' to refer to certain bulls they branded that became idols and subsequently were allowed to roam at will. The word 'Brahman' was adopted to refer to North America's first distinct Bos Indicus herd. During Australia's early days of colonisation, the Zebu cattle imported from India were either lost or absorbed by the British breeds. It took many years to overcome the marked suspicion and open hostility against the introduction of 'exotic blood' and the equally sluggish response to accommodating this new breed on the show circuits. Many cattlemen, with an inborn resistance to change, were reluctant to embrace this new breed because of perceived unsuitable temperament and inferior meat quality.

As Brahman characteristics became more apparent in our cattle, we discussed temperament and conformation and the feminine traits of the breeder compared with the masculinity and libido of the magnificent bull. The attributes of Australia's number one tropical breed were already apparent as our cattle were proving their adaptability to the environment, their disease and parasite resistance, and their increased reproductive capacity.

Jerome, our favourite bull, was by the renowned sire Jarocho. Even to an outsider, he was a beefy bull. A beautifully muscled and developed beast, he responded with typical Brahman curiosity to his new surroundings and new wives. Whenever we visited him, he turned towards his new human family with equal curiosity. Despite his inherent instinct to be master of his own domain, he stood his ground upon our approach. In John he recognised his equivalent and it was a moving sight to observe the two sires like two kings standing side by side in silent communication and intangible understanding.

Through hard work, Riveren was now clearly definable with paddocks and watering points strategically positioned to support our growing herd. Confidently, we submitted an application for perpetual lease tenure.

Until now we had held Riveren as a fixed term pastoral lease. A Land Board meeting to discuss our application was to be held at Riveren. Like other visitors, members of the board arrived with toothbrushes and pyjamas. Among them was Noel Buntine, a man who wore many hats. Apart from revolutionising the cattle and transport industries, he played a significant role in redirecting the beef roads programme. Because of his broad experience in pastoral management, Noel had been appointed inaugural chairman of the Northern Territory Land Board.

Security of tenure was on the agenda of all pastoralists. Although a recent report from the government pastoral inspector identified Riveren as one of the best-developed properties in the Northern Territory, formalities and procedures had to be followed. After touring sections of our property, we attended an official meeting around our dining room table. Noel congratulated us on our top operation, but reminded us of the necessary formalities that required the Board's recommendations go to the Minister for approval. As the books were closed and spectacles returned to their respective cases, John decided it was time to be seriously hospitable and called for a show of hands for beer or bundy.

During our conversion to perpetual lease, all relevant bodies and organisations had been contacted to ascertain objections to or interest in this proposal. Despite supportive responses all round, we subsequently received advice that interest had been expressed in an Aboriginal living area on Riveren. It was common knowledge that excision claims on all Northern Territory pastoral leases were being encouraged by the Aboriginal Land Councils.

When the Land Council delegation arrived, John recognised the elderly claimants as old time residents of Limbunya, the property to our north. It was a congenial reunion as they knew him too from Inverway stockcamp days. We escorted our visitors to the specified area. Upon arrival, the old Aborigines shook their heads.

'Dis humbug for John—too many bullocks here—we don't want dis place—humbug properly.'

Their escorts urged them to point to a substitute area on their map.

They shrugged. They wanted nothing. The genuine concern of those old men was uplifting.

The Pope whom John had known about all along was back in our lives. Becky was one of three School of the Air children selected to speak to Pope John Paul II on the radio during his Australian visit. Such was the importance of the media coverage that we had to travel the eighteen hundred kilometre round trip to the proposed venue at Mountain Valley Station for a practice run for film crew and cameras. Should inclement weather or faulty technology interfere with the much publicised event live on the day, there would be sufficient footage of the children already available. A month later we retraced our tracks as the most travelled Pope in history winged his way from the Vatican to our homeland. This time it was the real thing. It could have been a school lesson except that Becky and Jacqui wore new white ribbons in their hair and Angus too wore town clothes. All three knew not only their questions but radio technique backwards. When asked if she had butterflies, Becky replied, 'What do you mean? At home?'

As the RAAF Boeing 707 flew across the Northern Territory, the Pope held photos of the three children below. At the given signal, he pressed his microphone button to greet them. However, the infallible Pontiff omitted to conclude his message with 'over', thereby throwing out of sequence the two-way radio communication.

'Cut! We'll start again.'

Becky's question was last.

'Holy Father, what is the hardest thing about being the Pope?'

'The hardest thing about being the Pope is to see that many people do not accept the love of Jesus, do not know who He really is and how much He loves them. Jesus came into the world and He offered His life on the cross because He wanted everyone to be happy with Him in heaven. He is the Saviour of everyone in the whole world but He does not force people to accept His love. He offers it to them and leaves them free to say yes or no. It fills me with joy to see how many people know and love

Our Lord, how many say yes to him, but it saddens me to see that some people say no. Over.'

The same message of free will had been delivered to me at school, over and over again. God was never going to drag anyone to heaven. I pondered on this moving papal experience. To gain an audience with the Pope in Rome required detailed planning and yet here we were, in the middle of nowhere, communicating with the head of our Church.

This unforgettable flying visit and associated radio link highlighted to the world the remoteness of many Australian families. Becky answered a reporter's question by saying that the experience was special for her because no-one else in her family had spoken to the Pope. Her family was her world.

The industry and School of Air meetings in town were over. From Katherine, John would reach Riveren by air in two hours and Becky and I in our Landcruiser would hopefully be home in six hours. I glanced at my watch and hoped we would make it before dark. Eighty kilometres out of town I caught up with two roadtrains that covered the full width of the long narrow road as they snaked forwards. They set the pace and I hoped they were going on to Kununurra when I turned left to Top Springs and Riveren. No sooner had I resigned myself to a slow wait, than the driver in front gave me marginal room to pass. Timing and accuracy were critical as it was important to keep my inside wheels on the bitumen. I was now between the two double decker transports without any likely change of sequence until the turn-off another forty kilometres away.

The longest stretch of road was immediately ahead. The hilly ascent slowed the giant truck and I slowed too in order to maintain the gap between us. Away in the distance I noticed a roadside vehicle. To my absolute horror this bull catcher parked at the crest of the steep hill drove blindly onto the road directly into the path of the roadtrain. With the inevitable impact, tumbling bodies somersaulted through the air like rag dolls. It was incomprehensible that the driver had neither heard nor seen the roadtrain.

Within minutes we arrived at the frightful accident. Telling Becky to wait in the car I quickly joined the ashen roadtrain driver squatting beside two incoherent young people. They were as drunk as skunks. They lay moaning amongst spilled tins of food, cans of beer and large gas bottles looking more like torpedo weapons. The damaged petrol tank of the overturned vehicle dripped silently onto the debris as the couple grabbed one another in panic and bewilderment. They weren't making sense as I questioned their injuries. The badly shaken roadtrain driver talked to his mate who had just pulled up and together they waited to flag down the first vehicle townward bound. We needed help as quickly as possible.

The couple were young and out of control. He was angry and in pain as he told her to say she was the driver. As he continued to groan alarmingly, she yelled profanities that would challenge the reputation of any lady. When I told her to rest beside her friend, she started chanting like a crazed woman.

'I'm an epileptic! I'm an epileptic! I'm an epileptic!'

'Shut up woman and get me a smoke,' demanded her companion lying beside the leaked pool of petrol.

Our three hour wait for the ambulance was broken by the arrival of a bus load of tourists. When the driver stopped to offer assistance, his passengers grabbed cameras and traipsed haphazardly through the debris. They were as co-operative as my charges. The occupants of an army truck were next to join us. A horribly officious officer attempted to rearrange the injured. As we forcefully argued, I asked him to call in to Willeroo Station ahead to advise the employers of this couple of the accident. Peering indignantly through his gold-rimmed glasses, he spat out his words.

'Not possible lassie! I've got perishables on board. My one stop is my destination.'

He ordered his troops aboard and thankfully they departed.

As soon as the white doors with the red cross closed, I recommenced the journey home. It was now very late and my schedule was shot to pieces. I was in the situation we avoided at all costs. Travelling at night through these cattle-infested roads was for the foolhardy.

Our world was suddenly violated as we were thrown forwards then backwards to the sounds of the buckling door, crumpling bonnet and sizzling, hissing radiator. I did not see the beast and the impact was shattering. I held Becky tightly, knowing she was all right, but needing her to tell me so herself.

As we stood beside the smashed vehicle the thrashing sounds of terrified cattle crashing through the scrub reverberated all around us. Stranded in the pitch darkness, I voiced my thoughts.

'Thank goodness Josef Schwab isn't around anymore, Becky.'

She agreed wholeheartedly.

During his hideous killing spree, Schwab had shattered the innocence of the Outback and struck terror in our hearts. His first victims were father and son on a reconnaissance tour to establish a good fishing spot around the Victoria River Wayside Inn. Their wives waited in vain for their return. With the eventual discovery of two burnt bodies in a shallow grave, the search commenced for an unknown murderer loose in the great expanse of country where no police net would be effective. Another three people were stalked before being brutally murdered near Kununurra. The killer or killers would need fuel and food and everyone everywhere was on full alert.

I practised with Becky her dash to a hideout, one inside and another outside, in the event that a strange vehicle appeared. I had the rifle in place and cold fear in my heart. At night I locked doors for the very first time and was grateful for dogs that barked loudly at the very suggestion of a shadow.

At the Fitzroy Rodeo, scores of stockmen prepared to exchange working jeans for brightly coloured chaps. Peter Leutenegger was the experienced helicopter pilot mustering the rodeo horses at nearby Jubilee Station when he spied a well-camouflaged vehicle beneath a large Bauhinia tree. He and his passenger circled for a closer look before returning to Fitzroy Crossing to alert the police.

All the musterers on horseback and motor bikes were directed to evacuate the area instantly and the West Australian Tactical Response Group was flown in. When they ordered Schwab's surrender, he answered with a barrage of fire. As the gun dropped from his injured hand, the wanted man grabbed another, leapt into his vehicle and revved the engine. There would be no escape. The hurtled tear gas ignited surrounding grasses as well as ammunition inside his moving vehicle. Amidst deafening explosions and crackling flames, the man who was never going to be taken alive was mortally wounded. The collective sigh of relief ripped through the Outback like a Mexican wave at a cricket match.

The rumble grew louder as the lights enlarged. Two different roadtrain drivers sympathetically inspected underneath the dented, blistered bonnet of our severely buckled vehicle. The third set of lights belonged to a station manager returning from the cattlemen's meeting we had attended. He would continue home to find a chain then return to tow us to Montijinni Station.

It was midnight before I finally made contact with John on the radio telephone. When I asked if he would fly over next morning, he asked if I was joking.

'I'll fly over hopefully late tomorrow or the next morning. The buyers are looking for a lighter line of steers and if I'm short of numbers I might have to include Chocolate. Over.'

'You're the one who's got to be joking,' I retorted. 'If Chocolate goes, we all go. Chocolate is family. Over and out.'

Although newspapers and magazines were decidedly outdated by the time they reached us, we read each page with intense interest. Many publications were kept for school projects. Our latest edition of the weekly *Bulletin* detailed the *Bulletin* Mumm Cordon Rouge Champagne photographic competition, which invited black and white photographic entries depicting the theme 'Enjoying Life'. My interest was instantly aroused for two reasons. The bush must be represented and I was living in the most unrecognised part of our nation, apart from which we enjoyed life to the hilt.

I imagined the judges being flooded with images of crystal chandeliers mirrored by marble floors, or even ghastly graffiti scribbled on urban surfaces. Then there was Riveren. Here were a thousand winning images. Could I capture the one to beat all others? It was as though I was back in our original bough shed as I asked myself the pertinent question—where to begin?

In my backyard red croppy hills guarded endless straw coloured plains that were interrupted by ageless winding river beds. Overhead, steel blue skies contrasted dramatically with the giant thunderheads of the Wet Season. Tireless determined feet trod muddy or cracked soils, strong arms carried a motherless calf as committed families bonded by endurance left on this land an imprint for all time. The vibrancy of the landscape was matched by the tenacity of its inhabitants. Black and white images would give raw clarity, razor-sharp definition and a whole new dimension to my world. My camera became an extension of me.

The prize trip to Paris was not mine. It was awarded to a beautiful photograph entitled and depicting 'Family'. There could be no better or more powerful interpretation of the theme. However, my entry entitled 'Brahmumms' was published and this venture fuelled my pursuit of improved photographic skills and strengthened my commitment to sharing our largely invisible lifestyle.

During a stopover in Darwin, John caught up with Marie at the Beaufort Hotel and accepted a dinner party invitation from the friendly general manager, John Parche, and his wife Lyn. That night the Parches were also entertaining the popular television personality Daryl Somers. The cattleman had never seen 'Hey Hey It's Saturday' and Daryl Somers had never met a cattleman. When John rang to see if I had been able to fix a water problem and mentioned his dinner companions, I asked if I could say hello to the man I had watched for years and years on Saturday morning Sydney television.

Daryl spoke unashamedly of his love for the Northern Territory and admitted that he could not begin to imagine what it was like where we lived.

'Well Daryl,' I ventured, 'if you are ever passing by, be sure to drop in.' Like all invitations to visit Riveren, it was most sincerely extended. John just hoped that everyone we had invited to stay would not turn up at once.

The small cottage built at the same time as the tennis court begged for occupancy, according to John. I fancied placing it on hold for our retirement sometime in the next century, unless John's back dictated otherwise. John persisted.

'A married couple is what Riveren needs. Two sensible, reliable, experienced people who can manage without supervision. Can you imagine being able to go away for a decent break together?'

I could not. Apart from which Patrick's journey at Joey's was drawing to an end and his graduation was an absolute must for both of us. We had always tried to attend important family events, but the absence of both of us for more than a couple of days was extremely problematic. Other important functions that required the presence of only one or the other of us were more easily accommodated. With no long-term stability in our workforce, we were continually discussing our concerns and options for future stockmen. We were determined not to trap our children into their heritage on the day that they completed secondary education. With immovable reservations but genuine goodwill, I agreed that it was worth trying to find a married couple who could cope with the lifestyle and contribute accordingly.

We advertised through an agent and selected a couple with sound references and extensive rural experience in Queensland. They appeared self-sufficient and polite and their love of horses was evident from the beginning.

My brother Johnny, whose enormous capacity for caring had ensured he'd been a selfless and willing backstop to our boarding school children, was returning north after almost a quarter of a century. This time he was driving. It was an emotional moment when my old chaperone eventually pulled up at the front gate, beaming.

'What a journey! I feel like Burke and Wills.'

His vehicle was loaded with gifts, but his presence was the best gift of all. The rear windscreen was almost invisible behind the gigantic wire cage that was instantly despatched to the chook yard. Four timid young peacocks, unwinding and stretching heads in all directions, did a stocktake of their new home. With an air of resentment, the chooks gathered to inspect the long-legged intruders. Our dear friend Sally Warriner, insisting that every station needed extra 'watch dogs', had grasped this opportunity to despatch her gifts.

All too quickly we were to discover their other traits. John threatened permanent eviction if they shat in his shed. I argued that they would add beauty and atmosphere to our station. We agreed to disagree and review the situation in a month.

Johnny's questions were never ending. The enormous gaps in what he knew of our development were quickly filled and my little brother marvelled not only at our progress at Riveren, but at the forgotten beauty of the country. We walked down to Camel Creek and sat at the same site where my ex-patient from Ward 3 had proclaimed his vision and dream. It was now a reality.

Johnny gave me a big hug and smiled. 'Good on you. It must have had its moments.'

I shrugged. 'This poor bloody woman has learned thoroughly that there can be no privilege without hardship, no paradise without heartache. Together we have survived, and honestly, there is nowhere else I would rather be.'

He nodded. 'The Johns never doubted you.'

'So where are all those billions of annoying flies?' he asked. I explained that introduced dung beetles had really cleaned up the flies. The Commonwealth Scientific and Industrial Research Organisation (CSIRO) had sent out the beetles in boxes on our mail plane. We had dispersed them into fresh cow pads which were breeding places for pests like buffalo fly and the bush fly. The results had been quite amazing. Johnny could not believe it. Neither could we.

Our handling of cattle fascinated him and the response of intelligent and docile Brahmans to people left him speechless. Becky's show team were in serious training and most animals were following instructions, rather than Becky pleading and pulling them along. They were used to being washed and brushed, tied up and paraded. Precious persisted in lining up beside the smallest calf, in the hope that we might mistake her for one whenever the grooming brushes appeared. The cattle expressed their pleasure with the brush in various ways, either with neck extended or raspy tongues nuzzling hair or licking the salty sweat on our skin. Others raised tails or just emitted gentle snoring sounds of contentment.

Becky's preparation of the cattle for show presentation had been time and money consuming, and like everything else at Riveren it was family or no-one who made it happen. Becky had won the trust of the cattle; they knew her and responded to her presence before acknowledging anyone else. The only time she spent in the house was to eat and sleep.

Her hard work was rewarded when several months later, Riveren Spot was given the nod by the judge at the Katherine Show. To the delight of all, Becky won the gold medal for the best junior exhibitor. It was the first time the award had been made and she was the undisputed winner. The judge had watched her caring for her show team outside the show ring too and made special mention of the dedication and skills of one so young.

While Australians everywhere were celebrating their Bicentenary, we were celebrating a decade of independence. We were proud of Riveren, and of our involvement in Australia's Last Great Cattle Drive. We had donated cattle and loaned retired racehorses as drovers' mounts. Because Johnny's departure was timed to coincide with the launch of the Drive, we all travelled together to the point of departure at Newcastle Waters Station. This Bicentennial project had captured the minds and hearts of many Australians, both urban and rural. In its re-enactment of the pioneering journeys of the overlanders and drovers, it paid fitting tribute to blackfellas and whitefellas who rode together then and now.

Under the orders of Boss Drover, Noel Willets, the mob would travel approximately ten kilometres a day and take four months to reach the Stockman's Hall of Fame and Outback Heritage Centre in Queensland, which would be the beneficiary of the auction of the cattle. Noel was known as Piccaninny Willets as he had taken his first contract at the age of fourteen.

The second component of this project had attracted over eight thousand applications from young people worldwide. The successful fifteen to eighteen year olds promised the attributes so vital for the survival of our predecessors—self-discipline, stamina, and superior horseriding skills. Their two hundred kilometre treks (quite separate from the Drive) were planned along historic stock routes throughout the Territory.

The crowds had gathered long before our arrival. Hundreds of bushies, politicians and proud Territorians from near and far were joined by national and international visitors. The print and electronic media were having their own field day and the entire spectacle was overseen by renowned sculptor Eddie Hackman's incredible 2.5 metre bronze statue of 'The Drover'. The giant figure, carrying a pack saddle in each hand, stood in the Drovers' Memorial Park as a tribute to the drovers of the Murranji, otherwise known as the Drover's Ghost Track, which had been opened up by pioneer drover and one of Australia's greatest bushmen, Nat Buchanan.

Ted Egan, singer and songwriter, farewelled in song the cattle and their caretakers. As the whips cracked and the mob moved out, there was a mighty roar of good wishes from each and every bystander, who would be riding alongside in spirit.

With the gazetting of the Murranji and the north–south and the east–west stock routes around 1920, the township of Newcastle Waters had provided a meeting point and resting place, as well as telegraphic communication services and a base for the replenishment of supplies. At the old Junction Hotel many a tale was told and many a nightmare relived as the rum flowed freely between hardened men, who for months on end had survived on bore water and salted beef. There they drank to perished mates, some of whom had died through dehydration, illness or at the hands of hostile Aborigines.

That night that same hotel which had been closed for so many years reopened. We all flocked to the Junction Function, where there was talk of the past and talk of the future. We drank with a group of old drovers who reminisced about the way it was before the pub and store closed, before government services and Telecom were transferred to Elliott. We heard how Newcastle Creek flooded for weeks and sometimes months and how Elliott, being just thirty kilometres south on the Stuart Highway and instantly more accessible, became the replacement centre. We danced and talked and laughed, oblivious of the hour until the unmistakable crow from the rooster timekeeper left us wondering if it was worth unrolling our swags.

Hours later, the inevitable farewells could not be postponed. With nostalgic memories and numerous rolls of film, Johnny headed south. With sore feet and husky voices, we returned home to muster the steers.

The visit of Daryl Somers and John Parche from the Beaufort Hotel was in place. From Kununurra John flew them around the spectacular and mysterious sandstone hills called the Bungle Bungles, shaped like vacated beehives and keepers of many ancient secrets. They landed at the Wave Hill Cricket Club for smoko before continuing to Riveren. When Frank Dalton telephoned their departure time, Becky and I prepared for their arrival.

Upon landing at our aerodrome, our visitors were confronted by their first real sense of isolation and vastness. Driving along the bumpy, dusty road, they strained their eyes into the distance for some hint of civilisation. Five minutes later, John turned left into Back Paddock where a delightfully natural Becky and her mother in full cocktail dress stood surrounded by curious Brahmans. I retrieved champagne from the trough, glasses were filled and the welcome toast proposed, before I drove Daryl home to the school radio over which countless children scattered throughout the Outback awaited his personal greeting. In the meantime, Fleck, our former poddy calf, had demolished an entire bowl of potato chips and was slobbering on the white lace tablecloth in search of more delicious treats. As the cattle moved forward, long pink tongues sought the bubbles from glasses and this unsurpassable welcome would become a great talking point for many years to come.

The married couple in the cottage seemed settled. He broke in some colts while she was content to work in the garden. The immediate problem was that the blackfellas only recognised one Boss, and that was John, or in his absence me. Just who threw the first punch we never knew, but the inevitable fight between the new overseeer and one of the stockmen did nothing to resolve the situation. It became a matter of balance and careful planning, which really contradicted the reason for creating the new position: to give us a reliable and responsible back-up who could operate competently without supervision. The overseer's frustration at lack of recognition of his status by the stockmen was transferred to me. It became particularly difficult in John's absence, when the overseer not only did not consult me, but ignored me altogether. More than one kind of storm cloud was looming on the horizon.

In the meantime, we were grateful for the opportunity to attend together Patrick's graduation Mass and dinner. There was nothing in the world to equal the voices of adolescent schoolboys accompanied by the extraordinary Joey's band. With dynamic exuberance the words soared as the drum rolled, trumpets blared and cymbals clanged.

> *'And He will raise you up on eagle's wings*
> *Bear you on the breath of dawn,*
> *Make you to shine like the sun,*
> *And hold you in the palm of His hand'*

Forever after, those memories would shoot shivers down my spine, over and over again.

Isolated storms teased as the Katherine School of the Air Christmas party and break up approached. On stage that night Michael was Donald Duck, and sounded more like the lovable duck than Donald himself. Marie and a friend performed a mime rendition of 'Time of My Life'. Big John had only to change his surname to Wayne and with wig and sequined bustier I dressed as Joan Collins. We met Buddy Holly, Whitney Houston, Elvis, the Three Amigos, Zorro and many more as we joined the noisy throng at the 'Who's Who, Celebrity Do'. There was much to celebrate and the rain drumming on the rooftops only enhanced the enthusiasm of the bush families mingling with teachers and the town community.

John left for his meeting in Adelaide, Marie travelled with him as far as Darwin, while Patrick and his fellow school leavers left Sydney for the traditional party week at Surfers. In the meantime, Michael, Becky and I purchased four tyres, two batteries, two thousand doses of botulism vaccine, one dozen cartons of beer and our bulk order at the food outlet. With one trolley each filled to capacity with Christmas goodies we loaded everything into the car. Bags of ice were bought to cover the perishables in eskies and there was not a spare space anywhere in the well-stacked, fully loaded vehicle. As always, the plan was that the cottage couple would notify us at our motel of any rain which could prevent us reaching home safely. Last thing before leaving town I checked at reception. There were no messages, so we departed without further ado, despite the threatening weather in Katherine and the dark bank of clouds that filled the western sky.

For hours we watched the brilliant and breathtaking electrical storms in the distance. Throughout the towering, snowy thunderheads the lightning zigzagged relentlessly. Beneath this volatile vault, the blackness of teeming rain blanketed the landscape as though to block it out. I was thankful that we were on the ground and not in the air.

It was slow going from the Riveren turn-off towards home and though it wasn't raining at the moment, it was obvious that it had rained more or less continually since our departure.

'Big rain here, Mum,' commented Michael. The eyes that would have lit up with the possibility of getting bogged in the days when he was little, when his brother was equally fired up with excitement and their father was behind the wheel, now expressed concern.

The steering wheel was spinning beneath my grip as I replied, 'It must surely be drier ahead, otherwise we would have heard that the road was dicey.' As the mud increased and the vehicle slewed and swished and swayed at a slowing pace, I considered turning back. Suddenly we stopped. I fiddled with the ignition, but to no avail. The engine was completely dead.

Beneath the raised bonnet we peered and poked, prodded and prayed. Everything seemed in order. From the glove box, I removed the manual and looked up 'In Case of an Emergency'. With each passing minute the rumbling of thunder drew closer and the blackish sky overhead obliterated any suggestion of sunlight. There was an ominous feeling in the air.

'I'm going for help,' Michael announced, and even as I objected he ran off. I called him back, but if he heard he gave no indication. We were twenty-five kilometres from the homestead.

Knowing that her role in all this was incidental, Becky climbed nonchalantly onto the roof of the car, lay on her back and beneath the angry, growling sky read her latest library book. She was as laid back as she was horizontal.

Restlessly I paced around and around. As I thought about John in his five-star hotel in Adelaide deliberating with colleagues on a better and fairer deal for beef producers, I gave the mud-congested tyre a hard kick. I thought about the cottage couple and knew there would be no rehearsal necessary for the things I would say when eventually we were face to face. Above all, I worried about Michael. He excelled at athletics, rowing and rugby and knew Riveren like the back of his hand, so his getting lost or exhausted was never my concern. Patrick had walked fifty kilometres back home on the blistering January day that he broke down and was the only one on the station. They were Riveren bred.

The river crossing was my worry. Heavy rain brought immediate swelling of waterholes and this river was thirteen kilometres our side of home. I worried that Michael might not get there before dark and it could well be running a banker anyway. Knowing that Michael would be annoyed with himself that he had been unable to fix the car, I was fearful that he might take unnecessary risks to get us home before dark.

Becky clasped her book with both hands as the rising winds plucked at the pages. As I stashed some firewood under the vehicle, the first raindrops fell. Quickly the torrential rain cancelled visibility as the arrival of the Wet Season was confirmed. With noses on windows, mother and daughter peered out at the world of water and hoped all over again that one son and brother was safe.

The ferocious mosquitoes were undeterred by any tactics. They buzzed and bit as we nibbled fruit and drank water, thankful that at least that wasn't a problem with billabongs and gilgais springing up all around us. It poured until midnight and I hoped that Michael had reached home before the deluge. Heavy drizzle followed, guaranteeing a saturated country.

All through the wet night I had wrestled with the thought that this fiasco had been avoidable. It was breaking day when an apparition loomed in the distance. The overseer had walked out to see if I wanted anything. He told me that Michael was asleep after his exhausting run, there had been a further two inches of rain before midnight and therefore it had been too wet to get a vehicle to us. After a glance at the engine he confessed mechanical ignorance, but was more than willing to walk us home. Walk us home? My sleepless night and very real fears crashed through any emotional reserve to which I had been clinging.

'Why didn't you ring and tell me about the rain?' hung in the air unanswered. His indifference really needled me.

'You're unbelievable!' As I shouted furiously, he turned his back. I was yelling to myself. Away in the distance, he called some indecipherable words, before disappearing around the bend in the road.

'We're next Beck,' I said. 'Too bad about the turkey and ham. We need to get to a phone to contact Dad who will be worried about us if he tried to ring home last night. Home sounds good. Reckon you can handle the walk?' She nodded.

It was unbelievably hot and walking in mud was slow. All the gullies were running and each footstep grew heavier than the last until the clods of mud fell off, making room for more clinging clay to stick to our boots. The humidity was like a rock around our necks and fit as we were, Beck and I were both sweating profusely. We walked for two hours before she became tired. After a quick rest I urged her onwards. It was growing hotter and steamier every hour. We struggled on for another ten kilometres before I heard a distinctive sound. Faint and faraway as it was, the throbbing chopper was audible long before it was visible. I guessed that my knight in his new suit had at some stage discovered our plight and contacted Helimuster at Victoria River Downs to send a rescue helicopter. The pilot confirmed my theory. He ferried us home, then the overseer, and finally the defrosted festive foodstuffs.

Within a week John returned with Marie and Patrick. Everyone's blisters healed and the cottage was vacated. Record rains for December visibly revived the cattle, filled rivers and creeks and revitalised the initial shoots of growth emerging from drenched soils. There could be no greater joy than the prospect of a green Christmas.

It was wonderful to have Marie, Patrick, Michael and Becky home. On my birthday they urged me to go with John to inspect the artificially inseminated heifers. Suspecting a combined cake-making performance, I complied. We were only away for three-quarters of an hour and were alarmed to return to red eyes and trembling lips.

'It's Cuddles. We thought she was asleep under the house and didn't know why she wouldn't come when we called her. We crawled under and found out that she's dead. Cuddles is dead.'

When they handed me the biggest and most gorgeous birthday card I had ever received, there were messages of love from the four of them, interspersed with dogs' paws and cat's paws and peacock prints. Only Cuddles was missing. It was a kaleidoscope of messages from the inhabitants of my world.

CHAPTER 19

AN INLAND SEA

....

S he was gone. For me the whole homestead and the entire station were empty. Like a ship without an anchor, I meandered and tottered and vacillated. Our youngest had joined the schoolgirls in uniform at Kincoppal Rose Bay, Convent of the Sacred Heart. I was drawn to Becky's bedroom in the need to be close to her.

Our school room remained vibrant. Its walls were adorned with every imaginable art and craft work and gymkhana ribbons accumulated over the years when ponies Denim, Boxing Gloves, Tit and Whiskey carried their riders around barrels and pegs. Show awards and merit cards covered every spare space. However, the chairs and desks were unoccupied and after our eighteen-year-long journey the school radio had been returned to Katherine.

I had written the words of a school song and teacher Doug Fudge composed the accompanying music. That was our farewell gift of gratitude to the learning institution that was not just a school, but a way of life.

A degree of salvation was inevitable because of the very nature of our existence. There was no place for self-indulgence or self-pity. While I stood immersed in misery, John called out that he needed a hand with the floodgates at Revolver Creek. All the stationhands were busy on a new fence line and late rain had swollen the creek, washing down the section of fence that crossed the watercourse. In our kind of country many fence lines crossed creeks and despite reinforcement with flattened drums hanging from heavy cables strung from tree to tree, 'flood-gates' as they were called, seldom withstood the increased pressure and water level associated with heavy rain. Floodgates required constant maintenance during the wet season in order to keep cattle in the correct paddocks.

Grabbing my camera and extra film, I pulled on gumboots and hurried outside. John patted the seat beside him.

'So now you're about to rediscover Riveren. Considering your school commitments you've kept up well; however, there's so much to show you, new fences and laneways, roads and troughs.'

I took a deep breath knowing he was right, but as our wheels squelched and churned through the mud, I wondered if Becky was warm enough. Patrick had been interminably cold in Sydney and I had never known he was in the infirmary or why until afterwards. Was anyone checking Becky's bed at night to see if she was covered?

'Hello, gate here Terry,' John's voice intruded. When I jumped back in beside him, he squeezed my knee.

'She'll make it, just like the others. Stop worrying.'

For many years, we had been intimately involved with changes sought and wrought in the name of progress. Nevertheless, we were one of the few stations to still employ Aboriginal workers. Since their walk-off from Wave Hill all those years ago, everything had changed for all of us. Vincent Lingiari, with his unmistakable dignity, had won the respect of all people when he led the movement for self-determination. His appeal for equality sought the unity of all people. Vincent said he wanted everyone to be happy. His intentions were applauded by those who understood and by those who thought they did.

Though we had suffered from rapid turnover of workers for the last few years, some regulars returned to Riveren year after year. One such individual was Frankie McHale.

One evening Frankie seemed particularly pleased with himself. Beneath unruly fuzzy hair, his chubby features split into creases as he made a bee-line towards me.

'I'm a proper father now Terry, little girl eh. You can guess what I call my daughter?'

I was thrilled for Frankie. Ever since our discussion after Henry's death, we had been good friends. However this was far more difficult than Rumpelstiltskin's game. At length I shrugged and admitted defeat.

'Well I call her Ribreena, after this place here, my favourite place.'

We were all very touched.

Frankie loved Precious too, and reckoned he wouldn't mind a dog like her, especially after she had saved his life. He had almost trodden on the giant king brown lying in the shadow of a fuel drum, when the rotund blue heeler had pounced, attacked and killed. I discovered the triumphant dog racing around the house dragging from her mouth the ripped and bloodied reptile as though she was enacting some kind of a victory ceremony. She was so proud of herself and from that day became the 'snake dog'. Big snakes, little snakes, none escaped Precious. She ferreted them out from unlikely places and her cunning and fearlessness gathered momentum and praise simultaneously. John's comment that very few snake dogs live to old age simply provided food for thought, because there was no way this growing obsession of Precious could be controlled.

No sooner had I mentioned a mate for the snake dog than David Bradley, our good friend and vet involved in the Brucellosis and Tuberculosis Eradication Campaign, organised it. We all fell instantly in love with the velvety, jet black puppy who, though only weeks old, already stood taller than a mildly resentful Precious. There were very few Great Danes in the tropics and we were now the unexpected owners of one. There was no disagreement about her name, although Mandela was quickly shortened to Mandy. She was lanky and languid and although terrified of disapproval, she was the fussiest eater on Riveren.

Soon after, we acquired yet another pet. Before John left to destroy the adult feral donkeys in the trap paddock, I begged for any babies to be brought home. Now two very long ears were all I could see. As I walked towards the back of the vehicle, the gorgeous little donkey came into full view. Wounded in two places by the same ricocheting bullet, she was sore and frightened. Mandy was next to greet the latest new arrival, gently sniffing and inspecting the strange furry creature that was almost the same height as herself.

Donkey, or Donk as the boys called her, healed slowly. Initially she took her place beside the poddy calves, noisily sucking Denkavite from the bottle, or beer from the bottle, or whatever was on offer. She grew quickly and regularly challenged me in her game of 'chicken'. She was slow to learn that I was always first to move as she charged towards me across the flat.

Our response was guarded to the question, 'What would you like if you could have it?' The survey of needs by Telecom almost seemed unreal. Our lives were about to be totally revolutionised. Beside the radio-telephone tower stretched a taller one. The technicians followed to install the Digital Radio Concentrator System which allowed a radio signal to be transmitted from tower to tower built at strategic distances. Finally we had a normal telephone with a normal dial tone. No listening audience, no operator, no weather interference, no booking queue, no time limit.

I couldn't wait to share this most thrilling advance in our communication system. Mum and Dad were so surprised with the clear connection they thought I had arrived unexpectedly in Sydney. The three friends whom I rang next all responded similarly after initial greetings.

'Good heavens, this call must be costing a fortune,' and they hung up. Their conversations continued uninterrupted to friends and neighbours through normal communication channels, while I sat beside our new telephone and continued to talk to myself.

Almost a decade after the first day of play, the Wave Hill Cricket Club was officially opened by one of its greatest fans, Daryl Somers. We travelled over to join slightly fewer than one thousand lovers of cricket in the renovated Long Room. Sadly, the patron, Alan McGilvray, was unable to attend; however, number one badge holder and former Australian wicket-keeper, Rod Marsh, led one of the four competing teams over the weekend. Visiting umpires Max O'Connell and Tony Crafter were suitably impressed with the staying power of one and all.

On the final evening, we reluctantly farewelled the cricketers and their fans. Returning with us to Riveren were our good friends from Sinka Tinny Downs, Ted Egan and Nerys Evans, and of course the 'Hey Hey' guru who loved Riveren with a passion. The new stockcamp cook materialised minutes after our arrival. This man of silence known as Chatterbox stood at the gate repeating the word 'Shatterday' over and over again. His agitation and verbosity were puzzling. Presuming that he wanted the store which opened on Saturdays, I told him I'd open up in the morning.

'Nothing store,' he said excitedly, 'that Shatterday man there, look now.'

Daryl was absolutely delighted to meet the old black man with the long white beard, who had lived in town and regularly watched his show.

'Hello, Chatterbox. How long have you been at Riveren?'

'Might be six months now,' replied the man who had arrived four days earlier.

Six months later, Daryl telephoned to wish his friend Chatterbox a happy centenary. It was too late, for Chatterbox had returned to town. Upon his departure he delivered his final verbal outburst.

'See ya Boss, Missus. I might be pensioner. I'm gone now.'

Theatrical productions were automatically assumed to be a part of whatever I organised. Through the Beef Bash, the annual Cattlemen's Association dinner, I had created parades depicting the history of our industry, parades of lovely legs, and fashion parades. The combination of the serious and hilarious was understood and appreciated by fun-loving cattlemen and cattlewomen, who adopted and even expanded my scripts and instructions for their stage performances. I had also researched and presented on stage and in booklet form 'Twenty-Five Years of Katherine School of the Air'. Memories surfaced from teachers and families past and present as they reunited to ensure a mammoth and momentous celebration on stage that was documented for all time. In all, I had orchestrated a total of seventeen stage productions and industry dinners since *Dimboola*.

However, the most important production of my life was the joint celebration of John's fiftieth and Marie's twenty-first birthdays. In the bush-bedecked ballroom of the Beaufort Hotel, Patrick as master of ceremonies gonged our old station dinner bell to urge people to their seats. Each table or watering hole was symbolically named after a Riveren bore.

On stage Pat proudly stood beside Peg who, sitting in an old rocking chair, nursed an infant John replica. I invited everyone to rest easy in their saddles as we commenced our journey down an old cattle pad, retracing a small passage of history. Around the glowing embers of a camp fire, we shared the thoughts of a stockman named John as he sat silently sifting through the day already done and planning tomorrow's mob.

The chapters unfolded as the past loomed before us. Just as Michael and his young cousin Mitch depicted John at various ages and stages, so did Becky and her cousin Nicole portray Marie. There was no stone unturned and little left unsaid. The night of sheer magic galloped away as it transported two lives and more than one hundred onlookers through memories of love and hope, heartache and happiness.

It was a tribute owed John, a proven great stallion, and Marie, a very sound filly, for as long as I had known them.

Too few families were able to visit Riveren, so we were delighted when Dr Richard Condon, who had performed minor surgery on Michael in Sydney, his wife Phillipa and their young son Danny came to share the Riveren experiences we cherished so dearly.

Dick immediately assumed a role as John's useful helper, while Phillipa and Danny, armed with binoculars and notebook, joined me in the car twice daily as we observed specially selected cows set aside in Stallion Paddock for embryo transplantation.

Driving around, I explained to Phillipa that artificial breeding facilitated rapid genetic improvement and easy access to new bloodlines in a herd. Artificial insemination and embryo transplantation required the same detailed preparation and programme. As we were all interested in modern technology, this current trial was important to implement and evaluate. It promised the advantages of superior sires and cross breeding without the capital outlay on new bulls. As a fascinated young Danny watched the cows mounting each other, his mother recorded the appropriate ear tag numbers.

Observations complete, we all sprawled at random on the front lawn as behind us breathtaking skies shuttered the burnishing sun, changing our surroundings from pure gold to gentle neutrals. The unspoken bond that existed between friends was all powerful. We listened to chattering butcher birds, miners and pee wees busily preparing for night-fall. The ineffable peace was suddenly shattered by the telephone. The volume of the outside siren designed to reach the stockyards commanded an immediate response. I ran inside. It was Marie.

'Have you heard the terrible news, Mum?'

I explained that we had been out with cattle all day and only just returned.

'What is it Marie? Tell me darling,' I urged, willing her to continue.

'Dr Victor Chang has been murdered. Everyone is so shocked. No details yet, I just wanted you to know.'

Victor, resident medical officer when I met John in Ward 3. Victor, brilliant heart surgeon and charismatic humanitarian. Slowly I returned to the tranquil group to deliver the dreadful tidings. Nobody spoke. Disbelief reigned. Retired honorary surgeon Richard Condon, retired theatre sister Phillipa, ex St Vincent's patient many times over John, and I the graduate nurse struggled to absorb this nightmare. Tears silently fell for Victor's family and those patients whose need of his skills would be left unanswered. In the middle of nowhere a small but strong St Vincent's contingent stormed heaven with prayers for our former colleague and friend, and all involved.

In the specialised field of embryo transplants, James Loneragan was a recognised pioneer. He, his wife Liz, a biochemist, and family had promised to visit us ever since our initial meeting in the dormitory where Marie and Sophie had commenced boarding in Year 7. They finally arrived and it was marvellous to have a diverse group of people with cattle and kids as common denominators. It was school holidays and every bed was filled. From long-term drought, our trickle of visitors had reached flood proportions.

John's pride and joy, the shed, former home for the carpenters and ourselves, was now converted into a laboratory. Liz was adept with her microscope as she checked the viability of the fertilised egg or embryo in the frozen straws carefully removed from the container of liquid nitrogen. We had chosen big roomy cows that were not in calf for the conception and rearing of another breed. Our observation records had identified the cows in season and they were now in the yard. I recorded details of each sire and cow as James, using an insemination gun or pistolette, implanted an embryo into each recipient.

The outcome was something almost beyond contemplation. We had yet to see at Riveren a pure Simmental calf sucking on its mother, one of our Brahman cows. Embryo transplantation was heady stuff and to acknowledge new horizons, we celebrated accordingly.

Prior to their departure from their properties down south, I had mentioned the idea of a surprise black tie lunch in the paddocks to Phillipa and Liz. They had been instantly enthusiastic and agreeable. John and James, when presented with the idea, were sceptical, if not downright discouraging.

'Terry, if you think we're going to dress formally for lunch, you'd better think again.'

Phillipa chose that moment to float down the hall in a sweeping, coquettish, apricot chiffon ball gown. She was attended by her handsome, distinguished husband and cute young son, both in black trousers and braces over white shirts with black bow ties. Liz and Sophie joined the lounge room gathering, looking stunning in black with silver sequins. The giggles and groans from the verandah suggested that the Underwood and Loneragan teenagers had decided to cancel further objections. Outflanked, John decided on a clever compromise.

'Anyone over six foot three can wear shorts below formal shirts,' he announced.

Upon our arrival at Hut Creek Paddock, Jerome, the Brahman bull, and his cows were unconcerned by the large group of unusually clad people. The majestic sire immediately moved towards John who in consultation with James proceeded to estimate his testicular circumference and discuss other features of this most impressive bull. When the two giants in shorts moved away towards the cows to discuss their Brahman purity, Becky stood behind Jerome and continued to stroke him. As his tail lifted higher and higher with pleasure, a fearless Danny was lifted onto his massive back behind the large muscular hump and the little boy's smile denoted that the world was his kingdom. Jerome had always had an exceptional temperament. Most bulls would object to such close human contact. As we ladies strode in high heels and black stockings around and through cow manure, some of the heifers followed, attempting to nuzzle shoulders and hair. The biggest and quietest cow on Riveren, Tina, chewed on my old straw hat as though it was her own private portable hay bale.

Across the trough, I looked at my man as I mentally reaffirmed that every day with him was a bonus. John sensed my gaze and our eyes locked. Our awareness of the value of each moment had been brought home all over again with the senseless loss of Victor. I thought of our little angel, Martin, of Tony Noonan and my Dad who recently had been called to his just reward. The depth of loss cannot be measured or lessened by any circumstance. That day we all celebrated life and love and friendship, surrounded by inquisitive cattle and the backdrop of the beyond that stretched forever.

In Sydney another meaningful meeting of friends took place. Nursing mates assembled for the first time in thirty years. My close friend Ros had not only faultlessly followed her religious vocation, but was now the Mother Provincial of the Franciscan Missionaries of Mary in Australia. Thus it was at the beautifully appointed Missionary House at Point Piper that we assembled for Mass, dinner and an overnight stay that included very little sleep. There were so many stories to relate and share and those told by Ros of her missionary years in Indonesia were inspirational. In the chapel we renewed our graduation pledge to do all in our power to alleviate the pain of those entrusted to our care, to be generous, cheerful and eager to console. Then we sang the St Vincent's Hospital song. The faith, enthusiasm and dedication that changed our lives three decades ago bonded us still.

At the same time, Becky had returned to boarding school with a mature acceptance of the inevitable, and memories of another wonderfully happy holiday at home.

John was ready to leave Sydney immediately, but for me returning without children still meant leaving part of me behind. Our departure was delayed by a special dinner invitation from friends Jim and Sue, who had thoughtfully co-ordinated a surprise reunion with some almost forgotten mates.

My last image of Margaret and Michael O'Rourke had been the front page newspaper photo of radiant bride and beaming groom, undeterred by the drenching rains of a grey and gloomy city. Now as we gathered around the dining room table beneath a splendid crystal chandelier, the number of years from then until now instantly dissipated.

Margaret and I scarcely drew breath as our treasured common backgrounds of Albury childhood and St Vincent's nursing training were recaptured and relived. As the Hickey and Augustus families had been resolute 'pillars of the parish', she and I had knelt before the same statues in the same Albury church, beside the same confessional windows and sat at the same school desks.

At St Vincent's we had met our men. Michael, the seriously dedicated intern, now sat beside me as Professor of Medicine, with a warm, mischievous smile that confirmed his affinity with the land of the shamrock.

In an atmosphere charged with comradeship, entertaining raconteurs and reunited friends conversed with unflagging enthusiasm. Our senses were saturated. Surely every possible topic of conversation had been covered, when out of the blue Margaret leaned towards John and mentioned almost casually that her own family had had a stake in the far North. John was instantly all ears.

The subsequent discovery that her mother's brother, Charles Pite, had worked for the Quiltys was astonishing. His life, remarkably like John's, had centred largely around isolated stockcamps with long letters home revealing the nature of the young man and his challenges. After seven years he had planned to return home for the Christmas of 1934. However, in the untamed land that even today takes no pity on man, woman or child, Charles was tragically killed on the first leg of that flight home. He was buried where he perished, in an unmarked grave at Ord River Station, not far from Riveren by Outback standards.

We heard that Charles had followed in the footsteps of his two uncles, the McHale brothers, established in the North since the late 1890s. Half caste children proudly bore their name. When Margaret asked if we had heard of the McHales, John and I both spoke at once. Unbelievably we had discovered that 'little bit Irish way back' connection that Frankie claimed with such fervour; Frankie who had devotedly worked beside us for the past decade. The circles of Albury and St Vincent's and Riveren were getting smaller.

This magical thread could never be broken as the ghosts and mists of yesteryear surfaced to affect us all. The past was powerfully resurrected and seeds planted for future memories defying all prediction.

Another day was under way and as we headed towards our space and freedom, we felt certain that we would see Margaret Hickey O'Rourke again.

Goodbye Becky, little girl, keep your chin up. Goodbye Patrick, good luck at uni, and goodbye dearest Mum, I silently whispered as we wended our way north on the Pacific Highway.

Optimism swelled with the approach of every Wet Season. After abundant rains gave us a beneficial start, the follow-up storms formed and heavy daily showers continued to soak the country. Hay coloured grasses changed to green, the perennial Mitchell grasses grew and blossomed, the annual Flinders grasses appeared and newborn calves frolicked and played. An explosion of wildflowers of every hue was guaranteed. Our family would be united at home for Christmas and the time of year we loved best.

Many of the artificially inseminated cows were overdue. We put them in the laneway in order to keep an eye on them, as their calves were by superior Brahman bulls. No-one could have predicted the extreme weather over the following days. The deep cracks in the ground had long since filled, the creeks were running, the rainwater tanks were overflowing and still more water fell from the sky. It was too boggy for vehicles and so we walked daily, sometimes twice daily, the four or five kilometres to check the 'maternity ward'. Some of these Brahmans usually noted for natural mothering ability were wet and cold and confused, and subsequently ignored their newborn calves.

This family Sunday outing consisted of ploughing through knee-high mud to check the same mob. They were at the end of the laneway and although in the distance the calves seemed to be mothered up, we continued the full seven kilometres just to make sure. Beneath a bush lay a little calf just hours old with no obvious mother. We walked on until we found the cow that had freshly given birth, then ushered her back to her little one. She sniffed her calf. Then with total lack of interest she walked away. John suggested that perhaps our absence would assist more than our presence and so we trudged home. Towards dark the brisk winds strengthened and the cold rain continued to fall. Becky was desperately worried about the last calf. She and Michael decided to carry out a final check on horseback as the terrible night ahead would severely test any new arrival.

In rapidly fading light they found the desolate calf unwanted and unnourished. Michael dismounted from Simone. Tenderly he picked up the gangly, shivering mass and, talking all the while to the calf and Becky's horse Bliss, he lifted the calf and positioned it in front of Becky. Bliss, a lovely quiet horse, did not object to the extra passenger until they started moving. It was so slippery that the mare had trouble staying upright, but reassured by Becky she plodded towards the yards.

'Keep going Beck,' shouted Michael over the whipping winds, 'I'll hunt up the mother and a mate for her in the rear. See you at home.'

The calf had found Becky's sleeve and was sucking on it. The warmth of her body and the rocking movement combined to lull it to sleep. Becky's gentle voice and firm hands encouraged Bliss onwards through the greedy squelching mud. It was becoming wetter by the minute and several times the brave mare stumbled, once she fell to her knees, but somehow picked herself up and kept going.

The exhausted calf was undisturbed by the sounds of the yard gates closing. He awoke only when lowered to the ground and ushered towards his mother now standing in the crush. The basic sucking instinct surfaced as he nibbled before grasping his mother's teat to release the warm milk. As it spurted down his throat, his tail wagged joyfully and his tummy visibly filled. The cow was unconcerned as she was shepherded into the shelter of the stables. She lay beside her sleeping calf, chewing contentedly and seemingly oblivious of her baby and the wild weather outside.

Next morning a grey-coated sky greeted us all. As we unlatched the stable gate we found the mother in one corner butting her poor little calf away in complete rejection. The weak calf toppled and fell and the cow did the most extraordinary thing. She twisted back and sucked from her two front teats.

Becky prepared some Denkavite for the calf we'd named George, while I let the mother into the big yard to join a few mates. Perhaps there she would settle down and regain her sanity; however, that expectation was dashed even as we watched. She walked over to another lactating cow, one of the quietest cows of all, and drank from her as though a newborn calf herself.

'We'll bush that mongrel cow when it dries out,' decided John.

'I wonder if she'll rear other calves,' said Becky.

With a foolproof memory for individual cattle, she would monitor the situation.

'Moo!' George looked longingly at his mother in the distance. Then he responded to the trusted hands and familiar voice of his rescuer from the night before. He did not like the hard teat she gently placed in his mouth, but it gave warm milk and he sucked hungrily. Mandy and Precious, like professionally trained bodyguards, sat on either side of this newest family addition, licking the bubbles from his lips and keeping him warm.

A tropical depression hovered over Riveren and the heavens opened day and night. George bellowed loudly after his last bottle for the evening and we sat beside him for a while. The tin roof amplified the pelting rain and in silence we contemplated the weather over which we had no control.

George died even as the life-giving rains continued to fall. Unheard of amounts of rain became daily occurrences as we recorded falls of four inches, three inches and eight inches consecutively. We could hear the roaring of the creek over the roaring of the winds. The depression moved off the coast and uncannily returned to Riveren.

People from the weather bureau and emergency services rang regularly for rainfall readings, in order to forewarn others further downstream the mighty Victoria that the floods were far from over. Torrents of water continued to fill the already overburdened watercourse, a brown rumbling raging river that gouged new channels as it choked the old. A shallow lake formed between our buildings and all the roads were awash. Thankfully, our store and cold room were filled to capacity as the need to be organised for a big Wet was reinforced.

A further six inches of rain in four hours caused enormous damage as trees lining water holes snapped like matchsticks, changing the face of the waterways of Riveren. Creeks and rivers spilled across the land, depositing debris, later proof of the breadth and depth of the floods. Low clouds, high winds and ongoing downpours gave everything a sense of unreality. This immense expanse of water fuelled the depression that was not in any hurry to change its stationary status.

That night John and I lay in bed listening with disbelief to the incessant teeming rain. At daylight I measured a fall of six and a half inches. As I recorded the rainfall, I wrote in the diary. 'As far as the eye can see, it looks like an inland sea.'

CHAPTER 20

INEXTRICABLY LINKED

....

'Anyone would think we were breeding bloody peacocks,' muttered John as another mother with another brood crossed his path. True to predictions, the multiplication of these birds was indefatigable. Their common irritating characteristic was nightlong boisterous honking from the tree tops, the prelude to mating. In the ensuing weeks the mother was rarely seen, hidden in her cleverly camouflaged nest until hatching commenced. As soon as the babies were free of the shell, she vacated the nest and they followed.

'I know she was sitting on six eggs because I found the nest when I was checking the drip line watering system,' observed Becky as she counted five chicks. When the nest was rechecked, there was one egg intact. Becky kept an eye on the deserted egg.

Finally the baby broke out into an empty world, a world devoid of feathers and warmth and love. Becky gently picked up the scraggly chick and tracked down its mother and siblings.

They showed no recognition or interest in the clumsy feathered bundle that wobbled slowly after them. Becky tried repeatedly to mate them up until the weak little one fell asleep in the palm of her hand. That night she herded the new family into the 'hospital wing' of the chook yard and slipped the straggler beneath its mother's wing, where it gladly joined its family in bed. Mother was unquestioning and Becky and I breathed a sigh of relief.

However, next morning in her urgent quest for food and freedom, Mrs Peacock had fled. Only the late arrival was left. Several more attempts to reunite the orphan with its family proved hopeless. As Becky sat nursing her latest baby, Precious moved closer to sniff and inspect the fluffy, feathered bundle.

Precious quickly became completely besotted. It was hard to believe that this was the snake executioner sitting totally mesmerised as the baby bird nestled against her bulging, warm, blue tummy. We watched, hardly daring to breathe in case she pounced or rolled on or gulped down the tiny chick. With ironical timing, Mother and family stalked past without a glance in our direction. As though convinced of her new role, Precious repositioned herself. The little bird sat between her front paws, then later played in the tufts of grass under the watchful gaze of the doting bitch. Finally it nestled in between her back legs for a deep sleep. Precious assumed the role of motherhood with surprising tenderness, for she had never been mated.

The two were inseparable. At night the weary overweight dog stretched out long before the rapidly growing chick had finished somersaulting and slippery-dipping down a furry back and hind legs. Normal canine pursuits were put on hold and snakes slithered past safely at a distance beyond challenge. Mandy watched in puzzlement as her friend became full-time mother and guardian and mate to a scurrying, cheeping creature. It was difficult to dissuade Precious from her natural instinct to lick her baby, for this particular baby did not relish the wetness.

No-one knew why after weeks and weeks of this extraordinary relationship the little bird died. Precious could not understand why her baby lay motionless. We hastily buried the tiny creature that had brought so much joy to us all. As, teary-eyed, we erected the usual stick cross and placed bush flowers on the fresh mound, Precious sat on the grave with her head buried between her front paws. She was still there when the extended peacock family arrived to pay their respects. Forever after, Precious trailed each new peacock family in the hope that her baby would return to her.

We were shocked when Dorothy Sing rang to tell us that Sabu had been tragically killed in a road accident. Throughout the following weeks her incredible strength never faltered and Dorothy's private grief at losing her husband, best friend and mate could only be surmised.

People came from everywhere, blackfellas and whitefellas, all to mourn the passing of a good friend. They wore their Sunday best and almost every individual carried flowers or a piece of greenery. In his eulogy, John marvelled at Sabu's gentleness and dignity and his ability to cope with a complexity of problems. His outstanding horsemanship reflected his life as a true bushman, a man who interacted and coped with two peoples and two cultures. Sabu had epitomised a bridge, in many ways he was the bridge. Sabu, a part-Aboriginal man, had lived in both the black and white worlds with family and friends in both. He was born Mele, named by his mother of the Wardaman tribe; he was later called Harold, then Sabu by his foster father Tom Fisher, a Vestey station manager. When Dorothy and Sabu were married, his name was changed to Peter David. Sabu was like a brother to Ralph Hayes and a friend to all people. He was a true son of the Territory. His death was mourned by all who knew, respected and loved him. In four special young adults—the children of Sabu and Dorothy—his spirit will live on.

After he was laid to rest beneath a shady gum tree in the new Katherine cemetery, we joined the hundreds upon hundreds of people departing for the wake. I looked back for a final goodbye to see an old cattle dog sitting by the open grave. Even as I watched, he settled his head on his paws, reaffirming his intention to stay with his mate and master.

Too soon we mourned another lost friend. Noel Buntine's death was sudden and caused shock waves of disbelief throughout the country. The mighty pioneer who ran life's race at a scorching pace had an inimitable smile and style and had made a mighty contribution.

Sometime after the official burial service in Katherine, Noel was finally laid to rest. On the corner of the Victoria Highway and old Delamere Road to Top Springs, hundreds of people gathered for the naming of the Buntine Highway. A twenty-three tonne granite boulder with an inlaid bronze plaque featuring an inscribed B-model Mack roadtrain now marks the turn-off.

Yesterday and today will now forge renewed ties with the crossing of the Buchanan Highway and the Buntine Highway at Top Springs. Boss Drover and Roadtrain Pioneer will be thus honoured for all time.

It had not taken us long to discover the whereabouts of the small unmarked grave within sight of the Ord River Station buildings yet hidden from the road and world at large. We telephoned Margaret Hickey O'Rourke in Sydney and plans were completed for the Hickey family pilgrimage.

From their moment of arrival at Riveren we were struck by the warmth and love so obvious between Mrs Hickey, who still lived in Albury, and her four adult children. Knowing Margaret should have prepared us for the calibre of her family. They embodied a sense of honour, respect and devotion too seldom seen in the rush and bustle and preoccupation of the 1990s.

It was an incredible meeting between these five and Frankie McHale. This little bit Irish stockman, father of Ribreena, clasped the hands of his 'lations' from down south with undisguised emotion. They were equally overwhelmed. Beneath a cloudless pure blue sky in an unwavering landscape they stood together on warm red ochre soil, six people for whom the rest of the world did not exist. That was the way it was carved in their souls—we are all inextricably linked.

Next day John and I accompanied them on another special journey. Mrs Hickey and her children farewelled her brother Charles as they marked his grave with the headstone brought from Sydney. It was almost sixty years since he had perished at Ord River Station. As our friends continued west to visit the established family headstone which acknowledged the McHale brothers as Kimberley pioneers, we returned to Riveren to see if Michael had installed the new motor.

With top marks Michael had completed his Associate Diploma in Beef Cattle Management at Emerald Agricultural College. It was more than a natural progression to return home to stand tall beside his father. It was his calling.

Meanwhile, Patrick was nearing completion of his Bachelor of Commerce degree at the University of New South Wales. Although he missed home with feelings almost defying definition, Patrick coped with the crowds and lecture theatres and the culture of the city of Sydney.

After years of consideration, we had finally purchased a helicopter which Michael soon mastered. This machine would make all of our country accessible at all times of the year. The plane, although useful for aerial surveys, was housed in the hangar on an all-weather airstrip. However the road to our aerodrome was sometimes too wet and boggy for us to reach the plane.

The floodgate situation changed dramatically with the use of the chopper. The same big falls of rain that washed away floodgates usually made the roads impassable. Now the workers could land anywhere and fix cables and fences, hopefully before cattle had wandered through to another paddock.

However even the helicopter was outmanoeuvred by the Barons of the Bush. These rogue old piker bullocks were a breed unto themselves. They were masters of survival. For years they had hidden in the thick turpentine scrub on top of the jump up. With marvellous cunning, they had eluded man. At the sound of an engine, they lay immobile in the scrub and closed their eyes so that no-one would see them. They had avoided every muster and escaped the Brucellosis and Tuberculosis Eradication Programme shoot-outs. John decided their time had come.

By fencing off the main spring and pumping dry the ancient, almost inaccessible rockholes with the fire fighter, all cattle were forced to water at a trough. This watering point already had a trap yard incorporating spears erected around it. These spears were positioned to allow cattle onto water, but not back out again. Those that did not enter through the trap spears to water were shot before they perished. And so they were finally captured.

Their eyes reflected their untamed spirit. Their enormous curved and misshapen horns acted as hooks as they moved with difficulty up the loading ramps. Those wild old pikers were somehow noble in defeat. As we loaded them onto the double decker roadtrains, another notch was etched in our history. A month later at the Katherine Show, we were thrilled to receive the blue ribbon for our pen of dehorned Brahman steers. They had won first place in the live export steer competition for market suitability.

At the Darwin Performing Arts Centre I was preparing my inaugural photographic exhibition, entitled The Cattle Kingdom. Fifty black and white and twenty-six coloured photographs were catalogued and ready to hang. My excitement intensified as arrangements for the official opening by our good friend Daryl Somers were finalised. On the day before Marie was to leave Riveren to join me, she rang with news that brought me back to earth with a jolt. An aggressive king brown had bitten Precious on her lip, seconds before she killed it. The report that our lovable dog had initially staggered slightly, but now seemed all right was vaguely reassuring.

'Try not to worry, Mum,' said Marie, 'I've spoken to a vet and there's nothing we can do except wait and hope. You know I'll stay with her. I'll ring you soon with an update.'

Several hours later Precious died. There was no struggle, no distress. She lay down on Mandy's large mattress and with Marie and Mandy alongside, our faithful friend quietly sighed and closed her eyes. I cried and wished that I was home to help bury her beside Kyber, Ratsy, Bett, Cuddles and the peacock chick. People who think animals are replaceable are wrong.

My week long exhibition was more successful than I'd dared hope. It was encouraging to know that people were interested in and moved by my images that not only highlighted the dramatic changes in our industry and lifestyle, but paid tribute to the members of the cattle team.

With a new camera, I continued to photograph regularly, capturing from helicopter or stockyards extraordinary as well as ordinary glimpses of our everyday lives. Through my camera lens I hoped to take remote rural Australia to the rest of the world. It was another important tune to beat on my rural drum.

Just as I was walking out of my hotel room to return home, my sister-in-law Janelle telephoned.

'We're flying to Dunmarra first thing in the morning. Little Clinton Liebelt disappeared at lunch time yesterday. Everyone thought he'd be found by the aircraft or ground party today. They found his trail bike, but not him. Terry, you've been through it with Becky. Tell me what I should say to our friends Steve and Adele.'

Yes, I knew too well what it was like. Another savagely hot dry October was under way with daily temperatures in the high forties. There could be no worse time for someone to go missing. John and I headed straight to Dunmarra too.

Hundreds of people had assembled at 'Horrie's' Dunmarra roadhouse. Police, emergency services and countless volunteers were fed by teams of helpers. The little eight year old was lost in Murranji country, the Drovers' Ghost Track, with scrub and timber so dense and hostile that men and women on foot conducted line searches. Stockmen on horseback gradually penetrated the thick lancewood, spinifex and bulwaddy country, searching in painstaking detail. Overhead several planes and numerous helicopters with spotters aboard scanned the brutal country over and over again.

Ringers, acclimatised and tough, came from every station including Riveren to search. Bus loads of town people, schoolteachers, tourists, ministers of religion, nursing sisters and a doctor all joined in. Food, drinks, aviation fuel and diesel were donated by local businesses. The normal daily practices of hundreds of people were placed on hold in the desperate need to find one Territory child. His jeans and boots were found twelve kilometres west of the roadhouse, but still they did not find the little boy. Reports of fresh tracks renewed hope, even when it seemed impossible for anyone to survive the terrible temperatures in some of the harshest terrain known to man.

It was a week to the day since Clinton had gone missing and many searchers were recalled home. Some of the stockmen from Newcastle Waters Station ignored their instructions. They were so emotionally and physically embroiled that they could not leave until the little boy was laid to rest. With fresh horses and passionate determination they forced their way further west. Two days later they came across a white motorcycle helmet glinting on the parched ground. Soon after, Clinton's body was found by these young men.

The church in Katherine overflowed with people and tears. Clinton had wanted to be a ringer and his favourite Garth Brooks song 'Lonesome Dove' was played at the funeral. One young school friend placed on the coffin an envelope containing money for Clinton to buy a drink on his way to heaven. The little boy who had been petrified of the dark was now safely in the care and keeping of his Creator.

The congregation moved as one to the garden area outside the Katherine School of the Air. This small park was later dedicated to Clinton's memory. Steve and Adele eventually returned home to once again stand before the tree outside their bedroom window. On the morning he was last seen trying to give his Dad a hand to recapture two horses that had broken free, Clinton had carved into that trunk a face with a big smile.

We felt so much for those who lost their battles. We had been blatantly put on notice several times, but thankfully spared, over and over again.

John had written in the diary the countdown of days until my fiftieth birthday. He asked if I wanted another F Party. I thought it was time and a good excuse to see if we could cope away from home. We set in place plans to journey overseas with friends who were experienced travellers. However, nothing in the bush was simple. Many arrangements had to be made as cattle activities were in full swing. Also I was worried about my forthcoming encounter with water. Living on the edge of the Tanami Desert for three decades had provided neither the temptation nor the opportunity to further my swimming skills, pretty much non-existent following various childhood near-drowning incidents. The swimming pool, impossible to keep clean, had long since gone and the closest turkey nest was five kilometres away. So every day I drove to the above-ground man-made dam to swim practice laps.

Marie arrived home and the team was in place.

'Take care Mum and Dad, have a ball,' they waved us off.

We two bushies were wide-eyed throughout our adventures in exotic Morocco. We visited Berber villages, palaces and secret gardens, where roses growing in soil remarkably similar to Riveren's reached pumpkin-like proportions. Through the medinas and market squares we wandered. From Marrakesh we sighted the snow-capped mountains of the High Atlas and in Tangier we lunched and dined with fascinating local characters.

We were exhilarated by our first ever sailing experience as we encountered Old Man Sea in his every mood. The unseasonal Meltemi casually and carelessly tossed us about as through furious winds we churned towards Naxos for shelter. It was Greek Easter and high on the hilltop of this fabulous, fertile island we attended a moving midnight Mass. At Mykonos, beautiful people sunning themselves in the town square were arrested by our passing. 'Ah, Cowboy Dundee!' they exclaimed as they pointed to John, whose Akubra was a permanent fixture.

Steeped in ancient history and culture, we gained a whole new understanding of other countries and other peoples. We departed Athens in the rain and it seemed to me that the tears of the Greek gods fell as they fondly farewelled us.

The dazzling whites and brilliant blues of island Greece were painlessly exchanged for the familiar earthy ochres and spinifex greens, as were endless seas for never ending horizons. Marie, Patrick and Michael excitedly welcomed us back. Except for the absence of Becky, it was a wonderful homecoming on Mother's Day. Becky had not been home for her birthday or Mother's Day for five years.

Not only did we return to a gleaming, sparkling homestead and orderly surrounds, the entire station presented as though we had never been away. Marie, Patrick and Michael had enjoyed their responsibilities and our confidence in them was well founded. Moreover, home would always be our world and we were in no hurry to travel again.

While we were away, my photograph of stockman son Patrick had been selected as the face of Beef 94, the triennial week long Australian Beef Industry Exposition. While we had been enjoying the extraordinary fiftieth birthday celebration voyage, our children had not only represented us at this showcase event, but Patrick had been the key figure in the opening ceremony.

How quickly time had flown. The years of coaxing and supervising, praising and pleading, mopping up spilt water and nurturing a love of learning all of a sudden seemed to be just memories. My sturdy blond babies and toddlers had grown into reliable, caring, loyal and loving young adults.

The Royal Darwin Show was to be a Brahman feature show with a gala dinner containing a Brahman theme. The pleas for my experienced intervention were genuine and so I agreed to organise the function. It was to be my swan song yet again.

The Brahman Bash was a night filled with magic. Mrs Ann Chang, Victor Chang's widow, accepted without hesitation the invitation to fly to Darwin. She fell in love with the tropical city, the cattle team and perhaps most of all with Newcastle Waters Buster, a seven hundred and fifty kilogram grey Brahman bull, generously donated for auction by Ken Warriner. It was no secret that the owner, Kerry Packer, was the patron of the Victor Chang Cardiac Research Institute, which would benefit from the auction proceeds. Some years earlier he had been rushed to St Vincent's following a heart attack while playing polo. He had not forgotten the wonderful care he had received at the hands of Victor Chang and his team.

With typical Brahman docility, Buster paraded between the tables to stand majestically before the awed crowd assembled on the moon-blanched lawns. The bidding was lively and the dollars poured forth.

The main entertainment focused on the Brahman breed, described as the new dimension in beef production. I co-ordinated a cattle industry pageant in which various characters depicted the development, progress and changes within our industry. A suitably attired Nat Buchanan, boss drover, was followed by a camp cook and horse tailer. As my commentary continued we were joined on stage by the overlander, stockman, stock inspector, veterinarian and helicopter pilot, roadtrain driver, jilleroo and jackeroo, cattleman, cattle woman and cattle kids. With predictable imagination, the replicas of the battlers mingled with the appreciative crowd. As yesterday, today and tomorrow blended, sustainability was the buzz word. It was indeed a night where the Bush Telegraph and Cardiac Network united.

A popular national magazine gave written and photographic coverage to the Brahman Bash. Our astonishment was immense when a special person from our past subsequently contacted us.

Geoff Collits from Ward 3 had his cousin write on his behalf to express his joy at seeing his old friends in print. It was a detailed letter and Geoff affectionately recalled our hospital experiences before updating us with his personal news. At the time of his accident, his daughter Kerry had been an infant. Now we were looking at photos of Kerry's two teenage daughters.

Geoff's spirit had proven invincible. With the love and support of family and friends, this man who had become a quadriplegic at the age of twenty-one and lost his wife in a car accident several years later was coping extraordinarily well. He informed us that the Forbes locals had organised a two-day horse and sulky ride to raise funds towards the purchase of a special cushion for his motorised wheelchair. The participants had been undaunted by freezing temperatures and the weekend activities raised almost three times the required amount. John and I understood perfectly the high regard and admiration our friend from long ago attracted.

It seemed to be party time in the Territory, as days after the Brahman Bash, Sally Warriner telephoned John then proceeded to conspire with Marie to plan my fiftieth birthday weekend. I resisted but the Warriners persisted. Never in my wildest dreams could I have anticipated such a celebration.

My brother Johnny and three couples chartered a plane from Alice Springs for the overnight entree at Riveren. Next morning the Sydney Seven, as we'd christened them, preceded us in our Cessna, flying through stormy skies to Newcastle Waters for the main event.

Amidst a spectacular setting, the night of unheralded surprises unfolded. Everyone contributed to the floor show extravaganza as tap dancers, drag queens and ringers from the Top End rhythmically pounded and performed personally choreographed routines. For the very first time I was not only off stage and away from the wings, but the grateful occupant of the very best seat in the house.

One of the highlights was the presentation of my cake. As the giant pink sparkler-bedecked confection was carried in, I suspected nothing. The words to 'Happy Birthday' were suddenly overtaken by stripper music as a Drizabone-clad young man uncoiled from inside the huge cake. Shedding his outer layer, he revealed a bare body except for a crocodile pouch on a G-string. Scars and tattoos crossed his brisket and in long boots with jangling spurs, he headed towards me.

'Mrs Underwood, I'm not sure about this. I just wanted to be a jackeroo. I was in Patrick's year at Joey's; I thought he was a big bloke, but shit! Now I've seen your husband.'

'Don't worry, more pelvic thrusts will keep everyone happy,' I urged.

Without further ado, he hoisted me on his shoulders and we galloped around on a room muster, encouraged by a most enthusiastic crowd.

We danced and laughed as though there was no tomorrow. Only the blood red fireball seemed in a hurry as it suddenly confronted us to announce another day. It was an extraordinary weekend packed with treasured memories. Words seemed inadequate to express my gratitude to Ken and Sally, family and friends.

It was also a time for reflection. On our journey home I glanced sideways at John, who I had discovered on my first visit to Inverway so long ago was no longer the patient but the man who worked and understood his country. Still the latter, he was now husband and father, forever hard working and humble, a man who trusted everyone and believed in the intrinsic good in all people.

I thought about my children, too, and knew that forever after, the words spoken during their tribute to me at the party would quickly reorientate me in times of doubt or vulnerability.

'Riveren will always be the same for us, Mum, because of you.'

Throughout all the privileges of modern pioneering, we, as a family, have constructed and developed, agonised and rejoiced; as each sheet of iron was laid, each picket driven, each calf branded and each nappy changed. It has been said that, 'Day by day a child comes to know a little bit of what you know, to think a little bit of what you think, to understand your understanding. That which you dream and believe and are, in truth become the child.'

When I look at Marie, Patrick, Michael and Becky, I'm overwhelmed. I must have done something right.

St Vincent's Hospital beckoned yet again. This time it was neither repairs nor maintenance for any one of us that took us to Sydney. The Victor Chang Cardiac Research Institute was embarking on a fund-raising Million Dollar Dinner. John was adamant that we could not afford to go. I declared that we could not afford not to go. It was impossible to express our gratitude to St Vincent's Hospital—our home away from home—where the Sisters of Charity and a committed medical team had provided unparalleled care for us over all the years. Our attendance at this unique function would be one way to demonstrate our heartfelt thanks

The first person we saw upon our arrival was our dear friend Sister Bernice. During the evening I met the guest of honour, Diana, Princess of Wales, who was amazed to learn of our remote cattle station home and our connection with the hospital.

Throughout my life the intangible golden thread continues to interweave my Albury beginnings, St Vincent's Hospital and Riveren.

CHAPTER 21

HOW PRIVILEGED
WE ARE

....

For some people the gloss remains on the magic and mystique of the pastoral industry. The romantic notion of tasting the untamed Outback is cherished by many a dreamer who likes to imagine poking along behind a big mob of cattle towards a brilliant sunset, with regular time off for the thrills and spills of the rodeo circuit. That distorted vision continues to lure people to our country, but they are here today and gone tomorrow.

Our industry is making new demands even on old hands and to embrace change is to embrace viability. The yesteryear mentality of 'keeping the branding iron hot and ink off the cheque book' has changed to accept the need to spend a dollar to make more dollars. The control of this balancing act separates success from ultimate failure. Riveren has a property plan in place, taking into account the vagaries of rainfall and the variation of markets. We are continually upgrading our herd and replacing less productive breeders by introducing top quality Brahman heifers to stand with pure bred Brahman bulls. Just recently, Sunny gave birth to Dazzle and Thérèse's beautiful heifer calf was named Marie. From our selected pure Brahman stud herds we breed our own sires for our commercial herd. Right from birth, Riveren Frank bore a strong resemblance to his father, Jerome. We are all involved with the selection and distribution of males and females for home use and for our turnoff.

Work procedures on stations have certainly changed. Helicopters and aeroplanes have halved the workforce and increased the efficiency of musters. Today, good chopper pilots can show all the skills of pioneer stockmen by moving cattle slowly, keeping calves up with their mothers and dropping off cows with newborn calves. Today's stockmen draft off calves and brand them in a calf cradle. Yesteryear's ringer used a bronco horse to lasso the calf, pull it up to the bronco panel and either scruff it to the ground or use leg ropes to tip it on its side, depending on the size of the cleanskin animal. Today gas furnaces have replaced open fires and fire drums for heating brands. The males destined for turnoff rather than breeding are still castrated. All cattle are automatically dehorned. Horns are generally unacceptable, for they are not only dangerous but cause bruising during transportation. Efficiency has always been the name of the game, but as always must be assessed against the cost. Record keeping has become increasingly vital.

Michael is an advocate of artificial insemination. John, although keen to try the latest techniques, reckons it might be more cost effective to let the bull in the paddock enjoy doing what comes naturally. From beginning to end, management is continuing to change. It is no longer simply a matter of long hours in the saddle or verandah-style managers hanging in by the bash of their hats. The new approach is continually sifting the would-be's from the could-be's. Whereas twenty odd years ago we sold four to five-year-old fat bullocks, today we are turning off a younger, lighter animal. Land care continues to be an integral part of management. All of these changes affect the composition of present day stockcamps, as a multi-skilled workforce is needed to cope with the way it is.

The dramatic changes in communications have also revolutionised our lives. However, one age-old problem exists. If the telephone lines are not functioning at our end, we have no means of advising authorities or technicians that we are off the air. The phone that is out of order for us does not answer for the caller, who naturally assumes that we are out, and when communication is re-established, accuses us of never being home. The addition of an impressive facsimile machine to the office equipment has made possible instant exchange of written information and documents, a marked improvement on mail still delivered once a week by plane. It is governed by the same limitations, even though it is on a separate line. If one telephone line is out, they are usually both out.

The computer is in place. Our four children, all familiar with the world of computers, have been able to patiently lead their parents through the maze of new technology. Thanks to computer technology, our cattle, no longer sold exclusively in sale yards or from station inspection, can be marketed using a whole new concept. A registered assessor inspects the mob for sale then completes a description sheet or list of specifications. These cattle are listed and sold by a computer system known as Computer Aided Livestock Marketing. Buyers Australia-wide can bid on this mob.

The Northern Territory is coming of age. This last Australian frontier is also the gateway to Asia. In north-west Australia we are closer to Jakarta than Perth and closer to Singapore than Melbourne. Since the early 1990s, the Northern Territory livestock exporters have increased their trade by more than 500 per cent and in 1996 cattle numbers shipped through Darwin were very close to 400 000. Due to the infusion of Brahman bloodlines into our Riveren herd, we remain poised to meet the demand for Brahmans on boats to our northern neighbours. The Brahman, a magnificent, intelligent, curious and low maintenance creature, has revolutionised the beef industry and promised long-term viability.

Riveren too is coming of age. The tree trunks are massive and their huge leafy branches abound with bird life, high above the slippery dip and old swing. All those years of carting water have proven worthwhile. As another Wet Season remains ominously devoid of rain, the expansion of our property is timely. We have purchased from our northern neighbour, Limbunya, two adjacent paddocks, one thousand square kilometres in size. If necessary, cattle can be moved out there, reducing stocking rates and grazing pressure. Riveren, now three thousand square kilometres in size, sprawls the headwaters of the historic river named after a youthful Queen Victoria, twelve years before the naming of the Australian State. We have staked our future commitment.

Our herd stands at twelve thousand head. One particular bullock holds a special place in our hearts. Chocolate, weighing seven hundred and eighty kilograms, lives with selected cows and a single sire bull in Middle

Paddock. Donkey, in the company of her two heifer friends, Annie and Nougat, is happy in Back Paddock with another stud mob. She always responds to her name, eeaawing loudly as she nibbles fingers in search of food. Mandy still woofs as she bounds along on the tail of cattle, some of whom stare inquisitively at this strange friendly creature, taller than the calves she tries to engage in play.

Long-term drought, insecurity of land tenure, lack of viability and a younger generation who no longer want to put in the necessary effort are just some of the reasons why ownership of our vast pastoral properties has changed so significantly in recent years. Increasing financial pressures are sadly forcing many families out. Facing insurmountable obstacles, some have fallen away in abject defeat and with their spirits broken. Corporations have bought and sold all around us, and the continued commitment of giant investors remains a pledge of confidence in the future of our industry. With famous names like Durack, Quilty and Vestey becoming an echo of an age, one reveres even more the history makers. Three Underwood families continue to live and work adjoining properties, all of which comprised the original Inverway. At Riveren, we look forward to our future with a degree of optimism, thankful for our family commitment and the buoyant live shipping markets to South-East Asia. John's philosophy that everything is cyclical and a downturn possible is based on a lifetime of experience. He is a realist.

There are different pressures at different times for different people. We only have each other to bear the brunt of outbursts and breakdowns and there must be continual mending of emotional fences as well as those made from barb wire. Our world consists of one stage, Riveren, and we are the sole players. When things become tough, we have to keep going. We continue to make our own difficult decisions and must live with them. And always the ingredients have to balance, the tirelessness with the fearlessness, the courage and determination. I have grown in the belief and conviction that one must become of this country in order to survive. This land has claimed us.

However there remain changes and challenges ahead that would tax even our early pioneers. Our four children all have bush souls and remain committed to their roots in their individual ways. After five years of international travel associated with her hospitality consultancy business based in Singapore, Marie has returned to Darwin. She is now part of the Paspaley pearling team. Never far from home, physically or spiritually, Marie returns often to give a helping hand, lead cattle in the show ring and to absorb her beloved land. Patrick, also in Darwin, is using his commerce degree and accountancy skills in line with the needs of our industry. He too never misses an opportunity to head the thousand kilometres down the track to slam pickets into a fence line or brand a mob of calves. Becky, our baby no more, is at university in order to spring back into the industry in her chosen capacity. Through her degree in agricultural science, Becky is specialising in animal science. Michael, the first Territorian to win the Edgar Hudgins Memorial Scholarship from the Australian Brahman Breeders' Association, has returned to Riveren from overseas. His six months in the United States afforded him marvellous opportunities to visit Brahman ranches in four states, as well as participating at Brahman shows, schools and seminars. On the other hand, Michael's maturity and broad experiences equipped him as an effective ambassador for our Australian industry.

John and Michael, side by side, plan tomorrow. We have grasped our heritage with outstretched arms.

In this land of contrasts and contradictions we shall continue to give our all. There remains a glorious sense of freedom tempered by accountability. There is the controlling sense of discipline that is vital for survival. There is the majesty of this timeless land.

Beneath Mt Farquharson and beside the old Buchanan yards, we salute our predecessors, the trailblazers. We stand in their shadow with enormous humility and respect. We think also of friends who shared our journey and have already stood to be counted by handing in their spurs to the Supreme Boss. May they rest in peace. As we look to the future, the past must never be forgotten.

I look back on our achievements as we have worked, grown and developed: blacks and whites; young and old; side by side, in harmony with our land and its products. In this beautiful but unforgiving country, I remain contented and constantly challenged. Although Riveren is well developed and boasts a well-managed herd of Brahman cattle, there is much hard work yet to be done.

❖　❖　❖

One of the old Aboriginal stockmen rang up recently to ask how John was keeping. He told me that everyone still talks about that legend man, they talk about when John crashed his plane and nobody found him, when that John just picked up that wreckage next morning, put it across his shoulder and walked back home. Then he implored me, 'You look after that Boss for me please, Missus. John, my old Boss, is a good man. I miss him here in my heart.'

I understood perfectly. Every day I thank God for the gift of this wonderful man.

I thank God too for the gifts of motherhood. I thank God for the times when everyone returned safely at night; for helping me find enough empty containers to hold the bush flowers with two inch stems that were picked with two inch fingers; for all the stretching and sighing of my heart that began with the cry of our first born and proceeded awesomely to the first smile, the first step, the first heartache. Most of all, dear God, thank you for reaching down and helping us up the stairs, one by one.

Riveren has captured our bodies, hearts and spirits. It lies within the heart of Australia. How privileged we are to call it home. Riveren is where I belong.

I know it would not have worked anywhere else with anyone else.

In the middle of nowhere has become my everywhere.

GLOSSARY

....

BILLABONG   shallow catchment of water in area excluding creek beds

BILLY   metal container with wire handle, used to brew tea on open fire

BOGEY   bath or shower or clean up

BORE   a hole drilled for underground water

BOS INDICUS   Humped cattle of Asian or African origin suitable for the tropics and sub-tropics. Although there are over thirty distinct breeds named for the geographical areas in which they are found, the four main breeds that formed the development of the American Brahmans were the Gir, Guzerat, Nellore and the Krishna Valley. Today Brahman cattle thrive in seventy nations around the world.

BOS TAURUS	British and European cattle more suited to a temperate climate
BOTULISM VACCINE	a vaccine given routinely to prevent botulism, a disease which causes death in cattle
BOVINE	of or like cattle
BRONCOING	to lasso a beast with a head rope and pull it to a bronco panel to brand or castrate
BRONCO PANEL	two wooden panels designed to facilitate leg roping and casting of animal
BRUCELLOSIS	a disease which is characterised in cattle by abortion, primarily in first calf heifers
BRUMBY	feral horse
BTEC	Brucellosis and Tuberculosis Eradication Campaign. This was the national programme undertaken over many years to eradicate both diseases from the Australian cattle herd
BULWADDY	also known as hedgewood; extends its hardwood branches outward from the ground often interlocking with lancewood to form impenetrable scrub
CALF CRADLE	a ratchet locking device that restrains a calf for ear-marking, branding, dehorning and castration
CAMP OVEN	round vessel with fitting lift-off lid used for cooking on open fire and with coals
CLEANSKIN	unbranded beast
COMMERCIAL HERD	the bulk of the cattle herd whose progeny are sold

CONDAMINE BELLS	distinctive horse bells hung around neck, used to locate horses
CORROBOREE	traditional Aboriginal song and dance
CORRUGATIONS	folds and furrows in dirt road caused by heavy traffic
CRUSH	section of stockyard that restricts cattle movement
CULL	to remove from herd because of inferior quality
DEBBIL DEBBIL	Aboriginal pidgin for ghosts or evil spirits
DESTOCK	an eradication strategy involving removal of cattle for the purposes of the Brucellosis and Tuberculosis Eradication Campaign within an area suspected of being diseased with brucellosis or tuberculosis
DRY SEASON	from May until September when temperatures fall and cloudless skies overview natural haying of grasses. The season when cattle mustering activities are in full swing
EMU BOB	methodical collection by hand
FIRE FIGHTER	portable engine and pump used to pump water
FLOODGATE	section of fence crossing watercourse
GILGAI	shallow depression that holds water after rain
GREENHIDE	unprocessed bovine hide
HEIFER	young female bovine that has not calved
HOBBLES	straps used on front legs of horse to restrict movement

HUMPY	Aboriginal shelter or house
JACKKNIFE	a severe bend in the middle of a roadtrain causing the trailer to swing towards the driver's cabin
JUMP UP	a sudden rise in altitude onto a hill or plateau
KILLER	beast slaughtered for human consumption
LATERITE	volcanic rock closely related to basalt
LUBRA	Aboriginal woman
MICKEY BULLS	young bulls
MULUGA	Aboriginal word for Boss
NECK STRAP	strap around horse's neck to carry hobbles and assist catching and leading of horse
PICCANINNY	Aboriginal word for child
PICCANINNY DAYLIGHT	first light of day
PICKET	steel fence post
PIKER BULLOCKS	old-aged 'pensioner' bullocks
PLEURO-PNEUMONIA	or Pleuro, now eradicated, caused big losses of cattle in the droving days when affected cattle in close proximity with each other were subjected to hard conditions
PODDY CALF	orphan calf, non sucking causes stomach distension, hence 'pot gut'
RFDS	Royal Flying Doctor Service. Reverend John Flynn established the aerial medical service in 1928, renamed in 1942 the Flying Doctor of Australia and in 1955, the Queen granted the royal prefix. The service provides

communication, medical comfort and pastoral care over vast areas to geographically isolated Australians

RINGER	stockman
ROADTRAIN	prime mover and up to three trailers carting cattle
SPEARS	device to allow one way passage into a trap yard
STATION	Australian pastoral property
STUD HERD	selected superior cattle whose male offspring are used as bulls in the commercial herd
SWAG	bedroll and belongings rolled into canvas and tied with straps—'every ringer's suitcase'
TICK FEVER	or Red Water was a serious disease in northern parts of Australia affecting some domestic animals, cattle and buffalo. The organisms destroy the red cells in the blood similarly to the disease malaria in humans. The blood-sucking cattle tick acts as a vector transmitting the disease. With vaccines and drugs the disease can be controlled. Brahman cattle have been instrumental in a markedly lower disease incidence because of their tick resistance.
TRACHEOTOMY	opening made into the windpipe leaving patient unable to speak
TUBERCULOSIS	an infectious disease affecting animals by causing abscesses in a part or organ of the body
TUCKER	food

TURKEY NEST   man-made above-ground earth tank

UI   Aboriginal word for yes

WET SEASON   the hot summer period from October to
                     April when humidity, monsoonal influences,
                     thunderstorms and torrential rains prevail.
                     Annual rainfall averages vary from 800
                     millimetres to 1600 mm in the Top End to
                     less than 300 mm in central Australia

YAKKY   to call out, yell

ZEBU   common name for Bos Indicus cattle before
                     the adoption of Brahman

MEASUREMENTS

....

The story in this book spans several years, during which time Australia moved from an Imperial system of measurement to a metric one. Measurements are cited in Imperial or metric, depending on the year that individual events took place.

IMPERIAL TO METRIC

1 inch	=	25.4 millimetres
1 foot	=	30.5 centimetres
1 yard	=	0.914 metres
1 mile	=	1.61 kilometres
1 ounce	=	28.35 grams
1 pound	=	454 grams
1 ton	=	1.02 tonnes
1 fluid ounce	=	28.4 millilitres
1 pint	=	568 millilitres
1 gallon	=	4.55 litres
1 point (rainfall)	=	0.25 mm
1 square mile	=	2.59 km^2

CELSIUS TO FAHRENHEIT

0 degrees C	=	32 degrees F
38 degrees C	=	100 degrees F
Freezing	=	0 degrees C
Boiling	=	100 degrees C

CURRENCY

12 pennies	=	1 shilling
20 shillings	=	1 pound
1 pound	=	2 dollars